ADVANCE ACCLAIM FOR
THE MEANING REVOLUTION

"*The Meaning Revolution* makes the case that leadership isn't just about the mind. It's also about the spirit. Fred's book shows how when we set goals that reflect our values as well as our interests—when our teams strive to make a positive impact on the world together—we can achieve more than success. We can find greater purpose and meaning."

> —Sheryl Sandberg, COO of Facebook and founder of LeanIn.org and OptionB.org

"Welcome to the rigorously reasoned, deeply heartfelt, and always enlightening mind of Fred Kofman. Trained as an economist, with stops along the way as a management professor and consultant, Fred's official title at LinkedIn is Vice President of Executive Development. But I have a shorter name for what he does. I call him the High Priest of Capitalism."

> —Reid Hoffman, founder and former chairman of LinkedIn; board member of Microsoft (from the foreword to the book)

"'Transcendent Leadership' is exactly the kind of enlightened approach that today's leaders must embrace to win in the workplace and in the marketplace."

> —Doug Conant, founder and CEO of Conant Leadership; former CEO of Campbell Soup Company

"I believe culture needs to be about realizing personal passions and using the company as a platform to pursue those passions. Fred Kofman explores that notion even more deeply through vivid stories and truly profound reflections on business leadership and conscious capitalism. What is your noble purpose? Are your kids proud of your company's mission? Why might the biggest beneficiary of your business be your competitors' customers and employees? Read on!"

> —Satya Nadella, CEO of Microsoft

"As Fred Kofman makes brilliantly clea_____ ____ *M_____ Revolution*, real leadership is not about hitting your num_____ f purpose and meaning, and inspiring oth_____ lasting difference in the world around them.'

> —Arianna Huffington,

to being a highly accomplished scholar and business consultant, he is a deeply reflective thinker who has subjected his own life to the kind of bracing scrutiny that he recommends for others. The word 'spiritual' is overused, but *The Meaning Revolution* deserves that label. You can't read this book without asking yourself deep and invaluable questions about your life and your calling."

—Robert Wright, senior lecturer at Princeton; author of *The Evolution of God, The Moral Animal, Nonzero,* and *Why Buddhism Is True*

"A pleasure to read. Fred Kofman uses his academic training and consulting experience to show us that economic concepts are crucial to understand and improve organizations' leadership and culture."

—Jacques Lawarrée, professor of economics at University of Washington at Seattle

"In this brilliant follow-up to his seminal book *Conscious Business*, Kofman distills the wisdom he has accumulated in decades of work advising and coaching the leaders of major companies around the world. Beautifully written, this book illuminates 'the simplicity on the other side of complexity' that Oliver Wendell Holmes said he would give his life for. It is an essential guide to creating organizations that become sources of flourishing, meaning, fulfillment, and healing in a world that can no longer afford the unnecessary consequences of 'business as usual.'"

—Raj Sisodia, FW Olin Distinguished Professor of Global Business, Babson College; cofounder and chairman emeritus, Conscious Capitalism International

"Most of what comes from Silicon Valley today seems to imply scary outcomes for humans and society at large. But here comes Fred Kofman: leadership is a social technology, whose function is to increase the pride of belonging to a wider effort, restore people's self-esteem, and ultimately give the unreasonable nonsense of the world, especially the business world, a chosen, conscious meaning. Recounted with the passion of a practitioner and the precision of a philosopher, *The Meaning Revolution* is equal parts powerful and pleasurable to read."

—Laurent Choain, chief people and communications officer, Mazars, France

"The unique insights that Fred Kofman shares in this book have changed the way I lead and manage. They are at once simple enough to be immediately applicable and profound enough to merit a lifetime of practice."

—Mike Gamson, senior vice president of Global Sales Solutions, LinkedIn

"An exceptional, unbiased, and unfiltered deconstruction of leadership and management of people and organizations. Fred Kofman completely debunks the 'one style fits all' view on leadership and gives us an alternative view on what works where and how we can better manage and inspire people. A simple, direct, and profoundly helpful guide to extraordinary management and connecting to others through purpose."

—Mohammad Abdulla Al Gergawi, minister of Cabinet Affairs and the Future, United Arab Emirates

"This wonderful book is full of practical wisdom. Kofman's great skill is to be able to draw upon profound ideas about meaning, work, happiness, motivation, and even death; to give concrete advice about how we can live better lives and build better companies. Like the best teachers, Kofman is an engaging story-teller, and like the best guides, his stories carry weight because he has traveled this path himself and shown many people the way. *The Meaning Revolution* is a pleasure to read and will change the way you think about your job as a leader."

—John Weeks, professor of leadership and organizational behavior at IMD

THE
MEANING
REVOLUTION

THE MEANING REVOLUTION

LEADING
WITH THE
POWER OF PURPOSE

FRED KOFMAN

WH
ALLEN

1 3 5 7 9 10 8 6 4 2

WH Allen, an imprint of Ebury Publishing,
20 Vauxhall Bridge Road,
London SW1V 2SA

WH Allen is part of the Penguin Random House group of companies whose
addresses can be found at global.penguinrandomhouse.com

Penguin
Random House
UK

First published in the United Kingdom by WH Allen in 2018
First published in the United States by Currency in 2018

www.penguin.co.uk

A CIP catalogue record for this book is available from the British Library

ISBN 9780753548585

Printed and bound in India by Thomson Press India Ltd.

Penguin Random House is committed to a sustainable future for our
business, our readers and our planet. This book is made from Forest
Stewardship Council® certified paper.

MIX
Paper from
responsible sources
FSC
www.fsc.org   FSC® C018179

TO THE YOU WHO YOU ARE BEYOND
THE YOU WHO YOU THINK YOU ARE

CONTENTS

FOREWORD BY REID HOFFMAN

The most effective leader has no followers.

Benevolence, service, and love are the ultimate sources of economic value.

If you treat your employees as resources to optimize, you will never ascend from manager to leader. To make that leap, you must recognize your employees as conscious beings who yearn to transcend their limited existence through noble immortality projects.

Welcome to the rigorously reasoned, deeply heartfelt, and always enlightening mind of Fred Kofman.

Trained as an economist, with stops along the way as a management professor and consultant, Fred's official title at LinkedIn, where he has worked since 2012, is vice president of Executive Development. But I have a shorter name for what he does. I call him the High Priest of Capitalism.

In the tradition of Adam Smith, Fred recognizes capitalism as a kind of spiritual pursuit with alchemical moral power. To achieve long-term success in a free market, where individuals engage in voluntary exchange according to their own preferences, businesses and entrepreneurs must truly understand their customers' needs and desires. Then they must serve these customers in a useful and equitable way.

Capitalism, then, can be a crucible for empathy, compassion, and fairness. And the domain in which this takes place is the workplace.

But while many people ponder the meaning of life, fewer tend to think deeply about the meaning of work. In addition, capitalism is often portrayed as a domain where ethics and values can be put on hold in the expedient pursuit of profits. "It's just business" people often say when they want to rationalize ethical corner-cutting or outright sociopathic behavior.

That, however, is a short-sighted mind-set and a toxic one. Recognizing the concept of service that lies at the heart of capitalism, Fred encourages us to see the workplace not as an abstract realm of key performance indicators and profit-and-loss statements, but rather as a supremely humanized place, a place around which most people organize their lives, achieve their sense of self, and pursue meaning and impact.

Once we begin to embrace this key truth more consciously, we can begin to move from an "It's just (simply) business" mind-set to a "just (justice) business" mind-set, wherein we fully recognize how compassion, integrity, responsiveness, and service lie at the heart of any high-functioning organization.

This "just business" mind-set applies not just to how a company serves its customers but also to how it serves its employees. As Fred explains in these pages, great leaders define and articulate an organization's noble purpose and its values. Then they put those values into action in pursuit of that purpose, and inspire everyone else who works at the organization to do the same.

Here's how Fred put it at the Wisdom 2.0 Conference in 2015, describing Jeff Weiner's leadership style at LinkedIn: "A lot of leaders are rowing a boat. They're bringing everyone along with them, and saying, 'Come follow me.' But the way I've seen Jeff and other great leaders do it, they'll go and get on a surfboard. They don't say, 'Follow me.' They say, 'Come join us on this huge wave.'"

In the former vision, everyone's literally in the same boat, doing only what their leader allows them to do. In the latter, everyone's on the same wave and moving in the same direction, but they have much more freedom to improvise, to act boldly and creatively and set their own course of action.

Note, too, that it's a "huge wave."

What we see time and time again in Silicon Valley is how the companies that grow fastest, execute most consistently, and become the dominant players in their industries—the companies that do what I call "blitzscaling" or growing at lightning speed—are the ones that define their corporate missions in big, noble, and incredibly ambitious terms.

Google wants to organize all the world's information. Facebook wants to connect the world. Microsoft wants to make people and organizations more productive. Airbnb wants to help its customers belong anywhere. LinkedIn wants to enable everyone to have their best economic opportunities.

These companies commit to service on a global scale, and their big, clearly defined missions attract talented professionals seeking personal fulfillment through work that has real meaning and impact.

But a big, noble goal is not enough. You also need the right kind of culture in place.

Entrepreneurship, I often say, is like jumping off a cliff and building a plane on the way down. You have a plan, but your resources are limited and time is running out. In the first chaotic months of starting a new venture, your default state is that you're dead. To escape this fate, you have to reverse the downward course of your trajectory, and fast.

But here's the thing. Success—and especially blockbuster success—doesn't eliminate the danger of a fiery crash. When a start-up shifts from death plummet into blitzscaling mode, adding customers, increasing revenues, and growing the size of its workforce at dizzying speeds, a founder's job gets even harder and more complex.

In this phase of a company's development, an entrepreneur with a breakthrough idea must also become an inspirational leader. Micromanagement, after all, is not a mechanism for rapid growth. To scale quickly, an organization must give its employees the freedom to execute with speed, creativity, and risk.

Which ultimately means that the most productive organizations—the ones that create the greatest returns for society along with the greatest returns for investors—are the ones built on foundations of trust and integrity.

So read this profound book—but don't stop there. Just as the best leaders have no followers, and the best teachers have no pupils, the best books aren't just read. They're acted upon.

In these pages, you can find great inspiration in Fred's insights and actions. But it is in your own values, your own call to service, that you will ultimately find the sense of purpose that will compel you to work—and live—more consciously and productively, with the greatest possible impact.

The Meaning Revolution is a call not for followers but for fellow surfers.

Are you ready to catch that wave?

Chapter 1
A HOT WORKSHOP

YOUR JOB IS NOT YOUR JOB

> Success, like happiness, cannot be pursued; it must ensue, and it only
> does so as the unintended side effect of one's personal dedication to a
> cause greater than oneself.
>
> —Viktor Frankl

It was a sweltering July day in Vegas, so of course the conference room
was freezing. The participants of my "Conscious Business" workshop pulled their jackets tight and grimaced. They weren't just cold;
they were pissed off. They looked at me icily. I knew what they were
thinking.

I've been in situations like this many times. More often than not,
typical managers welcome me as warmly as they would an onset of
flu. It's as if we're all stuck in some Dilbert cartoon, and I can read the
thought bubbles appearing over everyone's heads.

What the hell are we doing here? one guy was thinking. *I've got work
to do!*

Another bullshit workshop, thought someone else. *I hate this stuff*.

I decided to play into their worst fears. "Let's start with an ice-
breaker!" I said in my cheeriest, most workshop-y voice. "Find someone you don't know and introduce yourself. Be sure to tell your partner
what your job is." I could hear their mental groans as they all turned to
their neighbors.

After three painful minutes, I asked for their attention. "Who

1

would like to share?" I asked sweetly, as if I were totally unaware of how much I was annoying them. Nobody answered, of course. "You two, please," I called on a pair. "Tell us your partner's name and job."

"His name is John. He's in legal," the woman said.

"Her name is Sandra," said John. "She runs marketing campaigns."

"Wrong," I said. Sandra and John looked puzzled, as did everyone else.

Then, Vegas style, I challenged everyone in the room to a wager: "I bet each one of you a hundred dollars that you don't know what your job is. And that it will take me less than a minute to prove it."

Nobody said anything.

"Oh, come on," I pushed them, "you really aren't sure what your jobs are?" I pulled out a roll of bills, with the $100 bill clearly showing on top. "Take the bet. If you win, I'll give you the hundred bucks. If you lose, I'll contribute the money to the charity of your choice. Raise your hand unless you really don't know what your job is."

A few people raised their hands, but most of them glowered, suspecting a setup. "Let me make it easier," I said. "Let's not bet money but time and energy. If I win, you stay in the workshop and participate fully. If I lose with more than half of you, we close this workshop and I'll take the fall with your managers. I'll tell them I just couldn't do it. They'll never know better; what happens here stays here. And to clinch the deal, you decide whether I win or lose."

People grimaced. Some shook their heads, determined not to play with me.

"Come on," I pleaded. "You're stuck with me. What have you got to lose, besides your confusion? If you win, you'll get rid of me right now. You can tell everyone the story of the idiot who messed up his workshop in the first five minutes."

Finally, I had their attention. Most of them raised their hands. I chose a woman sitting in the front. I peered at the name on her badge and thanked her. "Thank you for playing, Karen. What's your job?"

"I'm an internal auditor."

"And what's your job as an internal auditor?"

"To assure that the organizational processes are reliable."

"Okay, Karen, let's begin. Everyone, please look at the clock. Karen, did you play any sports in school?"

"Yes," she replied. "I played soccer."

"Great! As an Argentinean, I'm wild about soccer. What position did you play?"

"I played defense."

"What was your job?"

"To stop the other team from scoring," she said.

I turned to the rest of the managers. "The job of a defensive player is to stop the other team from scoring. Does anyone disagree? If so, please raise your hand."

Nobody moved.

"So now, somebody else answer me, please. What's the job of an offensive player?"

"To score goals," several people said in unison.

"Great, it seems we're all on the same page. My next question is, what's the job of the team?"

"To cooperate," someone said.

"To cooperate in order to do what?"

"To play well," someone else said.

"And why would the team want to play well?"

"To win!" came a shout from the back of the room.

"Bingo!" I replied. "The job of the team is to win the game. Anybody disagree with that?"

They shook their heads and rolled their eyes, annoyed at this exercise in futility. I saw someone faking a yawn. His thought bubble read, *What's the big frigging deal?*

"If the job of the team is to win," I continued, undeterred, "what is the primary job of each and every member of the team?"

"To help the team to win," someone else said.

"Right again! Do you all agree?"

Everyone nodded.

"Here's my last question: If the primary job of each and every member of the team is to help the team to win, and if the defensive player is a member of the team, what is the primary job of a defensive player?"

"To help the team win," a third person muttered, clearly intuiting where things were going.

"Yes!" I pointed to the person who said it. "Please say that louder."

"To help the team win," he repeated.

"Okay. Please check the time. It's been fifty-two seconds since we started this discussion."

People still looked puzzled, so I explained. "What is the primary job of a defensive player? Is it to stop the other team from scoring or to help the team win? You all agreed with Karen a minute ago that it was to stop the other team from scoring. I hope you'll agree with me now that it's to help the team win."

"What's the difference?" asked one contrarian.

"Imagine you are the coach of a team that's losing one to zero with five minutes to go. What would you tell the defensive players?"

"To go on the offensive and try to tie the game," someone asserted.

"Exactly! So how would you react if they told you, 'Sorry, Coach, but that's not our job'?"

"I'd fire their asses."

"Why? Doesn't that make it more likely that the other team could score a second goal in a counterattack? If the defensive player's job is to help the team to win, then going on the offensive is the right thing to do. If his job is to minimize the goals scored against his team, it is the wrong thing to do."

People were smiling. I could feel the tide turning. I pushed further. "So what's the job of the offensive player?"

"To help the team win."

"And what's the job of the water boy?"

"To help the team win."

Several people were giggling, but not everyone. "I still don't get the point about our jobs," someone said.

"In 1961, President John F. Kennedy was visiting NASA headquarters for the first time," I replied. "While touring the facility, he introduced himself to a fellow who was mopping the floor, and he asked him what he did at NASA. The janitor replied proudly, 'I'm helping put a man on the moon!'"

4

I let that sink in for a moment. And then I asked them, "How many of you told your partner in the opening exercise: 'My job is to help my company win?' How many of you realize that your primary job is to help your organization fulfill its mission ethically and profitably? How many of you heard your partner describe his or her job as 'contributing to increase the value (and the values) of my company'?"

In the now-not-so-icy silence, you could hear the proverbial penny drop.

BEATING YOUR NUMBERS, UNDERMINING YOUR TEAM

In 2014, Veronica Block called to cancel her family's Comcast Internet service. She was immediately transferred to a "customer retention" representative who argued with her for ten minutes about why she wanted to cut off the service. Every time Veronica asked the representative to simply terminate the service, the rep argued with her. The representative insisted that it was all about improving Comcast's service. "Tell me why you don't want faster Internet service," the fast-talking representative kept saying.

Frustrated, Veronica handed the phone off to her husband, Ryan, who had the presence of mind to record his eight-minute segment of the dialogue.[1]

The conversation was painful, wheedling, circular, and irrational. "My job is to understand why you don't want Comcast service," the rep argued, his voice rising.

"I don't understand why you can't just cut it off," said Ryan.

"It sounds like you don't want to have this conversation with me," the rep whined. "I'm just trying to give you information." Listening to the recording, you can practically hear the poor guy's manager breathing down his neck. "I'm trying to help my company be better," the rep says a little desperately. "That's my job."

"I can guarantee you right now," Block replied, "you're doing an incredibly good job at helping your company be worse."

5

The SoundCloud clip that Ryan recorded and posted on his blog was played millions of times. It resulted in stories in the *Washington Post* and the *Los Angeles Times* and on *Good Morning America* and the *Huffington Post*. It was definitely not the kind of publicity that Comcast was looking for, especially when it was trying to execute a widely hated merger with Time Warner Cable. Comcast later apologized for the singular behavior of its panicked employee, but not until after the damage was done.

In any case, his behavior is neither singular nor panicked; it is systemic and rational. As with most companies, Comcast's customer retention group lives in its own silo: everyone in that group is evaluated according to a checklist of key performance indicators (or KPIs). I bet you that this hapless rep's bonus and career depended on the number of cancellations that were recorded on his shift, regardless of whether or not it would be best for the company to stop those clients from leaving. He had a script that he had to follow strictly or he would be reprimanded. (And, most likely, his supervisor's performance would be affected, too.)

Here is what that rep was struggling with, without understanding it. To do the best for the company (in order to optimize the system), you must, at times, do something that's not the best for you or your particular area (suboptimize your subsystem). For example, to do the best for Comcast, the customer retention representative should have courteously terminated the customer's service, even though that was not what his area's performance is measured on. When he optimized for his subsystem (trying aggressively to retain the customer), he suboptimized the system (annoying the customer and eroding Comcast's brand). By doing "his job," the customer retention representative ended up doing a great disservice to Comcast through one of the biggest public relations fiascoes of the year.

In a normal organization, you don't get paid to do your job; you get paid to play your role. Your real job is to help your company to win; that is, to accomplish its mission profitably and ethically. At times, your job contradicts your role, since it requires that you sacrifice your agenda, change your priorities, or take a hit in your individual key performance indicators. You don't get rewarded for helping your company win, though; in fact, you might be punished for it, which is infuriating. *How can they be so stupid!* you may think. *They are setting me up so that when I do the right thing, I end up worse off.*

The point is that too often each individual, and each part of the organization, pursues his or her own interests at the expense of the whole. As the founding father of the total quality movement, W. Edwards Deming, observed: "People with targets and jobs dependent upon meeting them will probably meet the targets, even if they have to destroy the enterprise to do it."[2]

If only they tweaked this damned incentive system to make it more reasonable, you might think. But it turns out that a perfect incentive system is a mythical entity, like a perfect car. You must choose between comfort and performance, between crashworthiness and fuel consumption, between quality and economy. You can't have a family sedan that is roomy, safe, reliable, and economical and that performs like a sports coupe that is fast, responsive, nimble, and powerful. Organizational leaders have to make some hard choices: accountability or cooperation, excellence or alignment, autonomy or coordination. Unfortunately, collaboration conflicts with accountability, and collective performance conflicts with individual excellence.

Thus, organizations end up with an insoluble dilemma. It's like a blanket that is too short. If you pull it up to your chest, your feet get cold; if you cover your feet, your chest gets cold. On the one hand, individual incentives create silos; on the other, collective incentives destroy productivity. Most organizations stick with the devil they know—individual performance indicators—and accept the consequent impact on collaboration.

The good news is that there is a better way to address this problem. And that is through the use of meaning—the ultimate nonmaterial incentive. The bad news is that the kind of leadership that can engage people in meaningful work is much, much harder than you think.

THE INSPIRING LEADER

I define *leadership* as the process by which a person (the leader) elicits the internal commitment of others (the followers) to accomplish a mission in alignment with the group's values.

Leadership is about getting what can't be taken, and deserving what is freely given. The followers' internal commitment cannot be extracted by rewards or punishments. It can be inspired only through a belief that giving their best to the enterprise will enhance their lives.

In an organization you are part of a team—internal conflicts notwithstanding. As a team member, you cannot win unless the whole team wins. You may be an accountant, an engineer, or a salesperson. You may work as an individual contributor, a manager, or an executive. Beyond all professions, roles, and levels, beyond your personal targets and goals, you are a team member and you need to align your efforts toward the entire organization's collective success. You must cooperate with your colleagues to win as a team.

Traditional command-and-control leaders think that they can make people do this through the right incentives. They ask questions such as: How can I motivate my subordinates to achieve their individual and collective targets? How do I combine rewards and punishments to maximize results? How do I tickle their greed and fear in the right combination? Such managers may have an inkling that they can neither buy nor intimidate inspired performance, but they still believe that they can coax extraordinary efforts through carrots and sticks.

But this is ludicrous. Imagine a thief pointing a gun at you and commanding, "Give me your respect! Your support! Your friendship!"

Great leaders, wherever they are in an organization, ask themselves: How do I inspire my team or organization to work in unison? How do I encourage each person to take full responsibility for his or her individual performance while, at the same time, make the right sacrifices to reach our company's goal? How do I integrate accountability and cooperation? How do I inspire my team or organization to accomplish great, lasting, amazing things? How do I reach beyond the operational issues, beyond profits and losses, into something better and more beautiful, something that all our stakeholders will not only support but also wholeheartedly love? How do I make my life and the lives of those around me truly meaningful?

Unfortunately, typical management techniques fail to address these questions effectively, even in the hands of the best leaders. Standard management tools don't help good leaders to prevent silos, fiefdoms, and interfunctional conflicts that kill teamwork. In fact, such tools hinder teamwork.

If you hope to be an inspiring leader, the first thing you must understand is that such leadership has nothing to do with formal authority; it has everything to do with *moral* authority. Hearts and minds cannot be bought or forced; they can only be deserved and earned. They are given only to worthy missions and trustworthy leaders. This applies not only to organizations but also to many other domains of human activity.

Consider the case of parental leadership. As a father-manager, I want my children to do their schoolwork before they play. I incentivize them by threatening to take away their iPhones if I see them using them before their work is done. I add a carrot to the stick, promising that if they finish their homework they get ice cream for dessert.

By contrast, as a father-leader, I don't just want my children to do their schoolwork. I want my children to *want* to do their schoolwork. I want them to do it because *they* want to do it, not because I want them to do it and can impose consequences on them. I want to instill in them healthy habits because I love them and because I know that a work discipline will enhance their lives. But my knowing that is not enough. I have to help *them* know it, and know it so deeply that they will internally commit to it, and make the hard choices required through their own will.

As a father-leader, I have to integrate autonomy and control according to a higher principle: love. (Notice that I wrote "integrate" and not "balance." You don't "balance" right and left turns when going from home to work; you turn right or left at any point of your route according to a higher principle, which is your destination.) Only when my children experience me as trustworthy, and as totally on their side, will they listen to me. Only when my children experience me as a role model, as practicing what I preach, will they believe me.

As a leader, you don't want your followers to do as they are told. This is because you can't know what they ought to do to most effectively help the team to win. And even if you did want them to obey, you'd also want them to put their discretionary effort and experience into winning. You want them to act with initiative, intelligence, and enthusiasm; you want them to truthfully reveal the opportunities and challenges they see in their surroundings; you want them to give their best to the organization, in concert with everyone else. You can't extract this behavior by force. It must be inspired by enthusiasm and love.

To elicit this internal commitment in your followers, you need to reach beyond operational issues, beyond profits and losses. You need to latch onto something better and more beautiful—something that all your stakeholders will not only support but also wholeheartedly love and embrace. You need to make your life and the lives of those around you truly meaningful.

To be a great leader, you must understand that searching for success is, paradoxically, the wrong way to achieve success. Success is like happiness; it cannot be pursued directly. The more directly you pursue happiness, the less likely you are to achieve it. Pursuing happiness directly may result in short-term hedonistic pleasure, but it does not lead to authentic, soul-satisfying happiness. To achieve success you must live a life of meaning and purpose. You must pursue significance, self-actualization, and self-transcendence—not just for you but also for everybody who works with you.

A great leader makes the following offer: "In addition to compensation and benefits, I will provide you with an opportunity to infuse your life with meaning. I will provide you with a platform on which you can build a personal and social sense of worth. This platform will enable you to prosper not only materially, but also emotionally, mentally, and spiritually: emotionally, because we will relate to you as one of us; mentally, because we will respect your intelligence; spiritually, because we will join in a project that transcends our small egos and connects us to a larger purpose.

10

"In exchange," such a leader proposes, "I want your unbridled enthusiasm. I ask that you give your utmost energy in service of our great project. I ask that you exemplify our values and culture and hold others accountable for doing the same, and that you relate to your teammates with kindness, compassion, and solidarity. I want you to subordinate your personal agenda and collaborate with your teammates, doing whatever it takes to help the team to win. I ask that you put your heart, mind, and soul into fulfilling the noble vision that animates all of us, aligning your efforts with the rest of the organization."

MY ARGUMENT

If you want to lead a truly successful and enduring organization, I've got this message for you: Well-harnessed inspiration, born of deep understanding and compassion for our human nature, is not just a fairy dust to sprinkle to make people feel good; it's the solution to the hardest problems in business and in society today. It answers the toughest questions: How can I align self-interested individuals in the pursuit of a common goal? How do I get people who are fundamentally interested in their own agendas (*my* issues, *my* to-do list, *my* agenda, *my* KPIs, *my* compensation) to cooperate with one another in pursuit of a shared purpose (*our* children, *our* customers, *our* collective future)? How do I get them to do their best to accomplish their individual missions, but also to subordinate their missions to the larger mission of the organization, so that the whole team wins? How do I incentivize them in a way that will make them more engaged? What can I, or the organization, offer them that will satisfy their deeper emotional needs, and give them a broader sense of commitment and purpose?

In this book, I will show you how to resolve the conflicting agendas of self-interest and organizational mission into something much richer, more satisfying, and enduring. I will show you how to mobilize an organization into becoming a source of lasting goodness in the world, creating an enormous sense of accomplishment, service, and joy in all those associated with it. To do this, I will show you how to confront your own personal issues and assume the truly "response-able" mantle of leadership, in a step-by-step, practical way. But I will go deeper: I will show you how to move past your own deepest fears and anxieties to live a truly heroic life. It is only through becoming a moral hero that you will earn the authority to inspire greatness in those around and under you.

The Meaning Revolution addresses two fundamental questions: why organizations lose and how they can win.

1. WHY DO ORGANIZATIONS LOSE?

The most difficult organizational problem is aligning self-interested members in pursuit of a common goal. I argue this cannot be done through economic incentives. If the organization incentivizes excellence and accountability, it will disincentivize alignment and cooperation. If the organization incentivizes alignment and cooperation, it will disincentivize excellence and accountability. Incentives for accountability foster silos. Incentives for cooperation reward free riders who don't contribute fully.

The second most difficult organizational problem is to get the right information to the right people at the right time, and in the right format, to make the right decisions. This cannot be done through formal communications because each member holds both private and detailed local knowledge about resources, costs, opportunities, and threats. Even if an organization were able to convince all its members to eschew their self-interest and fully reveal everything they know for the benefit of the whole, that knowledge would be too complex and unstructured to be useful. It can't be communicated to the decision makers in a format that lets them compare alternatives and make the right decision.

These problems can't truly be solved. But they *can* be managed. In fact, most leadership and managerial techniques try to do just that. But they do it poorly. They go only halfway and fail to use tools that can make a massive difference. But even though the situation facing leaders today may seem desperate, it is not serious. It reminds me of the joke about the two hikers who were walking through the woods when they noticed a bear charging toward them. The first hiker removed his trail boots and put on his running shoes. The second hiker despondently said, "Why bother changing out of your boots? You can't outrun a bear." The first hiker replied, "I don't have to outrun the bear. I only have to outrun you."

The good news is that to win in the marketplace you don't have to be perfect; you only have to be better than your competitors. I guarantee that any competitor you face will be plagued by exactly these same unsolvable problems. So the goal is not to solve them but to manage them more efficiently. As the popular saying goes, "In the land of the blind (materialist), the one-eyed man (who sees the other dimensions of human existence) is king."

2. HOW CAN ORGANIZATIONS, AND THE PEOPLE WITHIN THEM, WIN?

It's impossible to travel one hundred meters in no time. It's also impossible to perfectly align all organizational members in pursuit of a common goal and to take full advantage of their local knowledge. Winning the race requires adding a new set of tools to your kit, something that takes you and your organization where others can't go.

By becoming a transcendent leader, you can address the essential problems of incentives and information much, much better than most leaders do right now. Transcendent leadership relies on the inspirational power of nonmaterial incentives—employees' personal sense of meaning, achievement, and self-esteem, as well as shared values and ethics, and their desire to belong to a community. The transcendent leader invites people to join a project that infuses their lives with meaning and significance. Such a project promises to leave a mark in the world that will far transcend the lives of those who carried it through.

The nonmaterial goods that are the pillars of transcendent leadership have a rare combination of two properties that enable leaders to address organizational dilemmas in ways that money and perks can't touch.

First, moral and ethical goods are, in the words of economists, nonexclusive. This means that if we work in the same organization, my enjoyment of our noble purpose, ethical values, and close community does not take anything away (and it may even add) to your enjoyment of these boons. Contrast this, for example, to a bonus pool, where the allocation of a certain amount to you means that such an amount is not available to me. While material goods are always under a budget constraint and create rivalry due to scarcity, moral and ethical goods are unconstrained and create cohesion because they are founded in shared cultural norms. In this sense, they are like what economists call "public goods" such as national defense, a lighthouse, or fireworks.

Second, in contrast to public goods, moral and ethical goods are "excludable." This means that if you are not part of the organization, both formally and emotionally, these goods are unavailable to you. Contrast this, for example, to the national defense or the Internet that everyone relies upon. Excludability creates a sense of boundary that defines a community of like-minded members who share a purpose and a set of ethical values. This shared purpose fosters the cohesion of the organizational members in a better way than any material good. In this sense, moral goods are like what economists call "private goods," like the stuff we buy and sell in the marketplace.

Economists call excludable, nonexclusive goods "club goods." That's because once you are a member of "the club," you can enjoy them without taking anything away from the enjoyment of other members. But you have to become a member of the club to enjoy these goods.

Moral goods allow leaders to discriminate between mission-driven (missionary) and money-driven (mercenary) employees. By offering the right mix between material and nonmaterial incentives, you can appeal to different groups of potential employees.

Compensation is always a "package deal." Like an iceberg, salary and benefits are the visible part. But they comprise less than 15 percent of our motivation. Over 85 percent of the reason people are engaged in their work lies under the surface. And that part is composed of respect, care, integrity, a feeling of belonging, a sense of achievement, a noble purpose, and ethical principles.

Abraham Maslow, the acclaimed psychologist who described humankind's hierarchy of needs, claimed that once we have satisfied our basic needs for survival and security, like food and shelter, our highest desire is the feeling that our lives matter, that we can make a difference, that we can contribute to make the world a better place for those around us and those who will come after us. We all want to live, to love, and to leave a legacy. An engaging organization enables people to achieve all three. It is the ultimate club of happiness and enthusiasm.

A BRUSH WITH DEATH

On February 18, 2004, Mark Bertolini, a senior executive at the giant health insurance company Aetna, was skiing with his family in Killington, Vermont, when he lost control, bounced off a tree, hurtled down a ravine, and broke his neck.

Prior to the accident, Bertolini was quite fit, so he had a built-in resilience that helped him recover remarkably rapidly. But afterward he was in constant pain. His doctors prescribed traditional painkillers that he knew could have turned him into an addict, so he turned to the less conventional interventions of yoga, stretching, and meditation. He felt better, returned to work, and was then named chief executive.

Bertolini took to wearing a shiny metal amulet around his neck instead of a tie. The amulet is engraved with the Sanskrit characters "soham," which means, "I am That," a mantra used to help control breathing in meditation. It signifies a spiritual connection with the universe. Everywhere he goes in the company, people take notice of the amulet and admire the fortitude of their leader.

The new CEO decided that what had helped him heal so well would be good for his employees and customers, too, so he chose to use his company as a laboratory. Two hundred thirty-nine employees volunteered for an experiment: one-third practiced yoga, another third took a mindfulness class, and the rest were in a control group. At the end of three months, the employees in the yoga or the mindfulness class reported significant reduction in perceived stress and sleep difficulties; their blood work also showed a drop in stress hormones. "The biostatisticians were beside themselves," Mr. Bertolini said.

Later, when Mr. Bertolini reviewed Aetna's financial performance for 2012, he noticed something surprising: paid medical claims per employee had dropped 7.3 percent, saving roughly $9 million in costs. Because productivity grew, the company raised its minimum wage for hourly workers from $12 to $16 an hour, and the company reduced out-of-pocket health-care costs, too.

"If we can create a healthier you, we can create a healthier world and healthier company," Bertolini told employees, who took his words to heart. Feeling happier and more satisfied at work, they bore twice as hard into their mission because their death-touched leader had reached a deep understanding that goes beyond material incentives.[3]

This understanding went right to the heart of the transcendent purpose: the "I am That." My guess is that Bertolini is able to extend *agape* (the ancient Greek word for "compassionate love") to all his stakeholders, enacting the commandment "love thy brother as thyself," because he feels, deep in his bones, that they and he are one, as each one of them is also "That."

Imagine working for someone like Bertolini—a living, breathing symbol of this kind of near-death understanding, wearing that symbol on his neck. How does he compare to the leadership of the company you're working in now? What would it be like to be in the presence of such an inspiring person? (A big health insurance company has a big advantage in terms of vision; its raison d'être is sustaining life and health.) The question is: Do the people in your company, division, or team believe this? Or are many just working for their paychecks?

Bertolini has a much greater understanding of leadership than most leaders have because of his brush with death. He is no longer detached, nor is he beholden only to the financial numbers. He's thinking bigger—much, much bigger.

"I am That" means that we—all of us, from the CEO to the janitor—are expressions of "That"—an enormous, vital, animating force. When you learn to tap into that realization, as Bertolini has done—you become what I call a transcendent leader. What would it be like to be such a leader, breathing this rich understanding of the meaning of the world, translated in a way employees, managers, and customers can understand?

THE TRANSCENDENT LEADER

I believe the most deep-seated, unspoken, and universal anxiety in all of us is the fear that our life is being wasted. That death will surprise us when our song is still unsung. We worry not just about our physical death, but also, perhaps more significantly, our symbolic one. We are afraid that our lives won't matter, that we won't have made a difference, that we will leave no trace in this world after we are gone.

If you're young and healthy, you probably don't pay much attention yet to this anxiety. It remains as a kind of white noise in the background, like the faint hum from fluorescent office lights. Every once in a while, if you have just dodged a bullet as Mark Bertolini did, you might reflect on what this amazing gift of life is *for*. You may ask yourself: Why am I here? or What difference am I making? What will my legacy be?

If you are fortunate enough to confront these questions, you come to realize that every ticking second, every opportunity to do good in the time you have left, becomes more meaningful. You want to make the most of the precious time you have, appreciating beauty and creating joy. What you don't want to do is spend your days performing work that feels trivial or without purpose. You want to wake every morning feeling that you are making a difference in the world. Once you tap into this realization, I've found, your true nature is allowed to shine through. You have the ability and reason to become a transcendent leader. You breathe this rich understanding of what a life well lived really looks like out in the world. You inspire people around you to work with a new sense of possibility. You have the ability to illuminate the organization in a way that reveals its ultimate gift: meaning.

Transcendent leadership dissolves the hardest organizational problems in a liquid mix of significance, nobility, virtue, and solidarity. It offers a way for those who follow its principles to address the core existential anxiety of every human being. That's why a leader who proposes a symbolic "immortality project," as humanist Ernest Becker called it—a project of enduring value beyond one's life—has an amazing way to engage the best in us.

In the past, these immortality projects took the form of military and cultural campaigns based on the attitude that "we are better than you because we can defeat and enslave you." But in the free market, our goal is not to eliminate the competition; rather, it is to provide so much value to stakeholders that customers choose us over the competition; competitors either have to follow or risk being left behind. Due to the voluntary nature of transactions, the free market allows each party to "opt out" unless he or she feels he or she is gaining value. The only way to profit is to make other people profit or do better. It transforms self-interest into service, and imperialism into trade.

It takes a special kind of person to be a transcendent leader. Those who embrace such thinking don't necessarily have to have a brush with death, but they do need to have looked deeply within themselves to understand the existential anxiety at the core of every one of us. They must face their own fear of death in order to create a significant and beneficent immortality project—a service-driven organizational mission that employees wholeheartedly commit to. Leaders must find their true selves through a "hero's journey" and share their hard-earned personal awareness with others, with humility, wisdom, and compassion.

Transcendent leaders work to align the individual purposes of those under them into a larger collective purpose that makes each individual larger as well. They understand that if you want to make accountability and cooperation occur at the same time, you need to inspire people and create a culture of commitment and connection to a larger purpose. When this happens, people look beyond their silos and their small decision-making issues. They align their best efforts with the organization's in natural ways that other systems can't lead them to do. It is the difference between rowing and sailing. A boat moved by mere muscle is no match for one moved by wind. A boat propelled by the wind flows in harmony with the natural forces. An organization that moves forward by formal authority is like a rowboat. One moved by a transcendent purpose is like a sailboat with the wind behind it, filling its sails.

Transcendent leaders are rare. But they do exist (and I profile a number of them in this book). They inspire followers not by relying on carrots and sticks (offering a nice salary, bonus, and tangible perks, or threatening them with demotion or firing them) but by appealing to the belief that they have spent their waking time doing some good in the world.

Transcendent leaders tend to be self-effacing. They embrace Lao Tzu's lesson: "The wicked leader is he whom the people despise. The good leader is he whom the people revere. The great leader is he of whom the people say, 'We did it ourselves.'" They encourage and empower their people to follow the mission, rather than themselves. In fact, I would argue that *the truly transcendent leader has no followers*—a point I'll return to later.

Companies and other organizations can become houses of meaning constructed on foundations of benevolence, service, and love. I believe this is the ultimate source of economic value. Connecting people to their highest purpose at work solves the biggest, hardest problem there is for those who work for organizations (how to achieve symbolic immortality), for organizations (how to align employee's self-interests in pursuit of a shared goal), for societies (how to foster peace, prosperity, and progress), and for humanity (how to coexist in tolerance and mutual respect and avoid conflict and self-destruction).

Transcendent leadership demands that we have the ability to look deeply inward—beginning with recognizing our own inevitable mortality—and the self-discipline to embody the principles that inspire others to passionate commitment. (I offer a sobering warning in this book, too. If you attempt to motivate people through high-minded talk without actually becoming a living example, your followers will end up cynical, disengaged, and angry.) I ask you to inspire others through a common purpose, a strong set of ethical principles, a community of like-minded people, a feeling of unconditional empowerment, and a passionate drive to achieve. These are not easy tasks, but meaning has nothing to do with ease.

HAPPINESS OR MEANING?

The pursuit of happiness and the search for meaning are two central motivations in every person's life. Both are essential to well-being and flourishing, yet only the latter is distinctively human. As the psychologist Roy Baumeister points out, "(We) resemble many other creatures in their striving for happiness, but the quest for meaning is a key part of what makes us human, and uniquely so."[4]

Happiness and meaning often build on each other, but not always. Living a meaningful life is different from, and can even be opposed to, being happy. Take the "parenthood paradox," for example. Parents of grown-up children may say that they are very happy they've *had* them, but parents who are still living with children score low on happiness. It seems that raising kids decreases happiness but increases meaning.[5] Or consider emergency volunteers, who often go through great ordeals and traumatic experiences in order to help those afflicted by accidents or natural catastrophes. Suffering negative emotions for the sake of a noble purpose brings meaning to their lives, but it doesn't make them happy.

What's the difference? Happiness, understood as pleasure and positive feelings, has more to do with satisfying your needs and getting what you want. Meaning, understood as significance and positive impact, is related to developing a personal identity and acting with purpose and principles. You might find that you feel happy if you find that your life is easy and you have achieved a measure of success, but you may not feel that your life has much meaning. On the other hand, reflecting about the past and the future, confronting adversity, and start-ing a family increase meaningfulness but not necessarily happiness. Higher levels of meaningfulness are related to deep thinking, which is connected to higher levels of worry, stress, and anxiety. However, meaning is associated with adaptation capabilities such as persever-ance, gratitude, and emotional expression.[6]

Meaning has two major components: making sense of life (cogni-tion) and having a sense of purpose (motivation). The cognitive com-ponent involves integrating experiences into a coherent narrative as if it were a story, taking a third-person perspective on one's life. The mo-tivational component involves actively pursuing long-term goals that reflect one's identity and transcend narrow self-interests. We are most satisfied when we engage in meaningful pursuits and virtuous activities that align with our best self. [7]

"Happiness without meaning characterizes a relatively shallow, self-absorbed, or even selfish life, in which things go well, needs and desire are easily satisfied, and difficult or taxing entanglements are avoided," wrote Baumeister. "If anything, pure happiness is linked to not helping others in need."[8] While being happy is about feeling good, meaning is derived from helping others or contributing to society. Yet what would you prefer to have written on your tombstone, "Here lies (your name), who strived to make his/her life happy by getting what he/she wanted," or "Here lies (your name), who strived to make the world a better place by giving what those around him/her needed"?

According to Gallup,[9] nearly 60 percent of all Americans felt happy, without a lot of stress or worry, in 2012. On the other hand, accord-ing to the Center for Disease Control,[10] about 40 percent of Americans have not discovered a satisfying life purpose or have a sense of what would make their lives meaningful—half of them (that is, 20 percent of American adults) suffer anxiety and depression disorders. Research has shown that having purpose and meaning in life increases overall well-being and life satisfaction, improves mental and physical health, enhances resiliency and self-esteem, and decreases the chances of de-pression. In contrast, the single-minded pursuit of happiness makes people less happy.[11]

As companies compete for talent, they try to give employees what they want, to make them happy: higher salaries, lower stress, more benefits, and fewer difficulties. But this strategy generally backfires. As the psychiatrist Viktor Frankl wrote, "The greatest task for any person is to find meaning in his or her own life." Most people divert their energy into trying to be happy, but "(i)t is the very pursuit of happiness that thwarts happiness."[12] What people really want, what makes us truly happy in the long term is not pleasure but meaning. And meaning is the offer of a transcendent leader.

WHO IS FRED KOFMAN?

Thirty years ago, after earning a degree and becoming a professor of economic development at the University of Buenos Aires, I came to the United States as a graduate student. At UC Berkeley, I focused on the economic theory of incentives as my field of specialization. At the end of my studies I took a job as assistant professor of management accounting and control at MIT's Sloan School of Management. My teaching and research there focused on the design and implementation of performance evaluation and reward systems. Thanks to MIT's strong ties with industry, I had extraordinary opportunities to collaborate with some of the most innovative companies in the world.

During my years in academia, I tried to solve the fundamental problem of organizations: that is, how to integrate individual accountability with group cooperation through financial incentives. I fulfilled my PhD requirements and achieved awards as "outstanding student instructor" at Berkeley's Economics Department and "teacher of the year" at MIT. I also received many requests from companies to consult for them in this area. But throughout the years I came to understand that such integration couldn't be just mathematical. The solution to the hardest organizational problem must also be spiritual; it needs to engage the "animating force" that gives human life purpose and meaning. So as a mathematician I failed; but I failed splendidly. My failure brought me to the unconventional path that gave my life a deeper meaning and has led me to write this book.

Thanks to my mentor Peter Senge, author of the groundbreaking book *The Fifth Discipline*, I began teaching leadership workshops for corporations such as General Motors, Chrysler, Shell, and Citibank. My work was well received, and I found that I enjoyed interacting with business leaders more than I did with MBA students—the former had been humbled by reality, while the latter still thought that management wisdom came from books and case studies. So after six years, I quit MIT and founded Axialent, a consulting company that, at its height, employed 150 people in seven offices around the world.

Ten years ago, I published a book called *Conscious Business: How to Build Value Through Values*. My purpose was to compile what I had learned about what anybody who works in an organization needs to know. That book, translated into a dozen languages, went on to sell more than a hundred thousand copies, and I have been told that it has inspired leaders around the world. Since then, I've thought much more deeply about what it takes to create and lead a conscious business. As a consultant, I've talked to a lot of managers, senior executives, and CEOs in companies all over the world about what it's like to be a conscious leader, and about how to address the most difficult organizational problems.

I left my consulting company in 2013 to join LinkedIn as vice president of executive development and leadership philosopher. My job at LinkedIn is to help the company to accomplish its mission of "connecting the world's professionals to make them more productive and successful." I do this by helping employees at all levels in the managerial hierarchy to develop into "transcendent" leaders—ethical leaders who wake up to their own sense of meaning and call others to pursue a larger, nobler purpose. I then help these leaders to inspire others to work cooperatively in the pursuit of that purpose, and to stay aligned in the face of competing commitments. It's an unusual job, even in an unusual place like Silicon Valley.

My approach to leadership training has very little to do with the standard things taught in business school—or any other school, for that matter. Instead, it asks that each one of us take a very long, hard, honest look in an existential mirror. It is part economics and business theory, part communications and conflict resolution, part family counseling and systems therapy, and part mindfulness and meditation.

Too many people feel that meaningful work is the province of non-profit organizations. I disagree. While we can help others and allevi-ate suffering through volunteerism or nonprofit work, I believe nothing holds a candle to economic development as a way to eradicate poverty and bring humanity to a higher level of prosperity, peace, and happi-ness. Entrepreneurs who behave ethically are the engines that propel the growth of humanity, creating value to all their stakeholders. That's what conscious business, and transcendent leadership, are all about.

WHAT IS "THE MEANING REVOLUTION"?

In *The Structure of Scientific Revolutions*, the physicist, historian, and philosopher Thomas Kuhn argued that normal science happens in pe-riods where there is an accepted paradigm that organizes the research. Over the course of this period, insoluble puzzles or anomalies crop up. Science then enters a revolutionary period in which scientists ask new questions, move beyond the mere problem solving of the previous paradigm, and change their mental models to point research in a new direction.

In economics, there is a puzzle involving two approaches to in-centives. From a "systems perspective," individuals must subordinate their local objectives to cooperate toward a global objective. Therefore, a manager should use *global* incentives. For example, a sales manager should compensate each salesperson as a function of the sales of the whole salesforce rather than his or her own sales. This will avoid raising artificial barriers between "my" customers and "your" customers, since they are all "the company's customers."

From a "principal-agent perspective," individuals must be account-able for the results of their work. Therefore, a manager should use *local* incentives. For example, a sales manager should compensate each sales-person as a function of his or her own individual sales. This will encour-age every salesperson to put their maximum effort without attempting to "free ride" on the effort of others and attract the best salespeople.

Economists have mathematically proved both systems theory and principal-agent theory. The problem is that the practical implications of these two theories are mutually incompatible. They cannot both be implemented simultaneously, and trying to combine them half and half is worse than either of them.

I propose to resolve this puzzle through nonmaterial incentives. *The Meaning Revolution* explores a paradigm shift from matter to mean-ing; from compensation, command, and control to purpose, principle, and people; from management to leadership. I propose that rather than seeing employees as machinelike entities driven by material incentives, you need to see them as conscious beings who want to achieve signifi-cance and to transcend their limited existence through projects that give meaning to their lives.

This book is about the work of going beyond being what I called a "conscious" leader in *Conscious Business* to become a "transcendent" leader. Although I provide some very practical advice throughout, I hold that transcendent leadership supersedes average managerial pre-scriptions because it is not only a way to *do* leadership or a way to *know* how to lead, but it is a way to *be* a leader who inspires followers to find what is most precious in their lives and commit to manifesting it.

There is no shortage of business books advising leaders at all levels how to get things done—how to organize change, hire the right people, execute strategy, and so on. They all offer good advice. But they miss something fundamental about the human condition, making them more suitable for operational managers than for genuine leaders. The very question of "How do you . . . ?" is managerial. The greater leader-ship question is "Who are you?"

Leadership emerges from our human need to make our lives mean-ingful. Nobody wants their accomplishments to just be a "flash in the pan." We all want to extend ourselves, touch others' lives, and have im-pact on the world; we want to rise above our physical limitations, even death, by participating in a transcendent project. But books about the importance of finding meaning are typically found in the self-help or the spirituality sections of the bookstore—not the most popular ones among business leaders. In addition, these books don't deal with the most fundamental and insoluble problems of personal accountability and organizational alignment in organizations. They do not address the basic questions of what inner and outer work you actually have to do to become the kind of leader whom people passionately want to follow, or what it takes to build a truly inspired workplace. How can we build a real, honest, human foundation for an enterprise—one that is so trustworthy that people will give just about anything to be part of it? And then, when everyone is committed, how do you work together effectively to win as a team?

In **Part 1,** I present the hardest problems any leader must solve if his or her organization or team is to survive and thrive. These are the Kuhnian anomalies that bring about the meaning revolution.

In **Chapter 2, "Disengagement,"** I discuss why most people lose their souls in the business world. I explain how the materialistic, produce-earn-consume view of work misses the most important dimensions of human existence. I argue that the most destructive organizational problems cannot be solved through the one-dimensional world of materialism alone.

In **Chapter 3, "Disorganization,"** I ask, Why can't organizations align their members in pursuit of a common goal? Here, I describe three issues: (1) most people are confused about what their "real" jobs are; (2) when everyone performs at his or her best, the organization often does not perform at its best; and (3) economic incentives designed to encourage cooperation work to discourage accountability—and vice versa.

In **Chapter 4, "Disinformation,"** I argue that nobody really knows the best way to proceed. I show how most people falsely evaluate costs and benefits from their limited perspectives. This leads them to make decisions that hurt the organization's performance. But even if they get over this hurdle and try to assess the global impact of alternative courses of action, they still miss the most important information: opportunity costs.

In **Chapter 5, "Disillusion,"** I issue a three-part warning for those who embark on the path of transcendent leadership: (1) what you do speaks so loudly that people in your organization will not hear what you say; (2) people will be hypersensitive and hypercritical—no matter how hard you try to walk your talk, you will be found wanting; (3) power corrupts—the more you try to inspire people, the more likely you'll betray them. If you fall into any of these three traps, you will poison the very culture you are trying to nourish.

In **Part 2,** I offer "soft," people-centered solutions to the hard organizational problems I present in Part 1.

In **Chapter 6, "Motivation,"** I argue that the hardest problems have a spiritual solution. How can you inspire accountability and cooperation at the same time? I demonstrate that while it's impossible to simultaneously incentivize accountability and cooperation through purely economic means, it is possible to inspire them through nonmaterial means.

In **Chapter 7, "Culture,"** I describe forces that leaders at every level must harness if they are to align their teams to win. I show how leaders can shape their organizations by defining, demonstrating, demanding, and delegating principled norms. A strong culture is built upon virtues such as wisdom, compassion, courage, justice, and love. Such virtues give leaders at all levels, as well as their followers and teams, the capacity to transcend their egocentric views and integrate multiple perspectives into a comprehensive worldview.

In **Chapter 8, "Response-Ability,"** I show how what I call absolute "response-ability" and accountability are an effective philosophy of business, and life. Assuming responsibility as a leader, and holding people accountable for their own choices, allows you to turn defensive behaviors into creative ones, and feelings of resignation and resentment into enthusiasm and commitment.

In **Chapter 9, "Collaboration,"** I show how even the most intractable conflicts can be solved through "escalating collaboration." This is an alignment process that allows intelligent discussion of trade-offs and rational decision making. In a system based on similar principles to those of British common law, leaders in the organization can let their decisions set precedents about their perspective that will guide future decisions at all levels of the organization.

In **Chapter 10, "Integrity,"** I show how honoring one's word is as critical as honesty for effective relationships, both in business and in life in general. A person with integrity keeps her promises whenever possible and still honors them if she is unable to do so. You make a grounded promise by committing only to deliver what you believe you can deliver. You keep the promise by delivering it. And you can still honor the promise when you can't keep it by letting the person you are promising know of the situation, and by taking care of the consequences.

In **Part 3,** I explain why the leader who wants to become transcendent must go beyond what I describe in Part 2. To marshal fervent followership, the leader must undertake what the mythologist Joseph Campbell called "the hero's journey."

In **Chapter 11, "Get Over Yourself,"** I turn around the traditional idea of leaders empowering their followers. I claim that followers empower leaders by committing to the mission a leader proposes. Perhaps the most important decision every human being must make is where to invest his or her precious time, his or her precious life. Followers "energize" leaders with their life force, just as investors energize a company with their capital.

In **Chapter 12, "Die Before You Die,"** I take a deep dive into the universal fear of death. I show why confronting that anxiety in yourself and others is the most important and useful leadership tool there is. Paraphrasing Zen wisdom, I claim that you must "die before you die, so you can truly live"—and *truly lead*. You must find what's unborn and undying in yourself and offer this as a mirror of meaning to those around you. I also show how the desire to be part of an immortality project is an open secret of leadership that historians, poets, and philosophers have mined from time immemorial.

In **Chapter 13, "Be a Hero,"** I explore the development path of leaders. The journey of the leader is fraught with trials that reveal, test, and sharpen his or her spirit. There's a natural pattern to human growth. It is a trajectory from unconsciousness to consciousness to superconsciousness. It is a process that forces you to face your biggest fears, find your greatest strengths, with the help of allies, and win the battle to shape your destiny and become the master of your life. Only after you have walked the path of the hero and vanquished your shadows can you bring the gift of true wisdom to your community. Only when you have found your deepest truth can you become a model for others and inspire trust.

In **Chapter 14, "Superconscious Capitalism,"** I explain that the market is a crucible that transforms self-interest into service, aggression into competition. This crucible is made of respect for the life, liberty, and property of others. If people respect one another, if transactions are voluntary and peaceful, then each participant must believe that he or she gains more than he or she surrenders. Adam Smith argued that even when the social good is not part of anybody's plans, market forces act "like an invisible hand" that shepherds people toward such a goal. I argue that rather than doing this by accident, transcendent leaders do it on purpose. Through respect, freedom, and service, they bring about a new, more conscious type of capitalism. This enlightened economic system fosters social cooperation and supports the development of humanity like nothing ever has before. Beyond fulfilling the material needs of human beings, it addresses our spiritual needs for transcendence and connection to something more permanent than ourselves.

In the **Epilogue, "What to Do on Monday Morning,"** I bring everything full circle, summarizing the book's essential lessons and advising leaders at all levels what to do on Monday morning, and beyond. It is my great hope that readers come away from this book inspired and empowered to make a lasting mark on the world—not only for themselves but also for those who follow them, for their organizations, and for the larger world.

And now, I invite you to join the revolution.

PART 1
HARD PROBLEMS

Chapter 2
DISENGAGEMENT

WHAT'S THE POINT OF WORKING?

> If management views workers not as valuable, unique individuals but as tools to be discarded when no longer needed, then employees will also regard the firm as nothing more than a machine for issuing paychecks, with no other value or meaning.
>
> —Mihaly Csikszentmihalyi

Marissa Mayer was a successful executive at Google before she became CEO of Yahoo in the summer of 2012. Although she was recruited to reinvigorate a dying digital brand, Yahoo still had a lot going for it when she arrived: the digital ad market was booming; the board welcomed her with a happy and cooperative attitude; the company had lots of cash and a billion monthly visitors.

But Mayer was in over her head. Within four years, Yahoo's finances dwindled, and it was finally announced the company would be sold off to Verizon in what *Forbes* called "the saddest $5 billion deal in tech history."[1] (Ultimately, the deal was sealed for $4.48 billion, about $350 million less than the original offer.[2]) Observers attribute this debacle to Mayer's incoherent strategy and her mercurial micromanagement style. "Mayer's legacy at Yahoo may be as the CEO who drove it into a fire sale," *Variety* declared.[3]

Forbes columnist Miguel Helft described an October 2015 off-site meeting for 120 of Yahoo's top executives that went "downhill fast" when the topic turned to employee engagement. "While Mayer was in and out of the room, Bryan Power, Yahoo's head of H.R., presented results from a recent employee survey that showed dramatic double-digit drops in metrics like morale and trust in the company's executive leadership. Various vice presidents began venting to one another, ending in outright heckling when another session—billed as an opportunity to improve communication—turned into a lecture from Yahoo's top brass that many found patronizing. Vice presidents started calling out their superiors for 'not listening,' 'not understanding' and 'not being interested in changing.' Some cursed. 'It was the most stressful and acrimonious professional meeting I've ever attended,' said one participant."[4]

Mayer's biggest mistake as a CEO was perhaps what *Forbes* contributor Mike Mayatt identified as a failure to understand Yahoo's culture, which he claims grew toxic under her leadership. "What Mayer has failed to grasp is that you cannot transform a culture you do not understand," Mayatt wrote. "A corporate culture is a fragile ecosystem with many interdependent mechanisms that must be nurtured in order to thrive. A strong culture is a performance accelerant capable of creating huge shifts in momentum."[5]

The problem with disengaging leaders like Mayer is that they don't just damage their organizations. Beyond that, everybody grows a little more skeptical of our institutions and their leaders, eroding social trust—without which an economy cannot function.

I met Marissa Mayer when she was at Google, before she went to Yahoo. At the time, I was consulting for Sheryl Sandberg, who was then Google's head of online sales and operations. Talking with Mayer was an eerie experience; in the hour-long conversation, she didn't make eye contact with me a single time. The interaction was so cold that I suffered from brain freeze. I do recall my thought at the end, though: *I would never work for this lady.* I couldn't engage with Mayer—or any organization she led. Her emotional disconnection would make it impossible for me to give my best. (This was in stark contrast with my feelings for Sheryl, who is both a friend and one of the best leaders I've ever met. I admire Sheryl's combination of personal warmth and professional acumen. While Mayer's brilliance is like a blue star in a faraway galaxy, Sheryl's is like an orange sun nearby.)

It's not that leaders like Mayer aren't smart and committed or don't want to do the right thing. (I recall being quite impressed by her intelligence and determination.) It's just that they have emotional blocks and intellectual misconceptions about what their most important job is—eliciting people's internal commitment to accomplish the organizational mission with effectiveness and integrity so that the team wins. As Harvard Business School professor Teresa Amabile has warned senior executives, "You may think that your job is developing a killer strategy. But you have a second, equally important task: enabling the ongoing engagement . . . of the people who strive to execute that strategy."[6]

Leadership is not a position; it is a process. Anyone who manages people, from a first-line supervisor to the CEO, and even anyone who coordinates people informally, needs to lead to be effective. People are not just "resources" that can be managed like other inanimate things. They are conscious beings who need to be inspired to contribute their best toward the organizational goals. Human beings require their own special kind of management.

As I was explaining this in a leadership seminar for a chemical company, a participant (who I later learned held PhDs in physics, chemistry, and chemical engineering) raised his hand. "I love molecules!" Boris (not his real name) exclaimed with humorous exasperation. Everyone looked puzzled. He went on: "Molecules are so well behaved. You apply a certain amount of heat and a certain amount of pressure to them, and you know exactly what they are going to do." We all laughed.

"The problem," he went on, "is that I did so well managing molecules that they promoted me to manage people. I don't get people; they are not well behaved. You apply a certain amount of heat and a certain amount of pressure, and you never know what they are going to do." Boris wanted to deal with people in the same way he dealt with molecules. It doesn't work. In contrast to molecules, people have minds of their own.

Like Boris, too many managers with scientific training miss this essential fact. According to the economist Murray Rothbard, these leaders practice not science but "scientism." "Scientism," Rothbard wrote, "is the profoundly unscientific attempt to transfer the methodology of the physical sciences to the study of human action." When we assume that conscious human beings can be as mechanically determined as molecules or other things that lack consciousness, we make a terrible mistake. "To ignore this primordial fact about the nature of man—to ignore his volition, his free will," Rothbard insisted, "is to misconstrue the facts of reality and therefore to be profoundly and radically unscientific."[7]

Even those managers who have some understanding of human nature and have the best intentions are not great as leaders. This is understandable: while they've been well trained in the technical dimension of management, they've been poorly trained in the human one. They don't know how to deal with these beings who have minds of their own. Despite their MBAs and executive education courses, they don't know how to win hearts and minds. So they fall into tunnel vision and narcissism. They rely on task-oriented, command-and-control directives, particularly in times of stress. They believe that soft skills matter less than their hard, cognitive ones, which they use as a bulwark against deeper, more introspective work.

This is not just a business phenomenon. Nonprofit organizations with noble purposes, such as hospitals, schools, and charities, are also burdened with managers who focus on the trivial and petty. They treat people badly; they fail to listen. They play politics, dragging people into the mud, casting blame instead of listening and taking responsibility for their behavior. They collect their paychecks and hold on until retirement. When such people are in power, the organization wilts. Everyone takes note, from janitors to executives. Employees shrug their shoulders and say, "If the boss can act like a jerk, why should I give a damn?" Cynicism and apathy set in like a virus. The infected organization dies off slowly, thanks to the leaders' ignorance and selfishness.

Such leaders can't possibly inspire others because they haven't bothered to look deeply into themselves and develop respect and compassion for others. They've lost their souls. Worse yet, they have turned into soul-eating zombies who undermine the people who work in their organizations. The only protection against them is disengagement.

THE TRAGEDY OF DISENGAGEMENT

According to the Gallup Organization, the news on the work front is sobering. For more than thirty years, Gallup has run in-depth behavioral economic research on more than twenty-five million employees across hundreds of U.S. organizations. Year after year since 2000, the percentage of those people who feel "actively engaged"—those with the most innovative ideas, who create most of a company's new customers, and who sparkle with the most entrepreneurial energy—hovers right below 30 percent. Another 50 percent of "disengaged" employees simply check out.

Engaged employees are emotionally committed to the organization and its goals. They care deeply about their work and their company. They are willing to put their discretionary effort in the service of the company's goals. They don't just work for a paycheck, or for a promotion, but for the organization's purpose—a purpose that they've made their own.

A story about Christopher Wren, the great architect who designed St. Paul's Cathedral in London, illustrates the difference between disengaged and engaged workers. One day, Wren was walking among the men working on the cathedral. Nobody recognized him. When Wren asked one of the workmen what he was doing, the man replied, "I am cutting a piece of stone." Putting the same question to another worker, the man replied, "I am earning five shillings two pence a day." When Wren asked a third man what he was doing, the man answered, "I am helping Sir Christopher Wren to build a beautiful cathedral."[8]

Then there is another, more dangerous group of employees in terms of the health of the organization—the actively disengaged ones, who compose the bottom 20 percent of Gallup's annual survey. Such people aren't just unhappy at work; they are busy acting out their unhappiness, undermining their coworkers and criticizing the organization. These workers feel so hostile that they're willing to resort to conscious or unconscious organizational sabotage. They become "detractors" who spread their negative feelings throughout the company and beyond.[9] Active disengagement costs the United States an estimated $450 to $550 billion annually.

Gallup has found that the workplaces where employees feel disengaged suffer nearly 50 percent more accidents and are responsible for nearly 60 percent more quality defects and incur much higher healthcare costs.[10] Moreover, 60 percent of millennials—the chunk of the U.S. workforce you would think has the most ideas and energy to offer—are disengaged, too. Gallup found that just 14 percent of millennials surveyed "strongly agree" that the mission or purpose of their company makes them feel their job is important.[11] Picture trying to cook in an oven with a crack through which it loses 85 percent of its heat, and you will have a mental image of the state of most companies today.

By contrast, Gallup has noted, work groups that are in the top quartile on the employee-engagement scale perform much better than those in the lowest quartile. Their customer ratings are 10 percent higher.[12] Their profitability and productivity as a group are 22 and 21 percent higher, respectively. They see at least 25 percent less turnover—in organizations where there is low turnover to begin with, engaged work groups experience as much as 65 percent less turnover. Highly engaged groups experience less absenteeism, and their work has fewer defects and safety incidents, too.[13]

The yearly losses around the world due to the engagement gap are in the trillions. According to Gallup's most recent State of the Global Workplace report, only 13 percent of employees worldwide are engaged at work;[14] the rest couldn't give a damn. Add it all up, and you have an astronomical waste of resources. On the other hand, engagement presents a gigantic opportunity to improve economic value for all stakeholders through greater productivity, efficiency, and service.

It's no wonder, then, that organizations everywhere are trying to increase engagement through all sorts of "engagement programs." The problem is that most of these programs are superficial, phony, hypocritical, and based on coarse manipulation of people's sensibilities to extract more from them.

Most of these programs center on an employee survey performed by the department of human resources. The survey leads to a flurry of activity, mostly composed of elaborate presentations. Writing in *Inc.*, a consultant named Les McKeown noted that "So-called employee engagement programs are misbegotten, unwieldy, ineffective rolling caravans of impractical or never-going-to-be-implemented PowerPoint presentations, usually spawned from an equally bankrupt exercise in so-called 'benchmarking' against alleged 'best practices' in other companies."[15] Sometimes these presentations turn into training programs that are evaluated on the basis of how many "heads" have gone through them—regardless of whether the owners of these heads were really present and learned anything that they actually put in practice to increase engagement.

To make matters worse, if a company really does implement a change based on an engagement survey, the results are generally counterproductive. Employees engage when they feel that their managers genuinely care about them, and when they believe that these managers want to provide a work environment that will promote not just their productivity, but also their connections with others and their personal well-being.

By contrast, if employees suspect that the changes aim to improve the company's ranking in the Gallup survey, or a manager's ranking in the company, they will disengage even more. When managers who for years have treated people as "less-than-human resources" suddenly adopt the superficial behaviors that they think will make them seem caring, more people feel manipulated. Employees see managers' claims of "we really care about you" as attempts to gain their favor through emotional treats, just like a dog trainer would do to his animal.

Imagine that your spouse gives you a surprise present for the first time in ten years of marriage without any explanation. The following week, you get a "spousal engagement" survey in the mail that asks,

"Have you received a present from your spouse in the last month?" Personally, I might suspect that my spouse was only doing so to raise his or her status in the survey.

Worse yet, any insincere managerial commitment has about the same staying power as a New Year's resolution that goes by the wayside in mid-January. Once the shiny new program loses its luster, managerial behaviors revert back to their previous state. But the organization's health and employee engagement tends to drop far below where it used to be after this yo-yo diet. When a leader comes across as a phony, making hypocritical attempts to manipulate people's sensibilities, such behavior is not just disengaging; it's enraging.

There's no way to open the future without closing the past. Unless the company's leadership does a serious examination of their previous disengaging behaviors, and convinces the workforce that they are committed to change that behavior in a serious way, any engagement program is dead on arrival. That's why, despite all the time, energy, and money spent on engagement programs, the statistics continue to be terrible. Engagement programs create the exact opposite results to the ones intended; every year the worldwide workforce is more disengaged.

THE DISENGAGING LEADER

A coaching client of mine—I'll call him "Bill"—told me a sad tale of how he became disengaged with his company. Bill traveled regularly across the world to lead a project in the Far East. "Before this project," Bill told me, "I had a pretty good relationship with my boss, the vice president of international operations. But something changed when I took on this assignment. The CEO had begun paying special attention to me, calling me directly, often bypassing my boss." Bill suspected his boss resented being out of the loop.

In one of his trips, Bill experienced severe stomach problems. He conducted his business meetings like a trouper; nobody noticed the pain he was in. But at the end of the day, he had to excuse himself from dinner and go to the hospital. There he saw a doctor who, after running some tests, diagnosed him with a bacterial infection. The doctor gave Bill antibiotics and, being the can-do kind of fellow Bill is, he went back to work the next day.

After the hospital visit, Bill sent his assistant the invoice for the emergency care to be processed for reimbursement. The bill came to less than $500, which he thought was quite reasonable. The next thing he saw was an e-mail from his boss (who had to approve the expense) asking his assistant (cc'ing Bill and the person in charge of benefits) to submit the expense as a claim to the insurance company. This reply was icily correct. What shocked Bill was not what it said, but what it didn't say: No "Hi Bill," no "You okay?" No nothing.

After the seven-day run of antibiotics, the infection was gone and Bill was back in physical shape. But he never recovered his emotional shape. "What absolutely floored me," Bill told me, "was that nobody in the e-mail chain wrote to ask me why I had to go to an emergency room in a foreign country and whether I was all right, let alone send me good wishes. There was only that terse business-like message about processing the insurance claim.

"I didn't get angry-hot; I got detached-cold," Bill reflected. "My thought was, 'These people are as dead to me as I'm dead to them.' First, I became totally numb and then mightily pissed off. I can't believe this company takes pride in 'treating people wonderfully,' as they stridently tell the whole world through their marketing campaigns, and when I'm in a health crisis, they treat me as a piece of machinery that needs to be repaired under warranty."

Bill reminded me of a movie clip I had shown in one of my workshops. In the movie *Modern Times*, Charlie Chaplin is a worker on an assembly line whose only job is to torque bolts with a wrench in each hand. Under tremendous pressure from the assembly line speed (constantly increased by "the boss"), he suffers a mental breakdown and is, literally, "processed" by the machines.[16]

"They displayed no feelings for me," Bill said. "They just wanted to process the insurance claim and move on. I felt like a cog in a machine; just another brick in the wall."

Against my advice, Bill gave up. He was so disengaged that he didn't even want to address the issue. "I don't want to talk about it," he told me. "What's the point in telling them that I'm disappointed that they didn't inquire about my health after they learned I was in a hospital in a foreign country? They'd come up with some lame excuse and pretend to be concerned. But that's too little too late. There are some common decencies I expect to receive from my manager without having to ask for them."

Although nothing materially affected Bill, he turned from engaged to actively disengaged, from promoter to detractor. "If someone asked me today if I'd recommend the company to a friend as a good place to work, I'd say 'absolutely not.'"

I don't know Bill's boss, but from his story I bet this VP was also disengaged—in fact, six months later, Bill told me the VP had also left the company. He may have been hurt by the fact that the CEO bypassed him to connect with Bill. I don't know the CEO, either, but I bet that he thought nothing of communicating directly with Bill. And I bet further that Bill's manager never told the CEO that he resented being bypassed. In fact, I'm sure that if the CEO asked Bill's boss if he minded, the VP would have lied and said, "Not at all." I've seen this story play out hundreds of times in the organizations I've worked with.

It is impossible to engage others if you yourself are disengaged. Research shows that emotions spread like the flu.[17] If you're depressed and unmotivated, I'm likely to feel depressed and unmotivated when I work with you. Any manager in the organization can start a chain reaction that alienates a large number of employees. And in organizational life, there are constant small, everyday frustrations that, left unaddressed, coalesce into thick layers of numbness that smother even the most passionate commitment. Imagine what happens when the majority of an organization, from a small team to a society, feels that way.

A bad manager is a great liability. Bill began quietly sending his résumé around and soon found a job at another company. The compensation and benefits were no better, but he left anyway, looking for an environment that he thought would be more conducive to his well-being. Bill's case is one of millions. People feel so helpless that they've stopped even trying to make things better.

Gallup argues that if companies want to engage their workers, they need to "focus on putting high-performing managers in place."[18] But where, oh where, are these so-called high-performing managers? I've worked with thousands of people in dozens of organizations over the years, and I can tell you that high-performing leaders—if we're talking about inspirational, truly engaging ones—are rarer than white tigers.

So here is the puzzle: If engagement is so crucial to organizational performance, and if the strategies to produce it are so simple and inexpensive, why aren't there more engaging leaders, and why aren't more companies dramatically increasing employee engagement?

My conclusion, to paraphrase the Beatles, is because "you can't buy love."

LEARNED HELPLESSNESS

During a visit to Angkor Wat, I treated my children to an elephant ride. As we prepared to climb onto the back of our elephant, we noticed that there were several others whose front right legs were tethered to a stake by only a thin rope. It was obvious that these powerful animals could easily break the ropes or uproot the stakes, but they didn't. They stayed quietly in their place. I asked our guide how they managed to keep the elephants tied by such flimsy contraptions.

He explained that when the elephants are young their handlers use a similar rope to tie them to stakes. Since they are small, that is enough to keep them from walking away. At first the elephant tries to walk off, but eventually it learns that such efforts are futile. So it just stays put, even when it grows strong enough to free itself. The elephant knows that it is trapped, so it never even tries to break free. The real binding is not physical but mental.

This was the perfect object lesson. "Like the elephants," I told my kids, "many people spend their lives believing that there are things they can't do because they had a bad experience in the past. Be careful not to fall in this mind trap. Test your limits regularly."

The American psychologist Martin Seligman coined the term "learned helplessness" back in 1967 when he was researching depression. Learned helplessness is the attitude of a person (or animal) who does not try to get out of a negative situation because the past taught him that he is helpless to do so. Seligman identified this behavior in humans and animals that repeatedly endured painful stimuli they were unable to avoid. After such experience, the experimental subject stopped trying to avoid disagreeable situations that he/she/it could effectively circumvent. In other words, the subject learned that it had no control over situations that affected it negatively, so it gave up trying.

Seligman was doing research on classical conditioning, the process by which an animal or human associates one thing with another. In one experiment, he rang a bell and then gave a light shock to some dogs. After a number of repetitions, the dogs reacted as though they had already been shocked when they heard the bell.

One by one, Seligman put the dogs from this first experiment into a large crate that was divided down the middle with a low fence. The floor on one side of the fence was electrified, but the other side of the fence wasn't, and dog could jump over the fence to avoid the shock. Seligman put the dog on the electrified side and administered a light shock. He expected the dog to jump to the nonshocking side of the fence, but instead, the dog lay down and didn't move. It was as though the dogs from the first part of the experiment had learned that there was nothing they could do to avoid the shocks, so they gave up even when the shocks could be avoided.

After the dogs didn't jump the fence to escape the shock, Seligman placed some dogs that had not been previously exposed to unavoidable shocks in the cage with the fence. These dogs quickly jumped over the fence to escape the shocks. Seligman concluded that the dogs that lay down had actually learned helplessness from the first part of his experiment.[19]

People aren't all that different from baby elephants and dogs. When we feel we have no control over negative situations, we simply give up and surrender to the shocks. We feel helpless, not only about the unavoidable situation but about our lives in general. Seligman and others have found a strong link between learned helplessness and clinical depression. I am sure that there's an equally strong link between learned helplessness and disengagement. That's why so many of us stop trying to make things better.

In my workshops, I ask people what they would like to change about their work. Almost all of them say they would like a better relationship with their bosses and colleagues, but too many of them have given up after so many empty promises and failed engagement programs. Just like Seligman's dogs, they've become resigned to the fact that they don't have control over their work relationships or their working environments. That's how learned helplessness sets in and people stop caring. (People who've given up dieting after trying over and over again for years often feel the same way; they simply stop believing it's possible to keep weight off, so they resign themselves to being fat.) These failures are not because it's impossible to improve matters, but because people have been given unrealistic expectations, bad preparation, and bad advice.

Learned helplessness is very dangerous. When people believe that no one—particularly their boss—cares for them, that they have no options or possibilities for growth, that their company is not a force for good in the world, and that there's nothing they can do to change this, they lose self-confidence, pride, belonging, and any reason to believe that what they do is important to others. That's how their work lives become meaningless; that's how they actively disengage.

It is harrowing to see what happens when learned helplessness sets in in an organization. People feel unable to question rules and regulations or take risks. Everyone feels like a victim of forces beyond his or her control and constrained by budgets and processes imposed by alien authorities. Nobody feels free to take the initiative or even ask questions. Everyone blames some kind of external circumstance for his or her inability to act; nobody feels accountable. This spreads to customers, who not only sense and respond to the unhappiness of employees, but become infuriated—just as the Comcast customers I described in Chapter 1 did.

IT—WE—I

We can think of the business world as a three-dimensional space. Let's call the three dimensions "It," "We," and "I." Just as every object can be measured in length, width, and depth, every organization can be measured in terms of It, We, and I. Over the long term, the It, We, and I aspects of an organization must operate in concert. Although it is possible to achieve good financial results in the short term with unhappy people, cold relationships, or wasteful processes, such an organization can't last. Strong profits will not be sustainable without equally strong interpersonal relationships and personal commitment.

"It" is the dimension of the impersonal. It focuses on the task, the systems and processes, the efficient allocation of resources and accountabilities. The It dimension concerns the organization's ability to have its members work rationally toward its goals.

"We" is the dimension of the interpersonal. It focuses on the relationships between the individuals, their interactions, the quality of their connections, and the kind of community they create. The We dimension concerns the organization's ability to have its members work collaboratively toward its goals.

"I" is the dimension of the personal. It focuses on the individual's values, beliefs, thoughts, feelings, aspirations, well-being, sense of meaning, and happiness. The I dimension concerns the organization's ability to have its members commit enthusiastically to achieving its goals.

I believe that one of the biggest detractors of employee engagement is that leaders see their organizations in only the impersonal dimension. "It" is all about increasing sales, reducing costs, gaining market share, and growing shareholder value.[20] In this dimension, the leadership's chief concern is for efficiency, effectiveness, and efficacy. This is the dimension in which all managers go through basic training; it's where most of them stay. The focus is on attaining the maximum output with the minimum consumption of resources. A successful It-dimensional leader will establish clear goals, strategies, and roles and provide access to the knowledge and resources people need to get their jobs done. When an organization's It quotient is low, employees' efforts are misdirected and often conflicting because the employees are disorganized and ill equipped. This saps their energy and kills their engagement.

Of course, the impersonal dimension is essential. Without a solid performance along its lines, an organization's very survival is at stake. If a company does not operate effectively, it will fail to draw energy and resources, and it will collapse.

It-dimension results are necessary, but they are not sufficient to engage people because human organizations transcend this dimension. Stripped of the other two dimensions, business becomes a purely mechanical activity in which success and failure depend exclusively on the rational management of rational agents. But in the three-dimensional reality in which we live and breathe, business success depends on the engagement of passionate beings who deeply care about their work. That's why it's helpful to understand the two other very real and equally essential dimensions to organizations: the We and the I.

The We is about the quality of interactions and relationships among the organizational members. Humans are social beings, which is why solidarity is so fundamental to long-term business success. Interpersonal success is required for survival. If people do not cooperate and respect one another, the organization will fail, as the example of Yahoo painfully illustrates. The We dimension is all about organizational behavior—an area that feels unfamiliar and uncomfortable to many who were trained only in the It dimension. It's about group cohesion, solidarity, trust, and mutual respect. In this realm, the focus is to create a collaborative community founded on a general sense that "we are all in this together." A successful We-dimensional leader will establish a collaborative environment in which people work together to accomplish audacious goals. These are the emotional elements of an engaging workplace. When an organization's We quotient is low, employees' efforts dissipate in the form of office politics, ego management, and passive-aggressive avoidance of tough issues.

The I is about the human need for personal achievement, self-actualization, and self-transcendence of each of the organizational members. This dimension is all about personal growth, meaning, and happiness. In this realm, the goal is to cultivate psychospiritual health. Every person, from the chairman of the board to the guy who unloads trucks at the warehouse, wants to feel whole, knowing that his or her life matters. When they feel this way, people are much more productive and creative. They are resilient when suffering setbacks and enthusiastic when facing opportunities. They trust themselves to respond appropriately to life's circumstances, to connect with others, and to deliver exceptional results. To get the best from its employees, the organization needs to provide them with opportunities for meaningful engagement.

McKinsey's research[21] shows that while the It and We dimensions (McKinsey calls these the "intellectual" and "emotional quotients," respectively) are absolutely necessary to create engagement in an organization, they are not sufficient. For years, McKinsey has asked executives what they found most often missing in creating a peak performance environment—one that inspires exceptional levels of energy, self-confidence, and individual productivity. The response is invariably "a strong sense of meaning." "By 'meaning,'" McKinsey reports, "they imply a feeling that what's happening really matters, that what's being done has not been done before and that it will make a difference to others." When an organization's I quotient is low, employees disengage; they put less energy into their work and see it as "just a job" that gives them little more than a paycheck.

To try to engage their employees, leaders living in the one-dimensional world of rational management tend to tell only It stories. The two most typical ones, according to McKinsey, are the turnaround story and the good-to-great story.[22] The first one goes something like "We're performing below industry standard and must change dramatically to survive—incremental change is not sufficient to attract investors to our underperforming company." The second one, "We are

48

capable of far more, given our assets, market position, skills, and loyal staff, and can become the undisputed leader in our industry for the foreseeable future." The two stories are usually complemented by "If we accomplish this, we will have more career opportunities, a higher paycheck, work security, and more benefits."

These stories are not bad, but they don't stand on their own. To create engagement, it is necessary to complement them with We and I stories. The We stories describe how "We are an extraordinary group of people, and we are all in this together." Take, for example, the U.S. Special Forces. Their esprit de corps is out of this world. They have endless stories about each member's heroic commitment to his comrades and the force. These stories inspire people in the Special Forces with a sense of belonging in a cohesive environment where "we" are proud to have one another as colleagues, working together for a noble purpose.

The I stories describe how "each one of us is improving the lives of our customers, benefiting society, and making a significant contribution to human progress." They assure organizational members that what they are doing is good and meaningful, that it will make a positive difference in the world. This is clearly an extraordinary source of engagement for the members of the Special Forces, who put their lives on the line every day for the sake of their noble ideals.

AN ENGAGING LEADER

The stories are important, but they cannot be decoupled from the storytellers. As the cognitive biologist Humberto Maturana observed, "Everything said is said by someone."[23] Leaders can't just tell the stories; they have to breathe them, feel them, live them.

A 2012 white paper published by the Dale Carnegie organization and MSW Research noted that the three key drivers of employees' engagement are relationship with one's immediate supervisor, belief in senior leadership, and pride in working for one's company. The behavior of the immediate supervisor is the most fundamental determinant of employees' engagement, but beyond that, it's senior leadership's "willingness to take their input, lead the company in the right direction, and openly communicate the state of the organization."[24] If an employee feels cared for and respected, and believes that the organization reflects his or her personal values, then engagement and loyalty follow. And when people feel engaged and loyal, they don't leave—saving the company the costs of recruitment and training.

Study after study concludes that a caring manager is essential to employee engagement. Employees want their managers to care about their personal lives, to take an interest in them as people, to care about how they feel, and to support their health and well-being. A manager's ability to build strong relationships with employees, build strong team interaction, and lead in a person-centered way creates an environment in which employees perform at their best.

Doug Conant is an example of such a manager. When Conant was recruited from Nabisco to become CEO of the old[25] Campbell Soup Company in 2001, the company was hemorrhaging both money and morale. It was the poorest-performing food company in the world. Core businesses, even the famous "mm-mmm-good" tomato and chicken noodle soups, were suffering. Surveying Campbell, Gallup found that 62 percent of the company's managers were not actively engaged in their jobs, and another 12 percent felt actively disengaged. Those numbers were the worst Gallup had ever seen for any Fortune 500 firm.

By 2009, everything had changed. Nearly all the old managers had been replaced; half the new leaders were promoted from inside the company, a move that increased morale tremendously. The most crucial criterion for new managers was to inspire trust in the people around them. As trust climbed, earnings climbed; so did earnings per share, putting the company near the top of the food industry. By 2009, Campbell was outperforming both the S&P 500 and the S&P food group. Sixty-eight percent of all Campbell employees said they were actively engaged, and just 3 percent were actively disengaged. That's an engagement ratio of 23 to 1, and Gallup considers 12 to 1 to be world class. It was a turnaround story beyond imagination.

Yet the recipe was simple. Conant put people first. "One of the first things I did," Conant told *Forbes*, "was make it clear I understood that

Campbell . . . needed to demonstrate its commitment to its people before they could be expected to demonstrate their own extraordinary commitment to it and its success."[26] Conant lived by his maxim, "To win in the marketplace you must first win in the workplace."[27]

Conant made showing that he cared about employees a priority, and he demanded that all the managers in the company do the same. He demonstrated caring by example. He always inquired after everyone. In the employee cafeteria—where he regularly ate his lunch in order to be with folks—he asked how the cooks were doing, how their kids were. He shook hands. He put an arm around people. The place felt more like a home than a big company—which made a lot of sense, since the brand is closely associated with moms and home. He knew the names of thousands of employees and personally wrote thirty thousand thank-you notes to them. He mentored hundreds of people. He sent roughly twenty thank-you notes a day to staffers on all levels. "And every six weeks," he said, "I had lunch with a group of a dozen or so employees, to get their perspective on the business, to address problems and to get feedback."[28]

Doug Conant was an authentically caring leader at Campbell. That's what made him an engaging one.

Chapter 3
DISORGANIZATION

TO WIN, EVERYONE MUST PLAY FOR THE TEAM

"Can't we all just get along? Can we stop making it horrible?"

—Rodney King

I had barely found my seat on the plane when the well-dressed, tired-looking, overweight businessman in his forties smiled and turned to me, extending a beefy hand. "Hi, I'm Greg."

He was clearly an extrovert. A salesman and former football player, I guessed. He must have been at least six foot two and weighed about two hundred and fifty pounds.

When I get on a plane, I just want to be cocooned. Contrary to what you might expect from a person who speaks to thousands of people all over the world for a living, I am an introvert. I rarely talk to strangers on planes—or anywhere else, for that matter, if I can avoid it. But Big Greg had beaten me to the draw. It was too late to plop on my headphones, lest I be considered rude.

I put my smaller hand in his. His eagerness and warmth were magnetic. I relaxed and smiled. "Hi, I'm Fred. Nice to meet you."

"Hi, Fred. Nice to meet you, too." He pushed the recline button and took a sip of his bourbon. "What takes you to San Francisco?"

"Work," I said. "What about you?"

"I'm going home for Thanksgiving after a long business trip. Can't wait to see my kids."

He handed me a business card. He worked for a big software company with a Silicon Valley address.

"Vice President of Field Sales," I observed. "That sounds like an impressive title. What does it mean, in terms of your job?"

He ran down a list of his responsibilities: "I look after the sales force, which means I manage their interactions with our clients in the field. I'm also in charge of training, operations, and administration."

"Sounds like a big job," I said sympathetically.

"Yup, lots of moving parts."

I apologized for not reciprocating. "I don't have business cards. I work for LinkedIn. I only connect to people online."

"What do you do?"

"I'm an organizational oncologist." (I take perverse pleasure in startling people who chat me up.)

"What does that mean? Are you a doctor?"

"Only in economics."

Greg smiled. "What a weird job description. What does 'organizational oncologist' mean?"

"I study why organizations die and what leaders can do to keep that from happening."

He took a thoughtful sip of his drink. "So tell me, Doc, why do they die?"

"Young organizations can die from many causes," I replied, "but organizations that disappear after being successful die from a cancer-like disease I call disorganization. There are entities in them that act like tumors. These entities try to capture ever more energy, ever more resources, and ever more power to the detriment of the rest of the system. These malignant bodies become parasitic and end up killing the host."

"Wow," said Greg, "I've never heard of anything like that."

"I guarantee these tumors are all over your own organization."

"How come nobody sees them?"

"Everybody sees them. If I tell you what they are, you'll immediately recognize them."

"Please tell me then. What are they?"

"People. You, your employees, your peers, your boss, his peers, every self-interested member of the organization can become malignant when the organizational immune system fails to keep them in check. And when these greedy cells lump into a department, a function, a business unit, or any subsystem of the organization, they can become lethal."

Greg laughed. "Where did you say you got your doctorate?"

"I didn't. But since you ask, I got it at Berkeley."

"Ah, Bezerkeley," he said. "That explains so much. And when did *you* go off the rails?"

"People typically think I'm a bit weird at first, I'll admit. Those who give me a chance to explain, though, change their minds. Either I have something interesting to offer, or I'm quite a con artist." I flashed my best snake-oil salesman's grin. "I've been able to fool some pretty smart people, including several Nobel laureates in economics and senior executives of companies like yours, for twenty-six years."

"Now that you mention it, there are some 'entities' in my organization that fit your description. They are killing me!" He finished off his drink. "Perhaps this flight will be much more interesting than my regular trips," he said, and added jokingly, "How about I give you a chance to fool me?"

The flight attendant came to collect our cups and asked Greg to put his tray away before takeoff. I muttered a line from *The Matrix* under my breath, "Hold on to your seat, Dorothy, 'cause Kansas is going bye-bye." (I always fancied myself as a Morpheus of sorts.)

I turned to look out the window. "I love how the city below seems to change as the plane climbs," I told Greg. "When you're on the ground it's all messy, but beautiful geometric patterns emerge as you look from above. I guess that's why I love the economic theory of organization."

HELPING THE TEAM WIN

"That was a bumpy start," Greg commented as we leveled off.

"Takeoff felt pretty smooth to me."

"I mean our conversation. This is not the usual way these chats go." I was clearly not his first victim, er, partner, in this kind of interaction.

"I usually don't talk to strangers about what I do. My ideas are too unconventional for most people. My experience is that only when people are facing a significant challenge are they willing to revisit their mental models. To save you and me an awkward flight, Greg, let me just ask you right off the start: Are you facing a significant challenge at work?"

He looked at me hard. "What, do you read minds, too?"

"Maybe," I said. "What's going on?"

He let out a long breath. "Our legal department requested we amend a contract we were about to sign with our biggest customer, and the customer did not agree. I was able to cool things off somewhat, but couldn't resolve the issue. The customer won't sign, and if we lose this sale, we'll never meet our forecast. There's only a month left in the year. A lot of my people will not make quota and will lose their bonuses. That's not going to make them happy, or eager to continue rejecting the calls of the headhunters that keep trying to poach them. And all because of those lawyers who don't give a damn about the business and only want to cover their asses with stupid clauses no reasonable customer would accept."

"Sounds like you have a serious challenge, Greg. If you're willing to think out of the box, perhaps I can help you find a way to deal with it."

"What do you think I should do?"

"I don't know what you should do. But maybe I can help you understand what's going on, so you can decide what you should do. Are you game?"

"Go for it."

"Let me ask you, Greg, what's your job?"

"I told you, I'm vice president of field sales."

"I heard you, but that's not your real job." I proceeded to walk Greg through what his real job—what everyone's real job in a company—is: to help the team win.

I could see that Greg was beginning to understand. After a thoughtful pause, he said, "I understand that my real job is to help my company win. But I get paid to sell. My KPIs (key performance indicators) are based on sales and revenues."

"You're not alone, Greg. Most people get paid to play their roles, not to help their company win. It's as though instead of using incentive systems to fight tumors, companies decided to nourish them. That's why so many die of cancer."

DOING YOUR JOB CAN BE HAZARDOUS TO YOUR CAREER

The flight attendant came by with our meals. As Greg tucked into his steak I wished him *"Buen provecho!"*

"What does that mean?"

"Buen provecho is Spanish for 'good profit.' It means, 'May you profit from the food.'"

"Gracias, amigo."

"Anyway, to continue our conversation," I said, "imagine a soccer team where the players' compensation and career prospects are determined by KPIs. The 'obvious' KPI for the defense would be goals allowed, where more is worse. The KPI for the offense would be goals scored, where more is better. Agree?"

"Agree," said Greg.

"If you were a defensive player, would you rather win five to four, or lose one to zero?"

"I want to say, 'Win five to four,' but I'm sure that's the wrong answer, again, Professor," Greg said.

"Try this another way," I said. "If you were a defensive player measured and compensated by the KPI of goals allowed, would you be better off when your team wins five to four, or when it loses one to zero?"

"Damn!" He was clearly beginning to grasp how deep the rabbit hole went.

"And if you were an offensive player measured and compensated by the KPI of goals scored," I continued, "would you be better off when your team wins one to zero or when it loses five to four?"

"Hot damn!" repeated Greg, slumping his shoulders. "Where's the trick?"

"I'm afraid it's not a trick," I said. "It's a trap. In the simplest example, with only two subteams and totally intuitive performance metrics, I can find scenarios where every player prefers his team to lose."

"Here's what I don't understand, Fred," Greg said. "To win a soccer match you have to score more than the other team, so the defense should try to prevent goals and the offense should try to score them. If everybody does their best, then the team should do its best, right?"

"Wrong. In order to optimize a nonlinear system, you must suboptimize its subsystems. If you optimize any subsystem, you will suboptimize the system."

"Oh, please," Greg said. "Is that some kind of economics tongue twister?"

"No, Greg," I replied. "It says that when everyone does the best for his position, the team does not do its best for its global objective. In order to win, everyone must play for the team. The team members must subordinate their individual goals to the team goal. At times the player shouldn't do the best for his position—which means his KPIs will take a hit. And that means that his compensation and career opportunities will also take a hit."

"You mean you'd punish people for doing the right thing?"

"I wouldn't, but your and everyone else's company does because they are run by the numbers. That's why I like to say that doing your job can be hazardous to your career."

He mulled over that last phrase. "'Doing your job can be hazardous to your career.' What does that mean?"

"Take a case where the team is losing one to zero. Suppose that the defense could go on the attack with a 50 percent chance of scoring. That is a risky strategy. Suppose further that the chances of the other team scoring in a counterattack are also 50 percent. For the team, losing one to zero or two to zero is exactly the same; they lose anyway."

I pulled out a notepad and a pencil and placed it on the tray table next to his now-empty plate. "Let's say that losing is worth zero points, and tying is worth one point," I said, scribbling a formula on the paper. "The expected payoff for the team of sending the defense to attack is $1/2(1) + 1/2(0) = 1/2$. But the defensive players have a different incentive system. For them, scoring doesn't matter. Remember that their KPI is the inverse of goals allowed, so goals scored benefit only the offense. Suppose that each goal scored against the team counts as -1 for the player. So, the defensive players' payoff is $1/2(0) + 1/2(-1) = -1/2$. For the defensive players, attacking is all risk and no reward."

"Wow, I never thought of that," said Greg. "What a raw deal. I just always thought that some players were just selfish."

"They might well be. But even if they are not, traditional KPIs will encourage them to act selfishly."

"Sales commissions encourage salespeople to act selfishly?"

"You bet. I imagine that your company pays commissions on sales revenue. Salespeople have, then, an incentive to sell the most expensive, highest-priced products rather than the most profitable, highest-margin ones, or the ones that are most suitable for the customer. If they focus on the ones that make the most money for them, they will make less money for the company, and perhaps create churn by pushing a product that the customer can't fully utilize. On the other hand, if they focus on the products that make the most sense for the company and the customer, they will make less money."

"It's like rewarding people for doing the wrong thing and punishing them for doing the right thing, isn't it?"

"Bingo!" I said.

Greg looked pleased.

"So if a company were a soccer team," I said, "sales would be the offense and manufacturing the defense. Winning would be maximizing profits, which happens by maximizing revenues and minimizing costs. So the 'obvious' KPIs for the sales organization would be focused on revenues and the ones for manufacturing would be focused on costs. Does that make sense?"

"Of course. I learned that in my MBA econ class."

"You must have had a lousy economist as a teacher."

"Why?"

"Because as we just saw with the soccer example," I explained, "you can't just partition the team—which is a complex, nonlinear system—into two subteams and then simply add their results. If you do that, you will incentivize each subteam to optimize their performance and sub-optimize the performance of the team."

"Are you saying my sales team should not be paid sales commissions?"

"I'm not saying anything yet, except that sales commissions have a dark side."

"Unless you make a lot of money on them. I've done pretty well." He grinned.

"I'm sure you have, but let me give you another example. What are the names of two of your sales reps?"

"Phil," Greg replied. "And Rachel. They're stars."

"So suppose that Phil has been working on an account for several months. At that point, he discovers that a key decision maker in the customer organization went to college with Rachel. Phil knows that Rachel would be more likely to make the sale. But if Rachel makes the sale, she gets the commission and the kudos while Phil gets zilch. If Phil wants to meet his personal sales quota and earn the commission, he will keep trying to make the sale himself with a lower probability than Rachel."

Greg smiled. "Terribly plausible."

"You see, Greg, instead of fighting tumors, your company is feeding them—just like every other organization out there."

As passengers finished their dinners, the flight attendants came down the aisle with a tray full of ice cream sundaes with chocolate sauce. I declined politely. Greg chose the biggest one, with a chocolate chip cookie on the side.

THE CONTRIBUTION CONUNDRUM

"I should have skipped dessert," said Greg regretfully. "I'm not burning calories like I did when I was twenty-five, and the pounds are piling up."

"What tastes good is not always good, and what is good doesn't generally taste so good. That's why we need to eat with our minds rather than our tongues."

"Easier said than done, Mr. Guru. Are you a health nut, too?"

"I just try to be conscious," I said. "I watch what I eat because I want to live a long and healthy life. Organizations get sick, too. They die from disorganization because their people do what is good for them personally, rather than what is good for the company."

"Amen to that!" Greg said. "I'm being killed by bureaucrats who couldn't care less about the company."

"You mean the bureaucrats in the legal department?"

"Those guys have no business sense. Every time we make a sale, they delay the contract for months. They insist on telling us all the things that we can't offer, request, or commit to do. And then they want the customer to accept these punitive clauses. It's a miracle that we get any contracts signed. But this time they outdid themselves. They're about to kill this deal and push the customer into the arms of the competition."

"My guess is that the legal team is tasked with minimizing legal risk, so they're trying to prevent anything from going wrong," I said. "Unfortunately, in their zeal to do that, they are also preventing things from going right."

"You got it, Fred."

"That's only half of the story, Greg. From their standpoint, what they see is that in your desire to make the sale, you are disregarding legal risks that can hurt the company."

"So who's right?"

"You're both wrong. The goal is neither to minimize risks nor to maximize sales. The goal is to help your company win. Which means to accomplish its mission ethically and sustainably, growing its economic value while benefiting your stakeholders."

"But there are no KPIs for that."

"That's why you have these ongoing feuds between different parts of the same team. KPIs and local incentives encourage people to not recognize each other as teammates. The obvious solution would be to compensate each employee according to his or her contribution to the global objective of the company."

"Are you saying that employees should be evaluated not according to how they do their job but according to how they contribute to the team? How can you do that?" Greg asked.

"Have you seen the movie *Moneyball*?"

"Yes! I love that movie. We use it to explain to customers how they can benefit from big data."

"It's a good example of how you can measure each player's contribution to the global objective. In the movie, the whiz kid economist from Yale finds that the most expensive baseball players are not the ones that most contribute to help the team to win. And some inexpensive players are more valuable than the expensive ones. So the manager of the Oakland A's sells the more expensive, less valuable players and buys the less expensive, more valuable players."

"Right," Greg said. "He took a lot of heat for it, but in the end the A's won the division championship, and with the lowest budget of the league."

"The real value of a player," I said, "is not measured by his KPIs but by his contribution to help the team to win."

"That may be possible in baseball, Fred, but how would you do that for a business? It's impossible to see what people do and keep stats so accurately."

"You are right, Greg. That's why bonuses typically depend on some combination of local and global performance."

"In my company," Greg said, "we have a mixed system like that for managers and above. Part of our variable compensation depends on our department's performance, to encourage us to work hard, and the other part depends on the company's results, to encourage collaboration with people in other departments."

"How is that working out for you?"

"Well, it seems to hit the spot. We all want to achieve our targets, but we also care about the company achieving its targets."

"But, Greg, does it work?"

"You don't think it does?" he said a bit resentfully. "How would you know? You don't work for us."

"Trust me, I'm a doctor," I said, trying to lighten things up. "What would you say is the impact of your personal effort on your company's global results?"

"I've got no idea. There are so many things that affect those results that it's hard to measure my personal contribution."

"Can we say it's rather small, relative to the company's total results?"

"Not great for my ego, but sure."

"And what would you say is the impact of your personal effort on your KPIs?"

"Much higher."

"You said that your bonus is based 50 percent on the global results and 50 percent on your KPIs?"

"Yes."

"So where would you put your efforts to maximize your payoff? To minimally move the needle of global results, or to maximally improve your KPIs?"

After a moment he responded, "On my KPIs."

"Of course. See, we're back to the individual incentive scheme. The 50 percent of the global results doesn't change things for you; you put in the same effort regardless. But it does change things for the worse in terms of your incentives."

Greg's brows furrowed. "Why? I understand that focusing on my KPIs may not be the best for the team, but I'd still be doing my best for my position."

"Sure, but you are less motivated. On the one hand, you'd only get 50 percent of the incentive you would have gotten in a pure scheme. On the other hand, you'd be dependent on many things that are outside of your control for the other 50 percent. That creates uncertainty, especially in the case of external factors like a recession, or if a big customer goes belly-up. And it creates conflict with other parts of the organization."

"You got that right," Greg agreed. "There was a lot of noise last year when the product managers and engineers blamed each other about late releases. Neither side got the bonuses they expected because they took each other down. And you should see the nasty e-mails between sales and customer support discussing the reasons for customer churn!"

"Would you prefer a fifty-fifty scheme or a hundred-zero one?"

"I guess the hundred-zero. But what if we changed the percentages to make people more focused on the global result? What if we made zero-one hundred? After all, we want everyone to play for the team, don't we?"

As the flight attendants picked up our trays, Greg pretended to look for his wallet. "I'll take care of this, Fred," he joked. "By the way, you seem less weird by the minute."

"Thanks, Greg, but we're only halfway to San Francisco. Why don't we split the bill?"

SPLITTING THE BILL

"Your idea of focusing people on the global result through team incentives is not a bad one, but I'm afraid it's better to stick with the devil you know," I said. "Here's why. Have you ever gone to a restaurant with a group and someone proposes that you all split the bill?"

"Yeah. My wife and I tried that several weeks ago with our neighbors. It was supposed to make things less awkward, but it looked like they would pay more because they only had soups and salads. Anne ordered fish and white wine and I had a steak and a couple of beers. So it ended up being awkward anyway."

"Restaurant owners love it when people split the bill like that."

"Why?"

"Because it ensures you all will spend more than you would have had you paid separately. If you do this with nine other people, each one of you pays only one-tenth of what you order. Nine-tenths come out of your friends' pockets. If you order a steak dinner with beer and dessert, they will pay nine-tenths of it."

"Yup," Greg replied. "As I said, it was awkward."

"It creates what economists call 'moral hazard,'" I explained. "There's moral hazard when one of the parties to a contract has an incentive, after the contract is signed, to act in a manner that benefits himself at the expense of the others. For example, subsidized flood insurance encourages people to build in areas prone to flooding that they probably would avoid in the absence of such insurance. Or financial bailouts encourage banks to participate in operations with risks that they would avoid in the absence of such bailouts. Moral hazard encourages individuals to do the wrong things because they can offload the costs and risks of their actions on others."

"There's a problem with your story, though. I was bothered by socking our neighbors for more money, so I insisted we each pay for our own dinners. I have scruples, you know?"

"But others don't," I replied with a smirk.[1] "That's all that matters."

"What do you mean?"

"Let's say that you, scrupulous Greg, order the least expensive item, but your unscrupulous tablemates order the most expensive items. How would you feel?"

"I would never dine with them again."

"What if you didn't have that option? What would you do the next time?"

"I wouldn't be the sucker that's left holding the bill again," Greg asserted. "I'd order expensive food, since that's probably what others would do too."

"Exactly! You are all on a race to the bottom or, more accurately, to the top-priced items."

Greg looked sheepish. "But what's the connection to bonuses and organizational cancer?"

"Bill splitting," I replied, "is not a bad analogy for a system where all the players get paid if the team wins, or all the salespeople get paid average commissions, or all the employees of a company get paid from a global bonus pool."

"How so?"

"Because it shields people from the consequences of their actions. In the case of the restaurant bill, it is the costs of their orders. In the case of the commissions, it is the benefits of their efforts. In the hypothetical case of Phil and Rachel, what happened?"

"Phil wanted to make the sale to earn his commission even though 'passing the ball' to Rachel had a higher probability of success," Greg replied.

"Here's the point," I said. "If you reverse the incentive from individual to collective, things tilt to the opposite extreme. If Phil and Rachel make the same commission regardless of who makes the sale, each of them would prefer to let the other make the effort. Everybody has an incentive to let someone else do the job since that person will bear the costs but everybody receives the benefits of his or her effort."

"That is a terrible system!"

"That is why companies tend not to use collective incentives once they become larger than a ground-floor start-up, where a tiny group of people can observe one another's behavior. Moral hazard is a bitch. Then you die of adverse selection."

AVERAGE PAY DRIVES THE BEST PEOPLE AWAY

"What's adverse selection?" Greg asked.

"Imagine that you are the best salesperson in the world, Greg. You are so good you could sell air conditioners in the North Pole. Would you prefer to be paid your direct commissions, or would you prefer to receive the average commission of a sales pool?"

"Direct commission, of course! The average would bring me down because I'm the best."

"Exactly."

"And now imagine that you are the worst salesperson in the world,"

I said. "You couldn't sell heaters in the North Pole. Would you prefer to be paid your direct commissions, or would you prefer to receive the average commission of a sales pool?"

"The average commission, because if I'm the worst, it would bring me up."

"Average pay drives the best people away," I said. "Superior sales-people who demand above-average pay will be repelled, while inferior ones will be attracted—thus bringing the company's average salesperson productivity further and further down. That's adverse selection. The company will end up in a death spiral of low-productivity sales-people who expend minimal effort."

Greg nodded. "Got it."

"In economics," I said, "we call this also 'the free-rider problem.' Without an immune system—by which I mean an incentive and control system—to check them, free riders will take advantage of others to hide their lack of talent, or industriousness."

"Collective incentives are even worse than KPIs."

"They are devastating, which is why organizations don't use them. And when they do, they run into big trouble. The way the Pilgrims did in the real story of Thanksgiving."

"What has Thanksgiving got to do with anything other than the season?"

"Thanksgiving is a cautionary tale about the dangers of collective incentives," I replied. "But very few people know the true story. Would you like to shock your friends and family when you see them on Thursday?"

"By all means, dispel my ignorance."

"In December 1620," I said, "the Pilgrims landed at Plymouth Rock. Three years later, they had a great feast thanking God for getting them through an earlier famine, and giving them now a bountiful crop. Do you know what created the earlier famine and then the bountiful crop?"

"The weather?"

"Nope; the incentives."

"What do you mean?"

"At first, the Pilgrims decided to abolish private property, which they thought caused greed and selfishness. Instead, they established a collectivist system in which all work would be done in common, with the rewards of their collective efforts evenly divided. They expected this to lead to prosperity and brotherly love."

"But it didn't work out?"

"Their experiment failed catastrophically, like all experiments in collectivism where there's no connection between effort and reward."

I opened my laptop and clicked on a document called "The Great Thanksgiving Hoax."[2]

"It created laziness, envy, and poverty. In fact, it killed most of them. Everybody resented working for others, so they didn't work very hard. For two years the harvest was not enough to feed them. More than half died of famine."

"The famine wasn't an act of God."

"No, it was an act of stupidity. But in the face of disaster, they came to their senses. The elders decided to divide the fields and gave each family a piece to cultivate. Whatever product they did not use for their own consumption, they could exchange with their neighbors."

"And this solved the problem?"

"Yes. Instead of laziness, envy, and resentment, they saw productivity soar. Their production was so great that they not only traded among themselves but also with the neighboring Indians."

"I never heard that side of the story."

"Feel free to share it with your family on Thursday, as you celebrate individual incentives."

"Ladies and gentlemen, we are beginning our descent into the San Francisco Bay Area. We will be landing in twenty-five minutes. Please return to your seats . . ."

"I can't believe we're almost there," Greg said.

I smiled. "Time flies when you're in good company."

"You said that there'd be a light at the end of this tunnel. I hope it's not an oncoming truck."

"Never fear, Doctor Fred is here."

"Well, Doctor, your diagnosis is depressing," Greg said glumly. "My company has a cancerlike disease because none of us is working in harmony for the common good. Everyone is behaving in selfish ways, so we become malignant cells that suck resources and make the company sicker. And it's all because of our KPIs. We can't play for the team, and if we try to change the situation by giving everyone the same incentives, that would only make things worse."

"Correct," I replied.

"I sure hope you have a prescription."

"Disorganization is not the kind of disease that can be cured with a pill," I said. "You can't solve the incentive problem. You can only manage it. The treatment requires behavioral modifications on the part of the leaders. If you have a tumor in your body, you need to change your diet and other habits to increase your chances of beating the cancer. If you have a tumor in your corporate body, you need to adopt healthy habits like having a shared purpose, clear strategies, strong interpersonal relationships, and employee engagement. If you and the other leaders make consistently healthy choices over time, you'll reduce risks and get better at recognizing the first signs of the tumor."

"You make it sound so easy, like a plan in a diet book. But if reading diet books were enough to lose weight, I'd be light as a feather."

"I'm not saying it's easy, Greg. It's actually quite hard. But it's possible. And the good news is that to win, you don't need to lead perfectly. You just need to do it better than your competitors. I guarantee that every competitor your company faces has exactly these same problems. So the goal is to manage the incentive problems more effectively than they do."

"So how do we do that?"

"That's an excellent question, with a very long answer. I'm afraid that unless you want to spend another few hours on the plane I can only give you a sketch."

"Okay."

"You have to turn your mercenary organization into a missionary one. You have to elicit the internal commitment of your followers to pursue a common goal, giving the best of themselves because they want to, because they find it intrinsically valuable beyond external incentives. You can only do this using another set of incentives; nonmaterial ones such as a noble purpose that people feel proud to pursue, ethical principles that people feel proud to enact, a community of like-minded people to which employees feel proud to belong, and a sense of power to make a difference in the world."

"You mean switching from money to nonmaterial incentives? That may be fine for volunteer organizations, but I don't think that would work in my business. Salespeople are motivated by commissions, not by dreams of changing the world."

"I think you're selling your people short, Greg. I'm sure that beyond the money they care about the meaning of their work. And to clarify, I don't mean switching incentives; I mean complementing them. It's not either/or, but both/and. To run faster than your competitors, you need to use your two legs, the material and the nonmaterial."

"How do you use the two legs, then?"

"We're close to landing," I said. "So I'm going to break my own rule and give you advice. I don't know if you'll be able to use it, though, as it requires some level of skill in conversation, but perhaps these ideas can help you deal with your colleagues in legal. You need to get together with your counterpart in legal to have a different kind of conversation. This conversation should start with an agreement about the outcome you are both willing to seek collaboratively."

"Fred, the problem is that we don't have a shared goal! I want to sign the damned contract with the customer, and Mike, the legal eagle, wants to stop me from doing it. How can we collaborate if we're totally at odds?"

"What if you said to him, 'Mike, my understanding is that we both want to help our company accomplish its revenue and profit targets with minimal exposure to legal risks. I believe we have a difference of opinion about what strategy would be more conducive for that, but we are perfectly aligned about the goal. Would you agree with that?'"

"Wow, that's really good!"

"Hopefully Mike agrees with this statement. But even if he doesn't, he has to accept it, or he'd be exposed as a jerk—not just to you, but to your boss."

"Got it," Greg said.

"Next, ask him to explain to you why he thinks that the contract is too risky as currently drafted to justify the revenue and profit it entails."

"But it isn't!"

"That's your opinion, Greg. If you want to move this ball forward, you need to bite your tongue and let Mike explain his reasoning."

"Okay. I get it. Go on."

"When he finishes, you need to summarize his position in the most supportive way you can and acknowledge that he has good reasons to be concerned about the contract."

"But he doesn't!"

"Greg, let me ask you, how is your current way of dealing with Mike working out for you?"

"Okay, I get it. I'll shut up now."

"After Mike recovers from the shock of you not being your crotchety old self, you can ask him for permission to explain your perspective to him. I bet he'll be ready to listen."

"We never got that far. In fact, we haven't ever talked face-to-face about this. It's been just e-mails so far."

"It's so easy to be better than your competitors. The bar is really low," I mused. "The next step is to explain your reasoning to Mike, but without claiming that you're right. You have to present your view as your view, instead of as the truth. The easiest way to do this is to start by saying something like, 'The way I see things, and I realize that this is an incomplete perspective, is that . . .'"

"I can do that."

The flight attendant came by and reminded Greg to put away his tray table and put his seat upright.

"Good," I said as he clicked the seat button. "Give it a try. I learned this way of conversation from one of my mentors, a Harvard professor named Chris Argyris. The first time I saw him at a graduate seminar at the Harvard Business School, he said that he had worked with over ten thousand managers, and not one of them had been able to behave according to what he called 'Model 2,' which is 'mutual learning.' Without extensive training, each and every one behaved according to 'Model 1,' which is unilateral control.[3] I must confess that at that time I thought that this was overstated. But twenty-five years later, after having worked with over ten thousand managers myself, I have to agree with Chris. I haven't found a single one who can do the apparently simple things that create a mutual learning conversation. But hey, who knows, you may be the first one!"

"Fat chance. Then what?"

"After you both understand the relative costs and benefits of your proposed courses of action, you try to find a way to meet all of your needs."

"What if we can't?"

"Don't be so quick to dismiss that option. You might be surprised how you might be able to come up with a strategy that takes care of your interests. But if not, I suggest you propose what I call a joint escalation."

"A what?"

"A joint escalation. You say something like: 'Mike, this is a very difficult decision that can have significant implications for the company. I appreciate your effort to negotiate a solution to our differences, but it seems like we can't make this decision on our own. The final evaluation of relative costs and benefits is above our pay grade. Someone has to bet the farm here, and it's not us. I suggest we go together to—' What's your CEO's name?"

"John."

" 'John, and explain to him the options and implications. He's the right person to make the judgment call. We won't ask him to mediate or solve our problem, but tell him we're there to give him the information he needs to make the tough call. If he wants to require the extra clauses in the contract with the customer, we'll do that. But if he decides that he's willing to bear the legal risk of leaving the contract as it is, are you ready to do the same?'"

"I love that. I'm going to give it a try."

"Will you write to me at LinkedIn and let me know how it goes?"

"Sure, it's the least I can do."

Then we felt the smooth touchdown.

Chapter 4
DISINFORMATION
WHAT'S REALLY GOING ON?

So oft in theologic wars,
The disputants, I ween,
Rail on in utter ignorance
Of what each other mean,
And prate about an Elephant
Not one of them has seen!

—"The Blind Men and the Elephant," John Godfrey Saxe

A king asked six blind men to determine what an elephant looked like by feeling different parts of its body. Each one of them claimed to know what the elephant was "like," but each one claimed it was like a different thing. The blind man who felt a leg said the elephant was like a pillar; the one who felt the tail said it was like a rope; the one who felt the trunk said it was like a tree branch; the one who felt the ear said it was like a hand fan; the one who felt the belly said it was like a wall; and the one who felt the tusk said it was like a solid pipe. The king said to them: "All of you are right, and all of you are wrong. You are right because each one of you touched an actual part of the elephant. You are wrong because each one of you imagined that the whole elephant was like the part you touched."

Think of the organization as the elephant and each of its members as a blind man who touches a part, believing that he can extend his experience to describe the whole. Everyone thinks that they know better than anyone else what is happening in their immediate surroundings. They are all right. Each person believes that his or her knowledge is sufficient to determine what the whole organizational situation looks like.

And, believing that, each person thinks he or she can make decisions about how the organization should move toward its objective. They are all wrong.

In a perfectly aligned organization, people in every division or department, in every subsystem, to use an economist's nomenclature, are committed to optimizing the system. Yet conflicts among its members still arise. "Aligned" means that everyone is playing to help the team win, regardless of his or her local performance indicators. But it doesn't mean that they can all agree on the best course of action, or on what each person should do to help achieve the shared goal. Because each person has different information and makes different inferences, they will often disagree as a group about strategic decisions. Worse, if each person assumes that he is right and that the other person is wrong, escalating clashes will inevitably rip the organization apart.

I call this problem "disinformation." And it makes it impossible for an individual to work in concert with others to pursue the larger organizational objective—even if everyone agrees on the objective. The problems of "disorganization" lead individuals to pursue their local KPIs and are not aligned on a common goal; with "disinformation" they are aligned on the common goal but disagree over the best strategy for accomplishing it. This is because people can only see a fraction of the possible impact that their actions would have on the global objective, so they don't know how their actions will affect other parts of the company. While they can sense the opportunities and risks that appear in their local environment, they have no idea of the opportunities and risks that exist in other places.

To make matters worse, the best strategy for the organization as a whole usually doesn't please anybody. Think about the familiar problem of setting a thermostat in a room with four people, each of whom prefers a different temperature (say, 68, 69, 71, and 72 degrees Fahrenheit). The temperature that would maximize overall comfort would be the average one of 70 degrees. But at that setting, every person would likely tweak the thermostat to make him- or herself more comfortable. Unless they all agree on the goal, and share truthfully their preferences, they will not be able to make a good collective decision.

Disinformation is a serious issue in its own right. It prevents rational decision making and coordination, and it creates conflict among individuals even when they are aligned behind a common goal. But it is deadly in combination with disorganization. These two dynamics together yield an incoherent and self-defeating pattern of organizational behavior. In the real world—where people are misaligned, and even incentivized by local KPIs to bias their outlooks and reports to give precedence to local performance—disorganization is more than enough to undermine an organization. But if it doesn't do the job, disinformation will provide the coup de grâce, blocking organizational effectiveness, success, sustainability, and even survival.

A WHALE OF A TALE

When we focus only on our immediate surroundings and experience, we lose sight of the larger environment and can make terrible decisions, putting others and ourselves at risk. I learned about the dangers of "tunnel vision" as I was diving in the Galápagos in search of whale sharks. I almost paid for the lesson with my life.

The whale shark is the biggest fish in the world. (The whale is bigger but it is a mammal, not a fish.) It can grow up to fifty-five feet and weigh up to sixty thousand pounds. Its mouth is over six feet wide. Fortunately, this gentle giant eats only plankton and has no teeth. Still, a smack of its powerful tail can kill you.

Divers dream of seeing a whale shark up close, but since it's a pelagic (migratory) species, it's never a sure thing that you'll find it. As I looked down from the deck of the dive boat that day, I wondered whether I would be lucky. But before I could possibly get a glimpse of the whale shark, I'd have to get past the hundreds of hammerhead sharks that circled lazily under the hull. *Yum, breakfast*, I imagined the sharks thinking. *Human wrapped in neoprene. Our favorite dish.* But I hadn't come all the way to the Galápagos to chicken out.

"Be careful down there!" the dive master told me and my six companions, right before sticking the regulator in his mouth and jumping over the side of the boat. We followed him into the cold, choppy, shark-infested waters.

I followed the dive master's instructions, descending slowly, ready to bail out at the slightest sign of aggressive behavior from the sharks. But the hammerheads reacted to us with utter indifference. For all they cared, we could have been sinking logs. They ignored us and kept swimming with their relaxed, elegant wiggle. Phew.

Minutes later, someone banging on a tank jolted me into high alert. It was the signal that someone had sighted a whale shark. I scanned all around for the massive shape, orienting myself toward the clanging. And then I saw it—a majestic, breathtaking, awesome creature. I was excited and relieved that the trip had not been in vain. From afar, the whale shark looked like it was barely moving, but when I got closer I realized that the enormous creature was swimming away rapidly.

I began to kick with my fins at full speed, totally oblivious to anything but the mesmerizing animal. I didn't realize that I was leaving my dive buddy behind—a diver's mortal sin that risks both people's lives. In a few minutes, I found myself right next to the whale shark. I moved beneath it, turned my body faceup, and swam just a few feet under its massive belly, my arms outstretched to my sides. My eyes welled up. I was in an altered state of consciousness, totally connected to this incredible life-form in its natural environment.

My fascination with the whale shark broke when I realized that I was sucking air harder and harder with every breath. I wondered what was wrong. I had been under water less than thirty minutes, so I thought I should have had plenty of air left. I checked my oxygen pressure gauge. What I saw horrified me: I had only about 100 PSI left in my tank, which means I was practically running on empty.[1] My dive computer marked fifty-eight feet. Worst of all, I found myself totally alone; there were no other divers around with whom to share air. I drew in the last fumes of my tank, feeling like I was squeezing a tube of toothpaste from the inside. *Relax*, I told myself, *you have enough to get to the surface.*

In recreational diving, if you stay within the limits of time and depth, you can come to the surface without stopping to let the accumulated nitrogen in your tissues "gas off." If you go beyond the limits and don't stop to decompress, the nitrogen condensed in your body by breathing at depth can literally make your blood bubble. This can cause rather unpleasant consequences ranging from "the bends" (pains in your joints) to death. Even when we stay within limits, recreational divers make a three-minute safety stop between twelve and sixteen feet to let the accumulated nitrogen exit the body as an extra precaution. Although strongly recommended, this safety stop is not required. *Guess I'll find out if the safety stop is really optional*, I thought grimly. I ascended as fast as I dared, disregarding the angry beeps of my computer telling me to slow down and make the safety stop.

I finally broke the surface, gasped a delicious breath of fresh air, and put on my snorkel. (The size of the waves made it hard to breathe without it.) I looked around and saw that the current had taken me away from the boat and the group. I was utterly alone, floating away in God knew what direction, among waves that made it impossible for me to see anything, or for anybody to see me.

I reached into my BCD (buoyancy control device, a kind of inflatable vest) and turned on the radio beacon that I had been given in case of an emergency. I also inflated my "sausage," a large, oblong orange balloon that stands about three feet above the surface, and hoped that the rescue team would find me. After the longest ten minutes of my life, I heard the engine of the *Zodiac*. Two crewmembers helped me climb in. We motored back to the mother ship.

The dive master was waiting for me on board. "What did I tell you in the dive briefing?" he asked sternly.

"To be careful," I replied sheepishly. "And I was. I paid close attention to the hammerheads and didn't see any of them making jerky or aggressive movements."

"It's not the hammerheads you had to watch out for, you knucklehead!" he chided. "They are not dangerous. Accidents happen when people get so focused on the sharks that they stop paying attention to air, depth, location, their buddy, and the group. You are the poster child for how *not* to dive safely!"

I learned a big lesson that day. I was so fixated on the hammerheads and the whale shark that I didn't pay attention to the most vital information. I was so captivated by the extraordinary risks and opportunities that I forgot the ordinary precautions, with potentially deadly consequences.

"It's not what you don't know that kills you," goes the maxim; "it's what you think you know for sure but isn't true." I "knew for sure" that I had enough oxygen in the tank since I hadn't spent more than half an hour underwater. But what I thought I knew wasn't true. In my excitement at seeing the whale shark and tearing after it, I had consumed the air in my tank at twice the normal rate.

This episode made me painfully aware of how often decision makers get so fixated on the risks and opportunities they perceive in their local environments that they disregard crucial information about other parts of the system. Put another way: we tend to put all our attention on the "sharks"—the objects of our ambition or aversion—becoming blind to the way our behavior affects the rest of the organization.

This tendency to focus on our own experience and interests creates tremendous problems. In a complex, highly interconnected system, any person's behavior has a significant impact on many others. However, because most of us consider only the local short-term consequences of our actions, and discount the global long-term impact, we make terrible decisions that put us, and our organizations, at risk.

WHO KNOWS BEST?

"People are going to die!" barked Bruce, the chief vehicle engineer. "I don't give a damn about your fuel economy numbers! This vehicle is already too light. If we take out any more mass, we might as well call them rolling coffins!"

Larry, the executive for regulatory affairs, shook his head vehemently. "If our fleet doesn't meet the CAFE (corporate average fuel economy) standards for gas mileage, there will be hell to pay. You may not give a damn, but the government does."

"You're going to have to get your compliance from some other vehicle," said Bruce. "This one is barely crashworthy as it is!"

"Listen, your vehicle is not going into production unless I sign off on it. If you don't make it lighter you might as well kiss it good-bye . . ."[2]

I overheard this argument back in the 1990s when I consulted for one of the major car manufacturers. I was helping the company with the cultural aspects of what they called the VLE (vehicle line executive) system. It was an effort to mirror Toyota's "heavyweight program manager" organization (which Toyota calls "Shusha"). At Toyota, the "Shusha" is the car boss, meaning that he makes the final decisions about the vehicle. That allows him to balance the power of the functional leaders—that is, the senior vice presidents—who want to optimize for their silos.

For example, design optimizes for "reach" (elegance); engineering for technology; manufacturing for hours per vehicle; procurement for material cost, and so on. In that spirit, safety engineers have a mandate to save lives, while fuel efficiency engineers focus on saving gas.

For safety engineers, the goal is to make the cars as crashworthy as possible to protect their occupants in the event of an accident. There are some things that have relatively little impact on the rest of the vehicle (such as safety belts). But most of their decisions significantly affect the whole vehicle. For example, one way to make the vehicle safer is to increase its mass. A tank, to take an extreme case, is the safest vehicle to be in in a crash, while a motorcycle is the worst.

But mass is "expensive" for many reasons. Beyond its direct cost, it increases the vehicle's fuel consumption and operating costs. It also increases pollution, which can create regulatory problems since there are legal limits to the fuel efficiency of vehicles. Moreover, a heavier vehicle requires a more powerful engine as well as a stronger suspension. Thus, the ride will be either rougher (due to stiffer suspension) or wobblier (due to less stiff suspension) because of the extra weight. This weight will also make the car take longer to accelerate and, perhaps more important, to brake. So even though the extra mass makes the vehicle safer in the event of a crash, it could be less safe overall because of the extra time and distance required for braking.

Larry and Bruce were each pursuing important goals. Bruce wanted to protect the occupants; Larry wanted to protect the environment. But they were at an impasse, and a timely resolution seemed implausible. While Larry and Bruce discussed what to do, the company was losing big dollars for every week that went by without a decision.

MASSIVE COMPLEXITY

Of course, a natural question arises here: Isn't it management's job to settle these kinds of arguments? After all, their job is to take in all the available information and make objective and informed decisions for the good of the whole. That's why they have the authority and get paid the big bucks.

The problem with this is that the experience of each "blind man" about the part of the "elephant" he touches is so rich and nuanced that it's practically impossible to describe accurately. A true description of the elephantine organization would have to include all relevant information about the organization in its present and potential future states: how it is structured; what its processes are; who its employees, clients, suppliers, contractors, and consultants are; what its resources are, such as raw materials, properties, plants, equipment, finished and semi-finished products, component parts, cash, lines of credit, and so on; what its liabilities are; et cetera. The list goes on, and on, and on. And that's less than half of it, as the list would also have to include the organizational environment in its present and potential future states.

Conveying what he knows, what he could do, what he would need, and what could happen, would require that the organizational member make gross simplifications that would render the information almost useless. The blind man can only communicate a thin slice of his knowledge to the senior managers who make global decisions. This does not suffice to make rational decisions about the best course of action. (And remember that we are making the heroic assumption that there is perfect alignment behind the global objective, and that no local departmental optimization is going on. If people are incentivized to achieve their KPIs, their information might not be trustworthy, because of their natural bias to benefit their own areas.)

People in maintenance, for example, may know that the plant can't continue to operate on three shifts for much longer. People in sales may know that customers are angry because there is not enough inventory to meet demand. People in procurement may know that there's a potential supplier in China that offers semifinished products. People in engineering may know that to process the Chinese products would require an adjustment of the plant equipment. People in government relations may know that regulators would frown upon imports from China—and so on, to an extent that absolutely boggles the mind. No one person, not even the CEO, can assess all the information necessary to create the best global strategy. No one knows what decision is best for helping the team win.

Not only is it impossible to integrate all this information into a common pool to fully evaluate alternatives, but circumstances are also changing all the time. The frequency and significance of these changes require substantial and constant modifications of the plans. As soon as knowledge is communicated, it becomes obsolete—which wreaks havoc on the firm's regular planning process.

On top of that, no one person can possibly take in and process the vast knowledge inherent in an organization. It's impossible to get a completely accurate picture of the massive organizational animal as a whole, even for those who sit at the very top. Just as the blind men touching the elephant wrongly (and arrogantly) extrapolated their experience to describe the whole elephant, senior executives, seeing the elephant from afar, wrongly (and arrogantly) think they can make out and factor in its granular features. Furthermore, they believe they can control employees through measurements, carrots, and sticks. The Nobel laureate Friedrich Hayek called this "the Fatal Conceit."[3] Many an organization has died from central planning and micromanagement.

YOU CAN'T PLEASE ALL PEOPLE

When I was a child in Argentina, I played soccer. My position was center midfield. My role was to pass the ball to the player who was best positioned to score. The offensive players would always raise their hand and scream "I'm open!" or "Here!" to get my attention. I could only pass the ball to one of them, so I had to decide which one of my teammates was most likely to help the team win.

No matter what my decision was, someone always blamed me for not passing to them, claiming they were well positioned. They didn't understand that my challenge was not to pass to a player who was well positioned but to the player who was *best* positioned, from my perspective.

We were aligned as a team, but we had many quarrels about my passing decisions. At some point, I realized that no matter to whom I chose to pass the ball, there would always be several other players who would be unhappy with my decision. They saw only their own opportunity; they couldn't compare it to that of the other players.

Many years later, when I was climbing mountains, I learned about what happens when one suffers hypothermia. If the body becomes dangerously cold, it will withdraw blood from the extremities and send it to the core, to keep it warm. That protects the vital organs at the expense of the toes and fingers first, the feet and hands second, and the legs and arms third. Sending blood to the core may be the best strategy for your survival, but I think that if the tissues of the extremities had a say in the matter, they would prefer to decrease a bit the overall probability of survival by keeping some blood flowing to them so that they, too, could survive. If hypothermia responses were up for negotiation and vote, the extremities would surely want to reach a "compromise" that would maintain their viability. The organisms that fell in this trap disappeared from the gene pool. The same is true for complex organizations that try to function democratically.

NO SUCH THING AS A FREE LUNCH

Even if one could calculate the global aggregate of every local impact today and in the future, one wouldn't know what the forgone opportunities elsewhere might be because there are always "opportunity costs." Basically, this means that every time you say yes to something, you say no to every other option you could have pursued with the resources you allocated to do the thing you said yes to. Even a free lunch has an opportunity cost. If you accept my invitation for lunch, you can't use the same time to answer e-mails, enjoy a book, exercise, call a friend or family member, or go for a walk.

Opportunity cost is the value of the best option not pursued. Whenever you make a choice among several mutually exclusive alternatives, you incur an opportunity cost—that is, the benefit that would have accrued to you by making the best alternative choice. Let's say you have three projects, A, B, and C, each of which requires the same $200 of investment. Suppose that you choose project A and eschew B and C because you have no resources left to fund them. Suppose further that project A ends up yielding $300, for an accounting profit of $100. Would you say that that was a good decision?

To answer such a question, you would need to know what the accounting profit of projects B and C would have been. Pursuing project A is a good decision only if projects B and C would have yielded a lower accounting profit. That can be extremely difficult to determine. Projects B and C never happened, so you can only estimate their accounting profits counterfactually. To expand the story of the blind men, people in organizations are not just trying to figure out what the elephant looks like by touching a part; they are trying to determine a probability wave of "quantum elephants" that will collapse into a "particle elephant" in the future (in my workshops I call this "Schrödinger's elephant").[4]

It's extremely difficult to compare the systemic benefits of a particular course of action with the ones of other alternatives that would have required the same resources. The knowledge of available choices and their value is distributed throughout the system. It is held by different organizational members who may not reveal it in order to further their interests. Furthermore, opportunity costs would be enormously difficult to compute even in a gross way due to the system's complexity. That's why people tend to use actual expenditures instead of opportunity costs. But using expenditures is mistaken, like the drunk who looked for his keys under the light but not in the place where he dropped them.

THE DUAL-ALLEGIANCE PROBLEM

Winning the business game requires that the organizational (global) strategy both inform local tactics and be informed by local information. The right interplay between strategy and tactics is very difficult to achieve. As I discussed in the previous chapter, local teams are often incentivized to optimize for their departments or division and compete with other teams. In addition, every manager except the CEO has a dual allegiance.

To get the best from her employees, a manager has to elicit their internal commitment. She needs to engage her employees to pursue the team goals. She does this by giving them a sense of purpose and a feeling of pride in their work. She also does this by creating an emotional bond of trust among her team members and herself. In addition, she provides opportunities for these members to experience achievement, autonomy, and mastery in their work, as well as supporting them to grow in their careers.

On the other hand, she has to subordinate her team goals, processes, and even her employees' welfare to the organizational mission. This means that she commits to doing her best to achieve the higher-order goal of her team; that is, the goal of her manager. For example, if LinkedIn is to function at its best, the managers of each business unit competing for scarce resources need to "put on their corporate hats," as it's often said, and share information truthfully, even if this information detracts from the likelihood that their local plans will be funded—even if it means that some employees might lose their jobs. Though managers need at times to "take a bullet for the (organizational) team," the ones who most often get shot are their reports—members of their division, department, or team.

In most companies, managers who bond with their teams try to defend the interests of the team to the higher-ups. But this can undermine organizational effectiveness and collaboration. Every level of the organization can end up working like the U.S. Congress, where representatives see their role as to defend the interests of their constituents. As we can see from politics, a collective in which each person represents different interests leads to all kinds of conflicts and operates incoherently.

If the manager takes her primary role to be a member of her manager's team and subordinates the team she manages, she runs the risk of breaking the emotional bond with her reports. They might consider her "disloyal" or that she "is throwing them under the bus" for the sake of her career. That will lead to disengagement and disillusion.

It's a terrible double bind for managers. They are damned if they optimize the system, because they will need to suboptimize their departments and their employees will feel betrayed. And they are damned if they defend the interests of their employees, because they will need to optimize their departments, thereby suboptimizing the organization as a whole. And then their manager and peers will feel betrayed. The way to break this bind, as I will explain in Part 2, is through transcendent leadership.

TO CENTRALIZE OR TO DECENTRALIZE: THAT IS THE QUESTION

Because organizations have to adapt quickly to changes in their circumstances, decisions are best left to the people who know the most about those circumstances, who understand the most about the changes that need to be made, and about the resources needed to make them. "This problem," Friedrich Hayek explained, "cannot be solved by first communicating all this knowledge to a (planning) board which then issues its orders." Hayek seems to be arguing in favor of decentralization. However, things are more complicated than that for the blind men trying to figure out what the elephant is. "The 'man on the spot,'" he continues, "cannot decide solely on the basis of his limited but intimate knowledge of his immediate surroundings. He needs more information to fit his decision into the whole pattern of changes of the larger (organizational) system."[5]

Put another way, local knowledge is too complex to communicate effectively to global decision makers, so it is best to let the ones who have it make the decisions. Take a war, for example. Field commanders know much better than generals what's happening in their theater of operations, so it makes sense to empower them to make decisions. But local knowledge is insufficient to evaluate the global impact of any decision. Wars are not won by a myriad of tactical successes; an army needs to fit all its units' tactical decisions into an integrated strategy.

Conversely, global knowledge is also too complex to communicate effectively to local decision makers. Generals see the big picture much better than field commanders do, so it makes sense to let the generals make strategic decisions. But global knowledge is insufficient to evaluate the best tactic in a particular time and place. Wars are not won just by brilliant strategies; an army needs to execute these strategies through specific tactical operations.

Hayek wrote in the context of what in economics is called "the socialist calculation debate." This was a dispute between free market and Marxist economists as to whether it was possible to allocate resources rationally in a centrally planned economy. For members of the Austrian school such as Ludwig von Mises and Hayek, the answer was a categorical no. They argued that the only way to do this was through the price mechanism of the free market, where people's individual decisions determine how much of a good or service should be produced and to whom it should be distributed based on their willingness to pay for it.

Hayek showed that free market prices give people the information and incentives they need to make economic calculations and act accordingly. For Hayek, the price system is like a dashboard that enables individual producers and consumers to watch merely the movement of a few dials in order to adjust their activities. Mises, on the other hand, argued that the pricing system in a socialist economy can't work because the government controls the means of production. And since that's the case, it's not possible to set market prices for capital goods. Mises's famous conclusion was that "rational economic activity is impossible in a socialist commonwealth."[6] He argued that this was so not only due to incentive problems (disorganization) but also due to information problems (disinformation).

Unfortunately, this doesn't help elephantine organizations. As they grow, organizations substitute the invisible hand of the market for the visible hand of management, to use the term of economic historian Alfred D. Chandler.[7] Within the organization, departments don't set prices for their services. If I work in the PR department, I don't charge for a press release about a new R&D center. In this sense, a capitalist organization resembles a socialist economy. Another economist, Murray Rothbard, explained how this decision-making problem is due to lack of market prices for intraorganizational transactions. In the absence of a market, it's impossible to calculate price. And without calculation, there is only economic irrationality and chaos.[8]

Some companies try to simulate a market using transfer prices between profit centers, but this system can't quite emulate a real marketplace. Managers are not real entrepreneurs with property rights and residual claims over the economic profits of their centers, so they're not really incentivized to maximize profits. Inside the company, there is no market for production resources, and therefore no prices. Without prices, economic calculation is impossible. Nobody, especially the planning department, can make rational decisions.

Although large corporations are privately owned and operate in a market economy, their CEOs and top teams find themselves in a situation analogous to that of the Soviet planning boards (or the characters of Asimov's story "The Machine That Won the War"[9]), trying to make decisions with highly unreliable information. Imagine trying to run a company without market prices, without profit and loss statements, and without a balance sheet. It would be a guessing exercise not much better than reading chicken entrails. Sadly, that's how most large companies make strategic decisions.

WHERE DOES ALL THIS LEAVE LEADERS?

As a leader, you must also elicit the internal commitment of each and every member of your team (and organization) to cooperate with each and every other member of your team (and organization) to accomplish the organizational mission. In other words, if people have a shared commitment to work together for the good of the team, then the issues of incentive-driven disorganization and disinformation can be managed much better than if they don't have such a commitment.

This means that leaders need to elicit people's permission (due to their moral authority, not just their formal authority) to make judgment calls. They need to have a "process consensus" as in a democracy, where people disagree on who should be the president but they all agree on the way in which that person should be elected. When leaders gather information from aligned team members who want to help the team win, and make decisions through a process these team members consider fair and are committed to implement, they can make better global decisions than their competitors. They can integrate more information under their decision rights and better consider trade-offs. This enables the team members to "disagree and commit" without holding bad feelings.

The leader needs to get people to share their information about local opportunities, risks, costs, and benefits, so that they can compare alternatives and make a rational decision. This requires that leaders put down their egos and adopt a position of humility, openness, and service to a higher goal. In doing this, they serve as an example for team members who can put their egos aside and give their best to implement a decision they would not have made if it were their call. Every team member needs to redefine "winning" so that it's not about who's right or most influential, but rather who has collaborated with the others to make the best, most informed, most rational possible choice in the circumstances—the choice most likely to help the team win. (In *Conscious Business*, I called this "adopting the spirit of the learner.")

This seems obvious when considered dispassionately, but it goes against some of the most basic drives of human beings. We want to be right in order to feel intelligent. We want to dominate others in order to feel powerful. We want to get our way in order to feel validated. We want to win (even against our team members) in order to feel that we are better (than they are). We want to protect and favor those closer to us (our constituents). In short, we want to prove to ourselves, to our followers, and to others that we are worthy, and we do this through behaviors that are the exact opposite of the ones required to play well as a team.

In Chapter 9, "Collaboration," I will define a process for managing these challenges much better than most companies do now. I have refined this technique with my clients for over twenty-five years, so I can guarantee it works. But there is a catch: it works only if, when you reach the head of the organizational elephant, you touch a transcendent leader.

Chapter 5
DISILLUSION

WHERE HAVE ALL THE LEADERS GONE?

What you do speaks so loudly, I can't hear what you're saying.

—Ralph Waldo Emerson

Martin Winterkorn, the former CEO of Volkswagen, was born in 1947 to ethnic German refugees who fled to Hungary after World War II.[1] Life was undoubtedly difficult for his parents, but their son was an intelligent, ambitious overachiever. Eventually Winterkorn earned a PhD in physics from Germany's illustrious Max Planck Institute, then worked at Bosch, and ultimately joined Audi. He rose through the ranks to become CEO of Volkswagen in 2007.[2]

Germans are extremely proud of their engineers—particularly those in the car industry, which is home to stellar high-export brands like Daimler, BMW, and Porsche. When he became CEO, Winterkorn yearned to make VW the world's biggest carmaker. This required conquering the U.S. market, where sales targets were brutal.

Winterkorn displayed a critical, exacting, and authoritarian streak of character. He was known for being both demanding and precise, and obsessing over "It" stuff. The *Guardian* newspaper reported a moment when, in the summer of 2013, Winterkorn found a tiny bump in the paintwork of a car. "The paint thickness exceeded company standards by less than a millimeter, but Winterkorn still lectured engineers about the waste," the article noted.[3]

Winterkorn had a habit of criticizing people and ordering them around, even in public. As a result, other executives feared their leader; woe betide anyone who told him something he didn't want to hear. "If you presented bad news," an employee told Reuters, "those were the moments that it could become quite unpleasant and loud and quite demeaning."[4]

So when VW acknowledged in 2015 a massive fraud in which eleven million of its vehicles worldwide, including nearly five hundred thousand in the United States, had passed emissions tests while emitting nitrogen oxide far beyond the legal limits, people around the world—and proud Germans in particular—were horrified. Winterkorn said that he was shocked, too. Though he took responsibility for the problems with the diesel engines and apologized repeatedly, he claimed that he was not aware of any wrongdoing on his part. He quickly put the blame on his people in the United States and resigned in order "to clear the way for a fresh start for the company."[5]

Upon admitting the wrongdoing in September 2015, Volkswagen stock dropped 30 percent, losing $18 billion in market cap.[6, 7] In addition, the automaker agreed to pay $4.3 billion in criminal and civil penalties, bringing the total cost in the United States alone to $20 billion.[8] In the first half of 2016, Volkswagen's share of the European car market fell by 10 percent, to its lowest level since the 2008 financial crisis. The drop was attributed to a consumer backlash the company suffered after the emissions scandal.[9]

The loss wasn't only financial. According to scientists at the Massachusetts Institute of Technology, thousands of people in Europe may die early as a result of the pollution from the cars fitted with illegal "defeat" devices.[10] The company's directors said that the perpetrators had caused "immeasurable harm" to Volkswagen and called for those responsible to be prosecuted.[11] This call was heeded as U.S. federal prosecutors pressed criminal charges against six Volkswagen executives, incarcerating the one they could lay their hands on in Florida (the others remained in Germany).[12]

Winterkorn may be innocent of wrongdoing. But he's guilty of "wrong-leading." He was a disengaging, controlling, and arrogant leader who promoted, and likely abetted, behaviors that drove VW over the cliff. He wound up resigning under an avalanche of criticism and accusations, leaving his company to face billions of dollars in fines and criminal investigations in Germany, the United States, the United Kingdom, South Korea, India, Brazil, Australia, France, Italy, South Africa, and Norway.[13]

When people are afraid to speak up, errors escalate into catastrophic failures.[14] When employees are afraid for their jobs, they will cheat to reach their targets.[15] Winterkorn's demanding standards, his inability to listen, and his public criticism of his own people influenced some of them to take illegal shortcuts, and many others to hide crucial information. I'm sure they all feared his wrath. He set the tone of the company, and the company played the tune.

It's probably safe to say that Winterkorn isn't the kind of man who spends a lot of time looking inward, though he may be doing more of that after the debacle. Perhaps through this reflection he'll discover what part his leadership played in VW's drama. But it's too late for him and for VW now.

Unfortunately, Winterkorn's management style is not unique. Employees and customers of the ubiquitous car transport company Uber suffered mightily under the leadership of its brash founder and CEO, Travis Kalanick. One video from 2010 showed him arguing with one of his drivers over fares.[16] In October 2014, the Better Business Bureau gave Uber an "F" rating for its unexpectedly high charges and lack of response to customer complaints.[17] In 2017, a former Uber engineer named Susan Fowler complained of sexual harassment by a manager, but the company did nothing; it turned out that such harassment was widespread.[18] In June of 2016, the company fired twenty employees as a result of the investigation. That year, the company lost $2.8 billion on $6.5 billion of revenue. After taking a leave of absence, Kalanick was forced to resign.[19, 20]

Employee complaints, as reported by the *New York Times* in February 2017, were shocking. "One Uber manager groped female coworkers' breasts at a company retreat in Las Vegas. A director shouted a homophobic slur at a subordinate during a heated confrontation in a meeting. Another manager threatened to beat an underperforming employee's head in with a baseball bat." The article offered this assessment: "The focus on pushing for the best result has also fueled what current and former Uber employees describe as a Hobbesian environment at the company, in which workers are sometimes pitted against one another and where a blind eye is turned to infractions from top performers."[21]

Kalanick and his band of merry men started as a pirate ship. They did really well with their unconventional methods of what LinkedIn founder Reid Hoffman calls "blitzscaling," which means scaling lightning-fast. They took over the market, surpassing the incumbent Lyft, but they failed to organize themselves as a disciplined navy. Although there are many reasons for this, I'll take the simple explanation "As above, so below." The organizational failure, I believe, mirrors the failure of the leadership team.

"SQUISH LIKE GRAPE"

In the 1984 movie *The Karate Kid*, an elderly Japanese karate master named Miyagi takes a bullied teenager named Daniel under his wing. After Miyagi asks Daniel if he wants to learn karate, the kid responds with a noncommittal, "Guess so." Miyagi sits him down. "Daniel-san, we must talk," he says in stern, broken English. "Walk on road. Walk right side, safe. Walk left side, safe. Walk in the middle, sooner or later you get squished, just like grape. Karate is the same. Either you karate do yes, or karate do no. You karate do 'guess so,' sooner or later you get squished, just like grape. Understand?"[22]

My warning to leaders is the same. "Either you leadership do yes, or you leadership do no. You leadership do 'guess so,' sooner or later you get squished, just like grape."

When people follow a leader, they let him or her into their inner sanctum. They give the leader the power to deeply influence how they think, feel, and act. They do so because they trust the leader to wield power fairly and compassionately. They believe that the leader will enable them to meet their most fundamental needs in the It, We, and I dimensions.

That said, hell hath no fury like a follower disillusioned. If people suspect that their leader has betrayed this trust, they will exact terrible vengeance upon him or her and on the organization—regardless of whether or not this suspicion is grounded. Leaders who want to inspire their companies through vision and values make a double-or-nothing bet. If they succeed, people will fully engage and the organization will soar. But if they fail, people will actively disengage and the organization will sink.

Disillusion is like a black hole. It's got tremendous gravitational pull. Almost every leadership effort, no matter how well meaning, is bound to fall into its event horizon. Unless you muster the energy to escape, this black hole will swallow you and your organization.

ENTER AT YOUR OWN RISK

When I'm asked to help with a culture change initiative, I warn the leadership team of the tremendous risk that they are about to undertake. I have seen too many leaders nonchalantly jump into the fray without having made a sufficient commitment to see things through. Inevitably, their initiative changes the culture for the worse.

For example, I worked with the leadership of a Fortune 50 financial services corporation for several years with the aim of creating a more constructive culture. At the outset of the project, I warned the executives that leadership and culture initiatives are like playing the futures market: the downside risk is not bounded by their investment. I explained that their participation in such a program did not mean just going to the workshops or expressing public support, but actually committing the time to resolve significant business issues by deploying the values and practices of their desired culture. "If you don't," I warned them, "you will cause great harm to the very culture you are trying to improve."

I also explained that although we were putting a lot of attention on the workshops and the culture change program, the most important messages that they would send to their people would come through their actions, both as individual leaders and as a leadership team. So we agreed that they would not only invest the time to participate in the workshops (which they did admirably) but also, more important, dedicate themselves to applying the material of the workshops, with my coaching assistance, to the tactical and strategic challenges facing the company.

The latter never happened. Indeed, my worst fears came to pass. During the hundreds of hours I spent on the project, I joined the leadership team in their business meetings exactly . . . zero times. Not surprisingly, even though the program was declared a success, the company's engagement scores sank to new lows over time. Because the leaders didn't walk the walk, the employees walked away from the company—if not physically, at least emotionally. (And as far as I know, the company hasn't done any work in leadership and culture since.)

It's embarrassing to confess to this failure. I am tempted to go along with the official story that declared this project successful because it met its performance metrics. But I have seen far too many organizations that, after implementing massive engagement programs, end up being run by "the working dead," disengaged people who have lost all vitality. This is why I can't emphasize enough the importance of integrity in the practice of leadership. If your actions don't match your declarations, you will elicit distrust and resentment instead of internal commitment.

No engagement effort will work unless it starts with the right "why?" Imagine a man proposing to his fiancée. He gets down on one knee, offers her an engagement ring, and asks, "Will you marry me?" The woman asks him, "Why do you want to marry me?" "Because married men have a higher life expectancy than unmarried men," he responds.[23]

How would you feel if you were the woman? What would you do? When I ask participants in my workshops these questions, they invariably say they would feel upset and wouldn't marry the guy. His answer is totally selfish and demonstrates a callousness that makes him unsuitable as a partner. He has no love for his fiancée, no concern for her well-being, her flourishing, her happiness. She is just a resource for him, valuable only as a means of achieving his ends. "If I were her," one participant memorably told me, "I would be thinking, 'What if you could live even longer by leaving me in the future? Would you stay with me if it were less convenient to you? What happened to "for better or for worse"'?"

But this is uncomfortably analogous to the situation of the vast majority of leaders who try to improve organizational performance through employee engagement programs. Although employees rarely ask their leader "Why do you want to engage me?" explicitly, don't doubt for a second that they are asking the question implicitly. Depressingly, the answer they presume is "Because getting a better score on the Gallup Employee Engagement Survey will make the company (and me) more successful."

How would you feel if you believed that your company wanted to engage you in order to exploit you? How would you respond to a program that tried to create a positive environment for you to yield more as a "human" resource? Would you feel engaged or enraged? Everybody I've asked leans toward the latter. Such reasoning feels selfish and objectifying. Even in a business context it strikes people as manipulative. Material exchanges, such as a salary for a service, yield no more than compliance. Engagement requires commitment; it can arise only from an emotional exchange.

It is an open secret in the consulting community that, although engagement programs are quite profitable for the consulting firms, they are rarely profitable for the client organizations. Yet, like a rain dance, whenever engagement surveys reveal a fundamental problem, the knee-jerk reaction is to apply a symptomatic solution. This never works. You can't cure cancer with a sugar pill.

WHAT YOU SAY IS NOT WHAT THEY GET

From the time we're children, we realize that talk is cheap. Growing up, we discover that it is possible to say one thing and believe or do another. We see the contradictions between adults' "espoused values" (what they claim one ought to do) and their "values in action" (what they actually do). We learn that lying makes us powerful when we do it to others, but vulnerable when others do it to us. We realize how easy it is to declaim high values without making any real commitment to them.

When I was in grade school, I remember visiting a friend one weekend. My friend got into a fight with his younger brother because his brother wouldn't let us play undisturbed. After his brother butted in several times, my friend hit him. The little boy started crying. My friend's dad intervened and spanked my friend in front of me. "This will teach you not to hit your little brother," he told my friend with a whack.

I was shocked. My parents had never laid a hand on me, and I'd never seen an adult hit a child before. The event stayed with me throughout the years because something bothered me at a deep level. As I grew older, I discovered that what I was most upset about was the hypocrisy of it all. If it was not okay for my friend to hit his brother, why was it okay for his father to hit him?

To survive in an environment fraught with these inconsistencies, most of us become skeptical of lofty declarations, at least until we see them turn into consistent behaviors over time. We learn our family's values by observing our parents' actions rather than listening to their words. What our parents say matters far less than what they do—especially when they are under stress and don't realize we are watching them.

Talk is cheap but behavior is expensive; that's what makes behavior a credible signal. You can easily declare lofty values, but to behave according to these values requires making hard choices and accepting their consequences. I remember bargaining with my mother as a little boy by saying, "If you promise you won't get upset with me, I'll tell you something." With a mix of amusement and resignation, she would say, "Tell me what happened. It will be okay." I was willing to be honest as long as I didn't have to pay the price of honesty. When you're four, it's charming; when you're forty-four, it's cheating.

Those who have power over us set the standards by example. The way our parents put their values in action told us what was really important in our families. Our teachers' behavior told us what norms we had to respect in order to survive and thrive at school. The same is true of leaders; their actions tell us what is really important in our organizations and how we ought to act to be a member of the community, to be "one of us." Unless the leaders of a company exemplify the values they espouse in daily business and, most important, in circumstances that test their mettle, their declarations are irrelevant at best and destructive at worst. The only way to get your organization engaged and aligned is to model the behavior that you expect everyone else to follow.

AN UNFAIR DYNAMIC

Leadership is not fair. Exemplary behavior is necessary but not sufficient to engage employees. This is because people perceive and interpret your behavior through the filters of their mental models. Even if you do the right thing you may be found wanting.

Let's say you lead in perfect alignment with your declared values. You should be on safe ground, right? Wrong. Even with as clean a leadership record as humanly possible, and even if you are perfectly consistent, employees might feel disillusioned. When people have been under the thumbs of poor parents, teachers, or managers (and who hasn't?), they suffer a kind of post-traumatic anxiety. After feeling betrayed by authority figures who raised their hopes only to dash them cruelly, they are afraid of being taken advantage of again.

Furthermore, when people see someone raise the flag of "noble purpose" and "values," the hair on the back of their necks stands on end, just as it does on animals sensing danger. They become skeptical of fine words as a way to protect themselves. Who can blame them? They don't want to be fooled again. So they consider any behavior that seems to them not perfectly aligned as conclusively damning evidence against the leader. "When leaders behave in ways that appear (to followers) to violate espoused organizational values," writes UC Berkeley management professor Jennifer Chatham, "employees conclude that the leader is personally failing to 'walk the talk.' In short, organization members perceive hypocrisy and replace their hard-won commitment with performance-threatening cynicism."[24]

Followers can't possibly know all the aspects of a situation in which the leader has to make a decision. They can't read the leader's mind, either, to know what he's thinking and feeling, so they fill in the blanks of their made-up stories, attributing dubious causes to his behavior. And when their story casts the leader as a "bad guy," followers withdraw their trust. They become cynical, and every subsequent negative event further cements their view. Even if leaders act reasonably, hypersensitive and hypercritical followers will suspect their motives.

ATTRIBUTION ERROR

"We are too prone to judge ourselves by our ideals and other people by their acts" as Dwight Morrow, U.S. Ambassador to Mexico, said in 1930.[25] We evaluate ourselves in the light of our intentions, but we evaluate others by their behavior and its effects on us. Whenever we do something that seems to mismatch our espoused values, we rationalize it, explaining that we didn't mean to do it or that we did it for a good reason. But when other people do something that seems to mismatch their espoused values, we harshly assert they are wrong, stupid, mean, or, in extreme cases, evil. We are prone to do this automatically, without inquiring about their motives, intentions, or ideals, and without considering the external circumstances that influenced them.

"Attribution error"[26] is the psychological bias that makes us judge ourselves much more benevolently than we judge others, because while we know what we think and feel, and what options we face, we don't know what others think and feel, and what options they face. So we make up stories to enhance our self-esteem and demonstrate that we are better than others. For example, if I'm driving a car and hit a tree, I would blame the accident on the circumstances, such as swerving to avoid a dog. But if you hit a tree, I would blame you for your careless driving. Alternatively, if I catch an eight-pound fish and tell you that it weighs ten pounds, I would excuse my exaggeration as a white lie. But if you do the same thing, I might call you a braggart.

Alleged leadership inconsistencies become "undiscussable" because followers share their conclusions only with others who agree with them. Followers fear (not without reason) confronting their leader in a way that would give the leader the opportunity to explain that there is no such inconsistency, or to recognize that they've slipped and need to correct their mistake. Followers justify their failure by criticizing the leaders for "not being open to feedback." A dialogue might go like this:

"You'd better not challenge these guys. They don't respond well to criticism."

"How do you know?"

"Well, look! No one challenges them. And remember Joe? He was fired."

"Why?"

"Don't know; he must have challenged them."

As this dynamic is repeated over time, people become resigned. They learn helplessness. Furthermore, they take their distrust of leaders into other organizations, where they start out with a negative bias. This makes it even harder for leaders to engage their employees. It's a terribly vicious cycle that spirals down into a difficult workplace experience for too many people.

This unfortunate and unfair dynamic makes your work as a leader much more difficult. First, like everyone else, you evaluate yourself by your intentions and excuse your own actions, so you are likely to project your beliefs onto your followers and miss their concerns. Your followers, however, assess you only in the light of your behavior's impact on them (which you don't fully understand), and their inferences about your motives (inferences that don't take into consideration your internal and external circumstances). Second, if you believe that people are judging you unfairly, you will be prone to discounting their concerns. You will tend to dismiss questions about your actions because, from your perspective, you are obviously right and they are obviously wrong. If you feel like you are being criticized unjustly, you can easily become avoidant, defensive, oppositional, and aggressive.

I experienced precisely this defensive impulse during a large weeklong workshop that I led. Among my goals, I told the participants, I hoped to get to know everyone better through a deep, small-group conversation during our lunches. Unfortunately, there were about ten more participants in the workshop than what could have made this daily plan feasible, so I had to come up with an alternative schedule.

To make up the difference, I thought it would be a good idea to sit with the people I hadn't had a chance to lunch with during a party the last evening. This turned out to be a bad idea, due to loud music and commotion, and the fact that there were no tables and chairs. The dinner was composed of hors d'oeuvres that people ate standing up. There was an area reserved for the people with whom I was supposed to dine, but in the midst of the loud music and the dancing all around us (and a couple of glasses of champagne), I totally forgot about trying to get to know my dinner companions on a deeper level. Oblivious as I was, I chatted superficially with those around me, but I never engaged with them in the deeper conversation I had held with everyone else.

The next morning as I was about to start the workshop, a member of my staff told me that the very people with whom I had chatted so pleasantly the night before had complained to her that I did not honor my commitment to holding our small-group dialogue. They were right, of course, but I was shocked by the fact that nobody had said anything about this at any point in the evening. I learned of their feelings only because one of the participants told a member of my staff, who then told me.

Even more embarrassingly, I had discussed with the whole group the importance of honoring one's commitments and holding others to account for theirs the day before. My immediate impulse was to confront them in front of the group saying something like the following: "Why didn't you ask me last night? If you had simply reminded me of my commitment I would have found a way to honor it. And why did you complain to other people rather than coming to me? I might never have realized that I broke my promise to you—and you would have never realized how much I care about you, and about honoring my word. I owe you an apology, without question. But you could have made things easier for me!"

This was one of those "integrity moments" on which whole seminars, and whole enterprises, can pivot. Fortunately, my meditation training came to the rescue. I took a deep breath, closed my eyes, and composed myself. I realized that if I expressed any of these defensive remarks to the group, I would betray my own values, lose their trust, and ruin the seminar. After calming myself, I entered the room, walked to the stage, and said this, instead: "It has come to my attention that I defaulted on my dinner commitment with the group last night. I'm embarrassed to confess that I totally forgot. I apologize for this breakdown and want to ask those whom I've let down if they could meet with me today at the end of the workshop. I would be very grateful if you give me a chance to make it up to you."

After the workshop that day, I had a very constructive dialogue with the previous evening's dinner guests. At one point in the conversation I said: "Without making any excuses, and for the sake of my own learning and yours, I'd like to ask you: What stopped you from reminding me last night that we were supposed to have dinner together? Have I behaved in a way that would make you wary of raising the issue?" They all laughed. "We thought you weren't interested in having a conversation with us after a long day," one of them said.

I'm glad that they complained to my staffer and that the situation got resolved. But I shudder to think how many times I've disappointed people, have never heard about it, and thus have been unable to set things right.

When leaders perceive that people around them are judging them harshly without offering a chance to explain, they can turn defensive and even Machiavellian. I've had to talk many leaders "off the ledge" after they read my 360 reports because they've felt unfairly criticized by some of the statements I had gathered. Their impulse is to call a meeting and confront those who rated them. I remember one irate vice president who barked at me, "Who the hell said this?" My heart went out to him; he felt people were unfairly drawing conclusions without giving him a chance to explain. I reminded him that he had agreed to maintain the anonymity of the respondents. He became even angrier. "All right," he snarled. "I will find out." I explained to him that the slightest whiff of punitive inquiry would destroy his reputation. He did calm down eventually, but it was touch-and-go for a while.

THE POWER PARADOX

If you wish to become a transcendent leader, after you vanquish disengagement, disorganization, and disinformation, you must confront the greatest and most challenging adversary of all: your own power.

In his masterwork *The Lord of the Rings*, J.R.R Tolkien tells the story of the quest to destroy the One Ring. The Ring not only confers power, but it also imposes serfdom on anyone who wears it. It's an allegory for what actually happens in our world every day: powerful leaders, even well-intentioned and idealistic ones, succumb to the lust to become ever more important, more respected, more admired—in short, more powerful.

For Tolkien, power is always evil. Many of his good characters ask if the Ring could be used to pursue a good end. Tolkien's answer is a resounding no; evil means can bring about only evil ends—regardless of whether the original intentions are good. That's why, when Frodo offers him the Ring, the wise Gandalf cries: "No! With that power I should have power too great and terrible. And over me the Ring would gain a power still greater and more deadly. Do not tempt me, for I do not wish to become like the Dark Lord himself! Yet the way of the Ring to my heart is by (. . .) the desire of strength to do good."[27]

Tolkien's allegory is not far off the mark. Research has found that power excites the same neural centers that respond to cocaine.[28] The feeling of power increases the levels of testosterone and its by-product 3α-androstanediol in both men and women. This, in turn, leads to raised levels of dopamine, hijacking the brain's reward system, which gives blissful short-term pleasure but leads to miserable long-term addiction. In other words, power literally goes to our head. It's addictive, and it can destroy your life if you succumb to it.

Take this as a serious warning. If you are able to earn the trust and commitment of your followers, you will acquire tremendous power. But this power will render you untrustworthy. American psychologist Dacher Keltner calls this "the power paradox." "Being nice is the best path to power," he writes, "but achieving power reliably turns people nasty. The seductions of power induce us to lose the very skills that enabled us to gain power in the first place." As Tolkien's friend the British historian Lord Acton famously said, "Power tends to corrupt; absolute power corrupts absolutely."

A great deal of research from social psychology supports Acton's claim: power leads people to act in an impulsive fashion and to fail to consider other people's feelings and desires. Power encourages people to act on their own whims, desires, and impulses. When researchers give people power in experiments, they are more likely to physically touch others in inappropriate ways, to flirt more aggressively, to make risky choices and gambles, to make rash offers in negotiations, and to speak their mind without social filters. They eat cookies like the Cookie Monster, with crumbs all over their chins and chests.

People who feel powerful are more likely to have affairs, to drive inconsiderately, to lie, to shoplift, to argue that it is justifiable for them to break rules others should follow. Power seems to lead to self-absorption. In experiments where people are asked to draw the letter *E* on their own foreheads so that others can read it, powerful people are more likely to draw it the right way to themselves, and backward to onlookers, as they no longer see the world from other people's perspective.

Perhaps more unsettling is the wealth of evidence that having power makes people more likely to act like sociopaths. Research has found that 20 percent of leaders in business and government demonstrate narcissistic and psychopathic tendencies; that's roughly the same proportion as prison inmates compared to 1 percent of the general population.[29] High-powered individuals are more likely to interrupt others, to speak out of turn, and to fail to look at others who are speaking. They are also more likely to tease friends and colleagues in hostile, humiliating ways. Surveys of organizations find that most rude behaviors—shouting, profanities, sexual harassment, and destructive criticism—come from individuals in positions of power.

Keltner claims that people with power tend to behave like mental patients who have damaged their brain's orbitofrontal lobes (the region of the frontal lobes right behind the eye sockets), a condition that seems to cause overly impulsive and insensitive behavior. He suggests that "The experience of power might be thought of as having someone open up your skull and take out that part of your brain that is critical to empathy and socially appropriate behavior." The paradox is that power is given to people to advance the greater good, but once people have power, they tend to abuse it.

There's plenty of empirical evidence in the business world to support Keltner's conclusions. A 2016 study from researchers at Stanford identified the following breaches of conduct in 38 events that made the news between 2000 and 2015:

- 34 percent involved reports of a CEO lying to the board or shareholders over personal matters—such as a drunken driving offense, prior undisclosed criminal record, falsification of credentials, or other behavior or actions.
- 21 percent involved a sexual affair or relations with a subordinate, contractor, or consultant.
- 16 percent involved CEOs making use of corporate funds in a manner that is questionable but not strictly illegal.

- 16 percent involved CEOs engaging in objectionable personal behavior or using abusive language.
- 13 percent involved CEOs making controversial statements to the public that were offensive to customers or social groups.[30]

These transgressions are costly. According to *Fortune*, when the CEO indulges in behaviors like these, the cost to the company due to losses in market capitalization (stock drops) is about $226 million in just three days.

There is a folk tale that goes like this: A scorpion wants to cross the river, but it can't swim, so it asks a frog for a ride. The frog says, "If I give you a ride, you'll sting me." The scorpion replies, "It would not be in my interest to sting you, since we would both drown." The frog thinks about this logic for a while and accepts the deal. It takes the scorpion on its back and braves the waters, but halfway across the river it feels a burning pain in its side and realizes the scorpion has stung it after all. As they both sink beneath the waves, the frog cries out, "Why did you sting me, scorpion? Now, we will both drown." The scorpion replies, "I can't help it. It's in my nature."

Unfortunately, power has a scorpion-like nature. Even though the narcissistic gratifications of authority and control are toxic to their interests, most people in power can't help themselves. They will inevitably sting their followers and drown together with them in a river of disengagement and distrust.

The Golden Rule prescribes: Do unto others as you would have them do unto you, and do not do unto others what you do not wish for yourself. Most people accept it in theory but violate it in practice. And they do it even more blatantly when they are in power. Is it possible to exercise the power of organizational leadership without being corrupted by it? Or is it like Tolkien's Ring that will enslave he who wears it as a servant of evil? More personally, if you attain this kind of power, how do you then use it for good?

If you want to lead an engaged organization, you must go beyond intellectual understanding. You need to have heroic integrity in the face of corrupting power, working honestly, respectfully, fairly, openly, humbly, caringly, and inspiringly every day. Without that, there is no chance of engaging your followers. These behaviors cannot be faked. Unless they arise from your core values and are enacted through skillful means, the odds are high that you will not succeed. And unless you are almost superhumanly disciplined and conscious, the danger is that you will betray your followers as you are tested by the corrupting influence of power and by the hypersensitive and hypercritical attitude of your supporters.

YOUR STAFF IS YOUR MIRROR

Your leadership behaviors are not just your direct actions. As a leader, you express your values through the choice of systems, strategies, and processes. You have the power to define—or at least significantly influence—how people get recruited, selected, and hired for your organization, how they get socialized and trained, how and why they get rewarded and promoted, and how and why they get reprimanded, demoted, or fired. Each one of these processes exists with your endorsement, and it communicates to your organization what is important, what is right, and what is just for you. Similarly, all the managers in your organization hold their office with your sanction, so their behavior reflects your values and beliefs more than anything you write or say—and perhaps even more than anything you do yourself.

I regularly hear leaders complain that they have inherited a dysfunctional staff or employee or lament that they have an extraordinary performer (in what we are calling the It dimension) who has "terrible people skills" (meaning he or she totally lacks the skills to care for the We and I dimensions). That may be so, but the moment these leaders accept their position with the power to promote, demote, hire, and fire, there is no place for them to hide. Whoever is part of their team is someone they have chosen, explicitly or implicitly. And that endorsement broadcasts their true values to their whole organization.

The It benefits of being a cantankerous rainmaker are obvious; the We and I costs are not. For example, the managing committee of a law firm had a rude awakening when they realized that their unwanted attrition was going through the roof. The firm was losing some of its best talent. They faced some tough decisions when they discovered that some of their best attorneys (as rated by their clients) were some of their worst leaders (as rated by their employees). In the attorneys' zeal to provide excellent service to their clients, they demanded perfection from their employees. In the short term, the firm's client satisfaction and revenues increased. But in the longer term, the attrition costs increased even more. People joined the firm because of its brand, and they left it because of its managers. After years of a chew-them-up-and-spit-them-out culture, the firm was in trouble. They called me because their loss of talent and declining reputation in the job market threatened their viability.

The management committee asked me to work with some of their most prominent "hard cases" to help them change. "Why would they want to change?" I challenged them. "They are getting consistently rewarded for their business results. They got promoted for their aggressive behaviors by leaders who were as demanding with them as they are with their junior employees."

After an awkward silence, one of the lawyers confessed, "We were—no, actually, we *are*—those demanding leaders." I suggested that the first step was for them to clarify what kind of culture they wanted, and how far they'd be willing to go in changing *their* behavior to become the role models for such a culture. I emphasized that such role modeling crucially involved defining the promotion and reward mechanisms of the firm and then accepting that some of their recalcitrant "best people" might decide to leave.

In golf, there is a variant of the game called "best ball scramble." The player plays two balls on every hole. He or she hits two shots, selects the best one, hits two balls from that spot, and so forth, until he or she sinks a ball in the hole. A variant called "worst ball scramble" is the exact opposite. The player hits two shots, selects the worst one, hits two balls from that spot, and continues hitting from the worst ball location until he or she sinks the two balls in the hole. Golf is hard, but worst ball scramble is wicked. It requires great consistency, since any mistake has compounding effects.

Leadership is like worst ball scramble in two ways. First, every leader is assessed according to his or her weakest areas. To elicit the internal commitment of the followers, a leader needs to be consistently great in the It, We, and I dimensions. He or she needs to demonstrate business acumen, social intelligence, and personal integrity. Any failure will compound to undermine performance in every other area.

Second, and more demandingly, leadership is a team sport. Every manager's authority is derived from the CEO, who therefore underwrites and is ultimately responsible for the manager's behavior. Any manager who behaves inconsistently with the purpose and values of the company places a black mark on the entire leadership team. All the managers need to be consistently great, since the leadership will be assessed by the performance of its weakest members.

It's a truism in business that people join companies and leave managers.[31] But even if people feel engaged by their immediate supervisors, they will disengage from a company that promotes and maintains bad leaders. Just as the score in the worst ball scramble depends on the worst shots, engagement scores depend on the behavior of the worst leaders. This puts a much heavier demand on every leader. She not only needs to be great, but she also needs to accept nothing less than greatness in each one of the other members of the leadership team.

THE NO-TABOO RULE: FACING THE MIRROR

Once you commit to truly leading, you and your team will need to review your behavior frequently. You will need to check the consistency of the signals the organization is receiving from you in order to avoid contradictions that destroy engagement. (Remember, what matters is not so much the message you think you are sending but the one that they think they are receiving.) You can do this only by empowering and encouraging your employees to challenge you when they experience any gaps between your espoused values and your actions—especially when you disagree with them. You must invite them to speak freely, and thank them for doing so. To lead effectively, you cannot have taboo topics.

Here's an example of what I call "facing the mirror." A few months after I joined LinkedIn, Jeff Weiner, the CEO, asked me to help him become the best leader he could be.[32] I suggested we start with a 360-degree assessment. I did an in-depth one using not only quantitative instruments, but also open-ended interviews with twenty people who interacted with him (board members, direct reports, midlevel employees, and so on). This type of assessment is quite intense, since I ask tough questions and give the client excerpts from the answers as raw data that we analyze together.

In Jeff's case, some of the questions I asked interviewees were:

"What do you most appreciate in Jeff as a leader?"

"What is the one change Jeff could make to be a better leader?"

"Do you see any gaps between Jeff's declared values and his actions?"

"What do you wish to discuss with Jeff but fear might upset him?"

The goal of this work was to help Jeff realize that the positive comments he heard regularly were not all that people said about him—especially when he wasn't there. The assessment would give him a picture of his stakeholders' perceptions of strengths and opportunities, plus open up conversations between Jeff and those close to him about topics that they could find difficult to broach. The report was an opportunity to discuss anything that could help them work better together.

Jeff had been hearing my theses about disengagement, disorganization, disinformation, and disillusion since we'd met each other in 2006. He understood how harmful these dynamics are for any organization, and he was committed to curbing them (as befits a transcendent leader). That's why he wanted to learn how to build on his constructive behaviors and resolve any perceived inconsistencies between his declarations and his actions, or gaps between his intentions and the experiences he produced in others, and to make those matters a subject of conversation.

On the positive side, people admired Jeff's inspirational energy and his ability to paint a very broad vision while at the same time understanding the crucial tactical details necessary to bring this vision about. They acknowledged his voracious mind that could organize vast amounts of information—and use it to ask good questions and provide convincing guidance. They were grateful for his coaching and his compassionate management.

It was harder to get information about Jeff's weaknesses. I explained to my interviewees that the goal was to help Jeff grow, and that required that he learn how he could satisfy his desire to always improve. They gave me some good material. Not surprisingly, Jeff's weaknesses were the shadow side of his strengths.

For example, Jeff's style of interaction, which at times could be perceived as intense questioning, came off as reluctance to accept disconfirming information. This habit deterred people from presenting information to him because they didn't want to be challenged by his sharp mind. Another issue was that his questions sometimes sounded rhetorical. People believed that Jeff would make up his mind about something but instead of asserting his position he would try to get people to discover it for themselves through Socratic questioning. This behavior seemed patronizing to some and closed-minded to others. Another (surprising) finding was that given Jeff's intensity, his kindness sometimes felt ominous to some people. "When he becomes so 'nice,' it's clear you're screwing up and he's holding himself back," said one of the interviewees. Yet another criticism was that Jeff's energy, charisma, and enthusiasm could create a reality-distortion field. "Jeff is so intense that others get swept up in his passion and lose their own perspective," someone reported.

The solution to leveling out a good leader's style is not to dim his or her light but rather to complement the leader's wisdom with compassion. The findings of the report became the subject of one-on-one conversations between Jeff and each of his team members, as well as among the leadership team as a whole. At Jeff's request, they gave him concrete examples of areas of misunderstanding, through which he was able to identify the specific behaviors (and his inner state while displaying them) that created barriers between himself and those around him. He was also able to explain to his team what he wanted to accomplish when he behaved in these ways. With all this information, Jeff and his team looked for ways to better meet everyone's needs.

It took a lot of courage and openness for the interviewees to give their feedback to Jeff, and an equal amount of courage and openness for Jeff to consider it and address it publicly with them. But the payoff was significant. Each one of the senior executives reported later that Jeff's was the best leadership team they'd ever been part of.

To add another twist to this story, before I had my debrief session with Jeff, LinkedIn's board of directors requested the senior vice president of our talent organization to prepare for them a CEO performance assessment. These types of assessments are typically done by consulting firms and mostly address hard skills (the It dimension). There may be some points about leadership capabilities, but the focus is mostly on business acumen.

When the SVP brought up the topic, Jeff suggested—in what I thought was quite a daring move—that the board use the report that I was preparing for him. I opposed the idea because my diagnostic is supposed to be used for leadership development, not for evaluation. It is too personal and too raw to be shared with anybody, let alone with a board of directors. In fact, I don't even give the report to the person who is the subject of the report in advance, as I've learned that most people need coaching support to process the information.

But Jeff insisted, so I created a summary report for the board that I presented with Jeff in the room. As had been the case with his team, there was a very productive conversation about how Jeff and the board could work better together, and also how Jeff was going to focus on becoming an even better leader by addressing the findings of the assessment. Several board members praised Jeff for his transparency and commented that his CEO assessment was the most constructive one they'd ever participated in.

Martin Winterkorn and Jeff Weiner represent the polar ends of the leadership spectrum. Winterkorn could not bear to look in the metaphorical mirror and do the kind of deep introspection needed to become an inspiring leader. He couldn't hear bad news or brook criticism; instead of owning his behavior, he attributed its bad consequences to others. He created a culture of fear that produced disastrous results. By contrast, Jeff had the courage to look at himself with the understanding that doing so is an absolute requirement for leadership. By doing so, he fostered a culture of radical transparency and integrity at LinkedIn. The most talented people in the world would probably not give their best to someone like Winterkorn; but in 2016, they voted Jeff the most admired leader in Silicon Valley.[33]

Once, while Gandhi's train was pulling out of a station, a European reporter ran to his compartment window. "Do you have a message I can take back to the British people?" he asked.

It was Gandhi's day of silence, a vital respite from his demanding speaking schedule, so he didn't reply. Instead, he scrawled these words on a scrap of paper and passed it to the reporter: "My life is my message."

The point is that it's not only that you can't just "speak" your values; you can't even just "act" them (understood as a pure business-like behavior). If you want to avoid the scourges of disengagement, disorganization, disinformation, and disillusion, you must fully "live" your values in a way that communicates to everyone all the time that this is your life-defining commitment.

PART 2
SOFT SOLUTIONS

Chapter 6
MOTIVATION

PURPOSE, PRINCIPLES, AND PEOPLE

If you want to build a ship, don't drum up people to collect the wood and don't assign them tasks and work, but rather teach them to long for the endless immensity of the sea.

—Antoine de Saint-Exupéry

An economist and a person who is not an economist are walking down the street. The noneconomist says, "Look, there's a $20 bill on the sidewalk!" The economist replies, "That's impossible; if it were really a $20 bill, it would have been picked up by now."

Just as nature abhors a vacuum, economists abhor a windfall. It makes no sense to us that a $20 bill would be on the sidewalk because someone would have scooped it up as soon as it fell.

Engaging employees is a huge productivity boost; it's like picking up thousand-dollar bills from the sidewalk. But the vast majority of leaders just let employees sit there, unmotivated and disengaged. This makes no economic sense. If American companies are losing an estimate of over $300 billion a year in productivity[1] plus the additional losses of talent, market share, and profits to disengagement, why aren't results-oriented leaders doing something about it? And if they aren't, why isn't market competition replacing these leaders?

A thought experiment can give you a sense of the tremendous competitive advantage enjoyed by organizations that engage their people. Let's assume that you work for one of these companies. How much more would another firm, known for its toxic culture, dysfunctional employees, soul-crushing work, obsessive and controlling management, and terrible brand, have to offer you to lure you away from your current job? And how much more would they have to pay you to work as hard, as cooperatively, and as creatively as you now do? Most people I ask this question refuse to give a number; they just wouldn't do it. There are things that money can't buy.

Given the enormous upside of engaging the workforce, you would think that when a manager does not motivate his or her people, the immediate supervisor would put pressure on him or her to change. And if that manager doesn't change, the senior manager should trade him or her for a better one ("either the people change, or you change the people," as the saying goes), and so on up the food chain through the CEO and the board. Unless they do so, the company's value would fall until the firm is taken over, or until it shuts down and some other (more engaging) organization acquires its assets.

Yet almost 90 percent of the global workforce (and up to 98 percent in some countries[2]) remains disengaged. Puzzling, isn't it? A disengaged organization competing against an engaged one is like a mule racing against a thoroughbred horse. So how is it possible that disengaging organizations, and their leaders and culture, still persist? They should be extinct.

There are two reasons for this Darwinian travesty. The first is the mistaken belief that money is what people want most—a belief that's deeply embedded in the way organizations are run. The second is a psychological cage in which most human beings are trapped. In Part 2, beginning with this chapter, I describe the mistaken belief and suggest ways to avoid it. Although this is by no means an easy task, it's the shallow end of the pool. In Part 3, I describe the psychological cage and show you how to free yourself from it.

Transcendent leaders know that human beings are moved not primarily by money once their basic needs are satisfied, but by meaningful purpose, ethical principles, significant people, and personal mastery. They understand that they can't dangle carrots or wave sticks in front of their people and get any more than rote obedience.

After thirty years of trying to solve the problems of disengagement, disorganization, disinformation, and disillusion through standard economic tools, I have declared defeat. These hard problems require a soft approach. The answer to the question "How do I motivate people?" might appear to be driven by economics, but it's really driven by psychology. This answer has to do with the human quest for meaning and transcendence. When a leader taps into this existential thirst—providing an opportunity for followers to create an individual and a collective identity, to become someone they feel proud to be, in a group to which they feel proud to belong—the leader gains access to the most precious resource: engaged human beings.

BAD WORK, GOOD WORK

The Gallup organization did the most extensive empirical research ever carried out on the subject of productivity and engagement. It examined over four hundred organizations, interviewing a cross section of eighty thousand managers, and about two million surveys. Using performance measures such as sales, profits, customer satisfaction, employee turnover, and employee opinions, they distinguished between bad and good workplaces.[3]

The first and second job experiences of the daughter of a friend of mine, a millennial just out of college, illustrate the Gallup research. The woman—let's call her Amy—first held a job for about six months in telesales at a software firm. She didn't care about the business, and she knew it wasn't a career job, but she took it to pay the rent. She was paid $20 per hour plus bonuses for meeting or surpassing her quota. Her job was to cold-call people who had previously used the company's software to sell them a new product. The job had nothing to do with Amy's desires or talents; she was just a cog in a machine.

Amy didn't really know what the point of her work was, other than pushing the company's product—which she had never used. She didn't know how this product would benefit the customers; she just parroted her scripted sales pitch in a skull-numbing litany hour after hour. She only knew that if she met her sales quota, she'd get a reward, and if she failed to reach it two months in a row, she'd get fired.

"My manager never praised me, only criticized me," Amy complained. "I never seemed to do anything right. I was stressed out all the time. I didn't have the tools I needed to do my work well. And I didn't want to ask, as I saw that when any of my teammates asked for help they'd get in trouble. I just put my head down and did whatever I had to do. I hated the job, my boss, my coworkers; and after a while, I began to hate myself."

To the great relief of her parents, Amy quit that awful job; and to their great delight, she found a new one where she feels totally engaged. She now works at an organization that connects people from the same neighborhood online. She believes that this organization is committed to achieving something good in the world. She feels grateful to participate in a noble purpose in the company of people who support her. She understands how her efforts fit into the big organizational picture, and she knows that her work touches many lives for the better.

Amy knows what's expected of her and is trusted to deliver it without being micromanaged. She has quite a bit of flexibility and autonomy regarding how she does her job and coordinates her efforts with her coworkers. She knows her manager is there to support her and to help her grow. The manager is always available and often asks Amy if she needs any tools, materials, or training to do her job better every day. Periodically, he'll engage her in a career conversation, encouraging her to plot a course that makes the best use of her talents and passions.

Amy gives her best, and her manager acknowledges her efforts with generous praise. Amy feels useful and tuned in to the work that best fits her. Everybody around cares about her, too. Some of her best friends are her coworkers. She's helping them and watching them thrive, and vice versa. If there's any disagreement among the members of Amy's team, they discuss the situation, trusting that their collective intelligence will lead to a wise resolution that integrates everybody's needs and perspectives.

Amy feels that she is part of an extraordinarily high-performance team, where everybody is committed to doing a quality job. She's proud of what she does, how she does it, what she does it for, and with whom she does it. Changing jobs or retiring is not even a remote consideration in her mind; she wants to rise in the organization to help it thrive.

According to a 2014 study of three hundred companies, 94 percent of millennials want to use their skills to do good in the world.[4] More than 50 percent say they would take a pay cut to find work that matches their values.[5] If you don't want to leave all those $1,000 bills on the sidewalk and engage the team you lead, you need to see through the illusion that extrinsic rewards are what employees care about most. You need to stop focusing solely on material goods and focus on nonmaterial ones.

THE FOUR PILLARS OF INTRINSIC MOTIVATION

Organizations that engage their people rely on what I call the "four pillars" of intrinsic motivation:

1. Purpose: Significance, meaning, impact, service, self-transcendence
2. Principles: Integrity, ethics, morality, goodness, truth, dignity
3. People: Belonging, connection, community, recognition, respect, praise
4. Autonomy: Freedom, creativity, achievement, learning, self-mastery

MONEY DOESN'T MOTIVATE

The problem in the first scenario above is that the software firm assumes that money is what primarily matters to workers like Amy. It's a mistaken belief that's been embedded in our culture ever since Adam Smith described the productivity of the pin factory in *The Wealth of Nations*.[6] Managers have been taught that monetary incentives and behavioral controls are the essential, if not the only, tools for controlling behavior in organizations. The assumption is like holy writ.

We humans care about material goods, for sure, but most of us do so only insofar as we have enough for ourselves and our loved ones. Then, the importance of additional money and the stuff it can buy drops precipitously—or as economists with a penchant for obscure language like to say, "The marginal utility of income decreases at an increasing rate."

According to management psychologist Frederick Herzberg, material rewards are a "hygiene factor."[7] This means that their absence or unfairness can cause people to disengage, but their presence doesn't make them feel engaged. As the management author Daniel Pink remarks, when it comes to motivation, the only reason to put money on the table is to take the issue of money off the table.[8]

Misunderstanding this fact about human nature has perverse consequences. For example, according to a 2013 survey by Gallup, two-thirds of American workers would continue to work, even if they had ten million dollars.[9] People want to work so much that the money barely matters. But then they go to work and feel disengaged, so they can hardly wait to leave at the end of the day. The sad fact is that organizations are designed, led, and operated to squeeze the most out of the workers, rather than to inspire the best in them—in spite of the overwhelming evidence that those who trade quality for quantity of effort end up with neither quantity nor quality.

Rewards and punishments certainly do induce compliance. If your objective is to get people to obey, bribing or threatening them may work. But if your objective is to garner their commitment, then rewards and punishments are useless. In fact, they are worse than useless; they are actually counterproductive.[10] People aren't like rats in a maze or Pavlov's dogs responding to a bell—although treating them as such will induce them to behave that way. Monetary incentives can't inspire people to care, to work for a common goal, or to support intelligent decision making. Monetary incentives are emotionally inert; they can fill pockets, but they can't touch hearts. Moreover, monetary incentives are easy to match, so they don't give any organization a competitive edge for recruiting, retaining, and engaging top talent.

It may well be the case that for the logical mind, two ways to motivate employees are better than one. But for the emotional heart, the math doesn't always add up. Sometimes instead of adding, reasons subtract from each other. In fact, forty years of psychological and economic research proves that "Adding financial incentives to situations in which people are motivated to work hard and well without them seems to undermine rather than enhance the motives people already have," the psychologist Barry Schwartz has noted. "Extrinsic motivation, such as the pursuit of money, undermines intrinsic motivation."[11]

The more a company uses material rewards and punishments to drive behavior, the less people will invest their discretionary and internally motivated effort.

There's an illustrative study by a behavioral economist named Uri Gneezy, who described a day-care center in Israel that wanted to incentivize parents to pick up their kids on time.[12] More and more of the parents—including Gneezy and his wife—were coming late to pick up their kids, regardless of the appeals of the woman who ran the center. So the center director established a small fine for lateness to give parents an additional reason to come on time. Being late wouldn't just break their commitment; it would also have a financial cost.

Surprisingly, lateness increased in the wake of the decision. Before the director imposed the fine, roughly a quarter of the parents showed up late. Several weeks after she imposed the fine, about 40 percent of the parents were late. Gneezy found that the parents interpreted the fine not as a punishment for a transgression, but as a fee for extended day-care service. And because the fine was small, they were happy to pay it. They lost the notion of an ethical breach. Being late stopped being "wrong"; it became a service that parents paid for. Essentially, the fines undermined what had been an ethical conversation about how the teachers needed to get home to their own families on time.

Financial incentives can dangerously reframe the question in people's mind from "Is this right?" to "Is this profitable?" Once lost, this ethical dimension is hard to recover. When the fines were lifted at the Israeli day-care center, the percentage of late parents increased to about 50 percent. This makes perfect economic sense. When the fee for extra care went down to zero, demand increased. Being late simply became even more convenient. The ethical concerns had been swept away.

There is a monetary principle in economics called Gresham's law. It states that bad money drives out good. For example, if there are two forms of commodity money in circulation—say, minted gold coins— that are legally set to have the same face value, the more intrinsically valuable commodity (e.g., the coins with higher gold content) will disappear from circulation as people hoard it. Thus, if "good" and "bad" money are required by law to be accepted at equal value, the bad money will dominate circulation. People who are spending money will hand over the "bad" coins rather than the "good" ones, keeping the "good" ones for themselves.[13]

There's a similar law in employee motivation: bad incentives drive out the good ones, as the example of the day-care center shows. The more a leader relies on financial incentives, the less he or she will be able to rely on engagement. And the less the leader can rely on engagement, the more he or she will need to rely on financial incentives. It is a vicious and futile cycle because financial incentives cannot possibly produce excellence. Financial incentives can never drive people to do good work because they want to, because they care, and because it is the right thing to do.

WHY MEANING TRUMPS MONEY

From an economic standpoint, meaning trumps money for three reasons. First, as I explained earlier, material goods are exclusive. There is only so much money to go around. So if I get a portion of the bonus pool as a reward for my performance, you don't. If you get it, I don't. If we both get it, the shareholders don't. This results in winners and losers—rivalry, turf wars, bickering, envy, and resentment.

Nonmaterial goods such as meaning, purpose, ethical pride, autonomy, and belonging are not exclusive. If you are inspired by the company's mission, it takes nothing away from my own inspiration. On the contrary, nonmaterial rewards expand rather than shrink the pie. The community that shares a vision enjoys a network effect that enhances the inspiration and sense of belonging for each of its members. If you are sincerely proud of the values our organization expresses and we exemplify through our work, that doesn't take anything away from my being proud as well. And if we are both proud, we take nothing away from the shareholders' pride, either. In fact, each one of us makes everyone else prouder.

Second, the value of material goods is disconnected from the way they're achieved. Whether I get the money because I deserve it, because everyone gets it, or because I game the system, the money is worth the same to me. As a pure economic being, I'm a "mercenary"; that is, I care only about how much I can get, by whatever effort-minimizing means I can get away with.

Nonmaterial goods, on the other hand, are highly dependent on the manner in which they're achieved. If I am a mercenary, I don't care about our company's noble purpose. Hence, the value of the nonmaterial aspect of my compensation is zero. If you are a "missionary," on the other hand, you care deeply about the company's purpose. Therefore, the nonmaterial aspect of your compensation is quite valuable to you. Furthermore, you can't enjoy the nonmaterial goods you haven't rightfully earned. For missionaries, an unearned nonmaterial reward is like a white-hot coin straight out of a smelter; it burns their fingers.

Third, material incentives are punitive and contingent on external factors beyond the control of employers. "If you achieve the results I want, you get a reward," the employer tells the employee. "But if you don't achieve them, regardless of the reason, you don't get a reward—and may be punished instead" (by being fired or demoted). This kind of statement appeals to two unrefined human emotions: greed and fear. Think of these two drivers as dirty leaded gasoline. They may propel your vehicle forward, but eventually they'll clog the engine and pollute the environment.

By contrast, nonmaterial goods are not contingent on external factors. What provides meaning is the pursuit of our noble purpose, while expressing ethical principles in community with people whom we appreciate and who appreciate us. These don't depend on any external forces, only on the actions of those who commit to them.

In my previous work, I've distinguished between pursuit of goals or success that is dependent on a contingent future and the commitment to process values—to success beyond success.[14] Success yields immediate pleasure, which is short-lived and subject to the anxiety of loss. You won a championship, but you may lose your title in the next round, quarter, or fiscal year. Success beyond success yields peace of mind, which is much more stable and free of anxiety. You may win or you may lose, but you can always do your best and promote ethical values.

I like to think of meaning, integrity, and belonging as a climbing harness on my way to a rocky pinnacle of success. It provides me with a sense of security and self-confidence, because I can trust that even if a challenge proves too difficult for my current capabilities, I will not fall. Holding fast to these values allows me to commit enthusiastically to noble goals, with the knowledge that I am guaranteed to succeed beyond material success. This knowledge lets me engage fearlessly and have a sense of perspective so I don't sweat the small stuff. It allows me to learn from any mistakes without self-recrimination.

In a story from Homer's *Odyssey*, Odysseus asks his sailors to tie him to a mast so that he can hear the sirens' song without harming himself. Meaning, integrity, and belonging are like that mast. It gives you the security to reject the dangerous songs of the sirens that will sink you and your followers into a sea of misery. It is a safety device to keep you on the path of righteousness, fending off the calls of your baser instincts. These values are the basis for the good life, a life well lived, the life that Aristotle called *eudaemonia* or "activity in accordance with virtue."[15]

In Chapter 1, I used the analogy of a blanket that's too short to explain the contradiction between global incentives to foster cooperation, and local incentives to foster accountability. If you pull the blanket up, your feet get cold; if you pull it down, your chest gets cold. There's not enough blanket to cover both ends of your body at the same time. However, through purpose, principles, people, and the granting of autonomy, there's a nonmaterial way to make this blanket large enough to keep you and your organization warm.

THE LEADER'S JOB

Eliciting people's internal commitment to pursue a common goal is the job of every leader. How do you do it? By making a transcendent offer that gives people a sense of significance: "If you give the mission your best," a leader proposes, "you will get not only material rewards but also pride, fellowship, freedom, and meaning in your life. You will go beyond yourself and connect with something larger and more enduring than your physical existence." And as you model ethical behavior and provide opportunities for employees to flourish, they will reward your company with their best efforts—which properly harnessed will turn into extraordinary growth and profits.

A transcendent leader seeks what he cannot demand—internal commitment rather than compliance, enthusiasm rather than obedience, love rather than fear. These are precious gifts, given only to a leader who is truly worthy of them, and who reciprocates with an equally precious gift: meaning.

To become a transcendent leader, you need to ponder what really motivates people. If you are a leader, invite your whole organization to answer these questions:

PURPOSE
- Why do we exist as an organization?
- What's our unique contribution to our customers and the world?
- Why would it matter to anybody else that we succeed?
- Why is our organization worthy of our best efforts?
- Does each one of us understand how his or her efforts contribute to our shared purpose?

PRINCIPLES
- What values do we want to express?
- How are we demonstrating a way of being and relating (to each other, and to all our external stakeholders) that we wish extended to all humanity?

- What behaviors will make us proud, regardless of the outcome of our efforts?
- Are we manifesting the true, the good, and the just in everything we do?
- What behaviors will foster collaboration while maximizing individual freedom and responsibility?

PEOPLE

- How do we create an inclusive environment where all those who share our mission and values feel like they belong?
- How do we connect to one another authentically?
- How do we ensure that everybody who belongs feels recognized, respected, and appreciated as a member of this community?
- How can we deepen our bonds of trust and solidarity?
- How can we better support one another to learn and grow?

AUTONOMY

- How do we foster informed choice and internal commitment so that each one of us can exercise discretion in service of our mission?
- How can we get better and better at the things that matter to us?
- What challenges are we taking on to test and stretch our abilities?
- What activities can help each and all of us learn and grow?
- What feedback mechanisms can support our improvement efforts?

PURPOSE

When my daughter Michelle ("Michi") was about seven years old, she saw me packing for a business trip. I was going to the insurance company Axa's headquarters in Paris. She pleaded with me to stay. "Please, Daddy, don't go," she begged. And she pierced my heart.

I was tempted to give her a perfunctory and dismissive response like "I wish I could, sweetie, but Daddy has to work," but I didn't do that. Such an answer would have made it look as if I were forced to make the trip by powers beyond my control, and that wasn't true. I opted instead to give her an answer more in line with my philosophy of response-ability, an answer that spoke to what at heart Axa's business provided to its customers: I was choosing to go because it mattered. Here is how I explained it:

"If I died, Michi dear, it would be a very bad thing," I said. "I would miss you a lot. I would not get to see you grow. And you'd miss me, too. We'd miss a lot of fun things I am planning for us to do together for many years to come."

She looked at me with big eyes, wet with tears.

"But if I died, it would be worse than that," I added.

"Why, Daddy?" she asked.

"Not only would I be gone," I explained, "but you and Mommy would have financial hardships. Mommy would have to work many more hours to pay for food, the house, the car, your school, and many other things all by herself."

By this time, Michelle was becoming genuinely upset.

"I've done something to make all this less bad," I told her. "Even though I can't ensure that the first part won't happen, the people I am going to work with on this trip will make sure that you and Mommy would be okay. I've made a deal with them so that if something happens to me, they will give Mommy enough money to buy all the things she'll need to take care of you without having to stay at work any more hours than she does now. The people who do this know that people like me want to protect their loved ones in case they are not there, so I pay them a small monthly fee, and in exchange they will pay Mommy the money she needs if I die. It's called 'insurance,' and it is a beautiful thing. It allows me, and many other people who love others who need them, to go out into a sometimes-scary world with peace of mind. I am grateful to them and proud to help them do this better and better."

Her eyes were still wet, but she smiled and said, "Go, Daddy, go."

During my meeting at 25 Avenue Matignon, I shared the story with Axa executives. "You are right, Fred," one of them commented. "We don't sell insurance; we sell love."

• • •

Deep down, every company has a noble purpose—it just needs to find it. I was proud to help Axa enable people to take care of their loved ones even beyond their physical existence—allowing them to face a risky world with confidence and peace of mind. And their purpose inspired me to give them my absolute best. I was proud to explain to my daughter what I really did. I could have told her that I was going to work to make money—Axa was certainly paying me for my services. But that would have been only a half-truth, and the less important half of it. The higher truth was that I was fulfilling my life mission by aligning myself with a company that helped people live better lives.

In my leadership workshops, I ask participants: "How would you describe to a seven-year-old child what your company does in a way that he or she would be proud of you?" I encourage them to open this conversation with their colleagues when they get back to their organizations. By discovering the human need that your company's product or service meets, you can connect your people to a noble purpose, one that can bring meaning and pride to you, your colleagues, and your family. How would you answer the question? What would your manager say? What about your colleagues, your employees, your customers?

We all want to work for organizations that understand how best to deploy their technology, their resources, and their talent for the greater good. We all want to create value, make positive social and environmental changes, and increase opportunities for those we care about. No one aspires to work for a company that harms its customers with its products or ruins the environment with its processes. What that means is that leaders who want to engage their organizations need to think about how they are making a positive difference in the world.

If you are to engage your colleagues, they (and their families) have to believe that the product or service you are offering is truly life promoting—as is the work process through which you produce it. This requires empathizing with your customers and understanding what's important to them. How does what you are offering allow them to meet their needs? It also requires empathizing with your employees and understanding what's meaningful to them. How does the work you are offering your employees allow them to meet their needs?

Paul Polman, the CEO of Unilever, once thought about becoming a priest and spending his life as a spiritual leader. It's not all that surprising; as the head of the world's third-largest consumer goods company, Polman has earned a reputation as a global business leader with a conscience. A tall, round-faced Dutchman with a twinkle in his eye, he is a standard-bearer for the noble purpose of business.

When Polman took over the company in 2009, he vowed to cut Unilever's environmental footprint in half by 2020, to double the size of its business at the same time, and to help one billion people achieve better health and well-being. Those are daunting—some would say crazy—goals, but Polman believes in what Jim Collins and Jerry Porras call "big, hairy audacious goals" (BHAGs for short). He also insists that "If you believe in something, you have to fight for that and have the courage to take the tougher decisions that come with it."[16]

At the heart of Polman's thinking is the desire to provide a concrete example of the business case for sustainability. For example, he worked with former UN secretary-general Ban Ki-moon to examine how business can work more effectively with the United Nations, and he helped create the Consumer Goods Forum, which has agreed, among other things, to stop buying palm oil, paper, soy, or beef from illegally forested areas by 2020. "We are trying to show that you can be successful as a business and at the same time show the financial community this should be one of the better drivers for their investments," Polman says. "We are growing and our share price is doing well. So we gain credibility. The more we can reinforce that link and show it to others, the more we can be a galvanizer in this world for good. That is what success will look like."[17]

Polman has aligned his huge multinational company in the service of a noble purpose. "Making sustainability a strategy and an operating model opens doors that are beyond people's imagination," he adds.

"Who will refuse that journey, who will refuse to jump on the train for a better world?"

A noble purpose, consistently managed, fulfilled, and modeled by leaders, can drive individual and organizational projects through an "invisible hand" as a benefit to society. A company with a meaningful project like Unilever's is not designed to "destroy the competition" or "be number one" but rather to create economic value (which is human value) through mutually advantageous exchanges with customers, employees, shareholders, lenders, suppliers, and other stakeholders.

PRINCIPLES

"You who are on the road must have a code that you can live by," Crosby, Stills and Nash sang. Although they referred to parents and children, they might have as well been referring to leaders and followers. Humans are ethical animals. We care deeply about what is good and just. Ask anyone why he or she did something and you'll get an ethical justification. From the five-year-old's "He hit me first!" to the fifty-five's "I have the right!," we seek to legitimize our actions by appealing to moral principles. To fully engage, we need a code that we can live by with pride. As a culture architect, every transcendent leader needs to define moral principles for the organization.

In his book *The Moral Landscape*, the neuroscientist and philosopher Sam Harris argues that "Questions about values . . . are really questions about the well-being of conscious creatures."[18] Good is that which fosters the flourishing of conscious beings and directs our attention to the set of attitudes, choices, and behaviors that influence it positively. Harris claims that human sciences can help us understand what any person should value, want, and do in order to live the best life possible, while at the same time supporting others in living the best lives possible. For him, there are right and wrong answers to moral questions, just as there are right and wrong answers to questions of physics.

The moral principles that have proved most effective in fostering human development are respect for self-determination and property rights. The founding fathers of the United States predicated as a self-evident truth that every human being is endowed with "unalienable" rights to life, liberty, and the pursuit of happiness—to which I'd like to add the search for meaning. Transcendent leaders hold these truths as the foundational principles of their organizational cultures. Their code is based on unconditional respect for every human being as an end in him- or herself rather than as a means for others' ends.

Transcendent leaders establish moral principles that respect individuals' self-determination. They give everyone, from employees to customers to vendors, the opportunity to make free and informed choices to promote their happiness, limited only by the equal rights to life, liberty, and property of everyone else.

They also establish effective principles that engage employees in pursuing a common purpose and using their dispersed knowledge intelligently. As I've noted, this is preciously rare. Most people in positions of managerial authority believe that they can best accomplish this through extrinsic motivation and control. These managers believe it is their job to stand between chaos and a well-functioning organization. They design structures, put processes in place, establish rules, and enforce them through sanctions. This is a mistake. To reiterate: the leader's job is to elicit people's internal commitment to collaborate to accomplish the organizational goal.

An effective organization functions as the result of the employees' individual commitment, regardless of the will of those in power. This allows it to achieve order without control; in fact, a certain measure of self-organization is essential for a company to maintain coherence in a volatile, unpredictable, complex, and ambiguous environment. Dee Hock, founder and former CEO of the Visa credit card association, summarized his ideas about self-organizing systems this way: "Simple, clear purpose and principles give rise to complex, intelligent behavior. Complex rules and regulations give rise to simple, stupid behavior."[19]

Too many leaders arrogantly (and ineffectively) try to shape the environment around them, rather than allowing the environment to help inform and guide their choices. By contrast, transcendent leaders are acutely aware of their limitations, which makes them humble. They are not intent on shaping the organization to their will. Rather, they become stewards of principles that foster alignment, collaboration, and use of knowledge to further the organizational mission.

Netflix, for example, has simplified its rule book to nothing. "Rules annoy us," they announce. "Rules creep into most companies as they try to prevent errors by less-than-stellar employees. But rules also inhibit creativity and entrepreneurship, leading to a lack of innovation. Over time this drives a company to being less fun and less successful. Instead of adding rules as we grow, our solution is to increase talent density faster than we increase business complexity. Great people make great judgment calls and few errors, despite ambiguity. We believe in freedom and responsibility, not rules."[20]

PEOPLE

Among the most significant sources of well-being at work (and life in general) are the good relationships we have with people around us. For most of our existence, humans have related most closely to those of our kin—a successful Darwinian strategy to replicate our genes.[21]

Abstract language, as noted by the Israeli historian Yuval Noah Harari,[22] has allowed us to vastly expand the reach of our communities, enabling cooperation and collective action at a much larger scale, reaching into the billions. This "memetic" kinship, to use the term popularized by the biologist Richard Dawkins to refer to mental genes,[23] allows large numbers of people to feel like they belong to the same group, creating a sense of identity that transcends any familial or racial distinctions. For example, people from different ethnicities will define themselves as American, as will those who came to America from diverse national, cultural, or religious backgrounds.

The same happens with companies. As Harari asserts, *Homo sapiens* came to dominate the world because we are the only animal that can cooperate flexibly in large numbers. This is due to our unique ability to conceive of and believe in objects existing purely in the imagination, such as gods, nations, money, and limited liability corporations. Harari claims that all large-scale human cooperation systems—including religions, governments, trade networks, and business organizations—derive from our distinctive cognitive capacity for imagining fictional entities: "Large numbers of strangers can cooperate successfully by believing in common myths. Any large-scale human cooperation—whether a modern state, a medieval church, an ancient city or an archaic tribe—is rooted in common myths that exist only in people's collective imagination."[24] Large numbers of strangers can cooperate successfully because, by believing in common myths, they stop feeling like strangers to one another.

Transcendent leaders are able to create social bonds based on a common narrative. Bob Chapman, CEO of Barry-Wehmiller, chose the common narrative of the family. Chapman didn't start out trying to be a transcendent leader. He took over his father's manufacturing technology and services company in 1975 when his father died suddenly of a heart attack. Chapman was a traditionally trained, by-the-numbers businessman; profits were everything, and he saw people as mere means to an end.

That was until one day, as he and his wife attended a wedding, he had a sudden "Eureka!" moment. As he saw the love with which the families of the bride and groom supported their union, he realized that caring for employees the way one cares for precious family is the job of a leader. So he set about treating every employee of Barry-Wehmiller and its subsidiary companies the same way.[25] "At the core of Barry-Wehmiller's philosophy is the belief that leaders shouldn't manage people; they should steward them," Chapman says. "After all, who in your life do you 'manage'? Your spouse? Your children? No, you care for them. You acknowledge the deep responsibility you have for them."

Chapman came to a startling conclusion: "We measure success the wrong way in this country. We measure it by the financial performance and growth of a company, and yet we've got people whose lives are being destroyed every day by the way in which many companies operate." So he made his core resolution: "We are going to measure success by the way we touch the lives of people. All the people: our team members, our customers, our vendors, our bankers. For every action we take, we need to understand the impact it has on all the people whose lives we touch." Chapman's concern was not only the interests of Barry-Wehmiller's direct stakeholders. "If every business did that," he added, "the world would be a much better place than it is today."[26]

The sense of community at Barry-Wehmiller is palpable. "Those who work [at the company] talk of their 'love' for the company and each other," Simon Sinek writes in *Leaders Eat Last*.[27] "They proudly wear the logo or the company's name as if it were their own name. They will defend the company and their colleagues like they were their own flesh and blood." This devotion has paid off. Since 1998 the company has grown from $38 million to $2.4 billion and more than eighty companies. Sinek also found that Barry-Wehmiller "continues to outperform their competition year after year. Twenty percent year after year compounded growth the past twenty years."[28]

I understand the appeal of trying to establish a lifetime relationship with a sense of belonging, but I worry that in doing so leaders may set themselves up for a misunderstanding. In a family, parents can't fire their children for financial or performance reasons, or because there is a slowdown in the business or the economy. In a company, managers do lay employees off for these reasons. Employees who believe in the family analogy could feel betrayed—and justifiably so.

Reed Hastings, the CEO of Netflix, says, "We're a team, not a family." He challenges his managers to ask themselves, "Which of my people, if they told me they were leaving for a similar job at a peer company, would I fight hard to keep at Netflix? The other people should get a generous severance now so we can open a slot to try to find a star for that role."[29]

Like LinkedIn founder Reid Hoffman, I believe that the metaphor of a sports team is a better analogy for a company. By that, I mean it has the following characteristics:

- *A specific mission* (to win the games and the championship) for which the team members come together.
- *Flexibility in composition*. The players change over time, either

because they choose to leave or because the coach decides someone else is best suited for that position.

- *Common principles* of trust, mutual investment, and mutual benefit, which prioritize team success over individual glory.
- *Success for all.* When the team succeeds, individual members do, too.
- A *commitment to winning* (purpose) together (people) through fair play (principles) and high performance (mastery).

This doesn't mean that a company doesn't care about relationships. While a professional sports team offers only limited employment for its players, the employer-employee relationship still benefits when it follows the principles of trust, mutual investment, and mutual benefit. Teams win when their individual members trust one another enough to prioritize team success over individual glory. Such an approach is perfectly compatible with individual incentives. The team's success is the best way for individual team members to succeed.

Instead of creating bonds of loyalty as in a family, both leaders and members of a sports team seek the benefits of alliance. "As allies, employer and employee try to add value to each other," Reid Hoffman suggests. "The employer says, 'If you make us more valuable, we'll make *you* more valuable.' The employee says, 'If you help me grow and flourish, I'll help the company grow and flourish.' Employees invest in the company's *adaptability*; the company invests in employees' *employability*."[30]

My son Tomás beat me at Scrabble for the first time when he was seven years old. I felt more joy and pride on his behalf than if I had won myself. I was happier to see him succeed than to prevail over him—which I was certainly trying to do.

Because I love Tomás, I am committed to supporting his well-being and development. Seeing the beloved person flourish is the greatest joy, a joy worth spending intense efforts and taking great risks.

The Greeks called this kind of love *agape*.[31] "*Agape* has to do with the mind: it is not simply an emotion which rises unbidden in our hearts; it is a principle by which we deliberately live." We are not responsible for our feelings—we can't help how we feel—but we are responsible for our *agape* because *agape* is not a feeling but an act of will. *Agape* is a commitment, independent of our likes and dislikes.

Transcendent leaders extend *agape* beyond their family and friends, to the stakeholders in their organization and beyond. This is the key to preserving personal bonds in the workplace, without falling into dangerous confusions between family ties and professional relationships.

AUTONOMY

Every human being craves autonomy. We all want to be the sovereigns of our lives. When we work for others, we can sell our physical and perhaps even our mental energy, but we never sell our emotional energy. We may sell our bodies and our minds, but we never sell our hearts and souls. The latter we give only as a gift, to those who deserve them. Whoever attempts to curtail our self-determination through authority will never get our best.

There's tremendous power in giving employees autonomy and the opportunity to use their own best judgment. Nordstrom, for example, has a simple statement of purpose for its new employees: "We're glad to have you with our company. Our number one goal is to provide outstanding customer service." And then they present an equally simple rulebook: "Rule #1: Use your good judgment in all situations. There will be no additional rules. Please feel free to ask your department manager, store manager, or division general manager any question at any time." Nordstrom does not rely on complex procedures and controls to ensure quality service. They rely on hiring and training employees who care about their customers, and then inspiring these employees to demonstrate their care judiciously.

Lee Cockerell, the COO of Disney World for many years, created the rules that Disney theme parks operate by. Their "cast members" were given responsibility to handle customer complaints immediately at the park, without having to go to a manager. After this happened, complaints plummeted and customers were delighted. There were a few instances when an employee overcompensated, such as giving a golfer a free complete set of clubs in response to a complaint, but that was part of the growing pains of giving employees increased responsibility. And the upside was a huge uptick in engagement and less turnover.[32]

In contrast to top-down command-and-control management, employee autonomy is a gold mine; it's a much better motivator and driver of productivity than money because each of us wants most of all to feel respected and supported in our growth. Allowing employees to make their own decisions, and to learn from the consequences, encourages workers to be more engaged and more loyal to the company. Having the chance to design their work gives people a sense of personal power and self-respect. They see themselves as self-determined beings who exert a great measure of control over what they do.

In 2005, a couple of management consultants came up with an idea called "Results-Only Work Environment" (ROWE) based on the idea that employees have total autonomy over where they work, how they work, and when they work. Employees are measured only on the results they produce—not the amount of time they spend at their desks, the number of meetings they attend, and so on. In a ROWE organization, employees have total autonomy.

The idea has proven itself in companies that require less physical space and where employees are highly self-disciplined. ROWE-certified organizations (SpinWeb, GAP Inc., American Family Insurance, and others)[33] report that employees use fewer sick days and take less time off, because they can better work around appointments, illnesses, and other events, and that employees are healthier, happier, and have less work-related stress. ROWE increases employee satisfaction and decreases turnover, thereby reducing hiring and onboarding costs; and then they have a major increase in productivity.

"Pay doesn't have the power it used to when up against the ultimate benefit of autonomy—control over one's time," says Jody Thompson, one of ROWE's creators. "This levels the playing field and creates a workforce that is focused on what's relevant to the business. It's the workplace for adults. Managers manage the *work* (clear, measurable results), not the *people* (my time and place)."[34] When people are engaged, managing them is not necessary; when they are not, it is not sufficient.

"Autonomous motivation involves behaving with a full sense of volition and choice," researchers Edward Deci and Richard Ryan write, "whereas controlled motivation involves behaving with the experience of pressure and demand toward specific outcomes that comes from forces perceived to be external to the self."[35]

Deci and Ryan, along with Paul Baard of Fordham University, carried out a study of workers at an American investment bank. As Daniel Pink reports, the three researchers "found greater job satisfaction among employees whose bosses offered 'autonomy support.' These bosses saw issues from the employee's point of view, gave meaningful feedback and information, provided ample choice over what to do and how to do it, and encouraged employees to take on new projects. The resulting enhancement in job satisfaction, in turn, led to higher performance on the job. The researchers found that the benefits that autonomy confers to individuals extend to their organizations."[36]

An organization offers its employees far more than money when people within it are given a meaningful purpose, autonomy, challenging work, collaborating colleagues, and opportunities to stretch and grow while they express their values in action. Business is based on win-win exchanges, on trading for mutual benefit. To get employees engaged in your organization, you must give them something that they find more valuable than any alternative use of their life energy.

During one of his visits to MIT, I had the opportunity to host Russell Ackoff, Wharton Emeritus Professor, organizational theorist, and founding father of systems thinking.[37] In a casual conversation, he made a comment that has stuck with me throughout the years. "Money to a company is like oxygen to a human being. If you don't have enough, you have a serious problem," he said. "But if you think that life is just about breathing, you are missing the point." Nobody wants to just breathe. Nobody wants to live to work or work to live. In our hearts, every one of us wants to be fully alive, to contribute something worthwhile to the world, and to experience the enormous satisfaction that comes from being purposefully alive.

Transcendent leaders see through the cultural and psychological illusions that alienate people. They understand that the vast majority of us are not moved primarily by money. We are moved by meaningful purpose, ethical principles, and connections to other people. We value autonomy, mastery, and learning. We are at our best when we're in the creative and playful flow and when we're challenged to stretch ourselves in the face of exciting challenges. We don't live from the outside-in, seeking to fill our emptiness; rather, we live from the inside-out, seeking to express the fullness that we are. To get our best, companies must recognize us and treat us according to our true nature.

The connections between positive leadership behaviors, employee well-being, and productivity are as scientifically grounded as the connection between wholesome habits like diet and health. But if you have developed unhealthy leadership habits, adopting the habits of the transcendent leader is as hard as it is to quit eating sugary foods. That's why, to become a transcendent leader, you need to undergo the personal transformation I'll describe in Part 3. It's not a fad or a crash diet; it's a new way of eating for life.

Chapter 7
CULTURE
DEFINE, DEMONSTRATE, DEMAND, AND DELEGATE

> Culture is a segment of the meaningless infinity . . . on which human beings confer meaning.
>
> —Max Weber

Among the annoyances many of us endure when flying, from surly TSA agents to gum stuck in seat pockets, overbooked flights take a special place. Airlines do this because they assume that some people won't arrive at the gate on time. So when all the passengers show up, the gate attendants have to entice some of them to surrender their seats and reschedule their flights with travel vouchers, gift cards, or cash. This arrangement works if enough people have flexibility, but what happens when this is not the case?

On Sunday, April 9, 2017, a nightmarish incident took place on UA 3411, a completely full United Airlines flight bound from Chicago to Louisville, Kentucky. Despite the offer of up to $1,000, people refused to voluntarily surrender their seats to accommodate four off-duty crewmembers who had to get to Louisville for another flight the next day. When selected to give up their seats involuntarily, three passengers grudgingly deplaned, but a sixty-nine-year-old Vietnamese-American doctor, David Dao, refused to leave, claiming he was needed at a Louisville hospital. That's when United's employees decided to deploy their muscle. The crew engaged security personnel to thuggishly drag the screaming doctor off the plane. Cellphone videos taken by other passengers showed Dao's face bloodied as his glasses fell from his face.[1]

The videos went viral; they were seen by hundreds of millions of people around the world. The outrage they drew was universal. Everywhere there were calls for boycotts.[2] Twitter and Facebook were filled with snarky comments such as "not enough seating, prepare for a beating." The late-night comedian Jimmy Kimmel created a fake ad starring a United flight attendant wearing brass knuckles who said, "We'll beat you so badly you'll be using your own face for a flotation device."[3] The PR disaster got worse when United's CEO, Oscar Munoz, congratulated the crew's behavior in dealing with the passenger, whom he called "disruptive and belligerent"[4] (presumably for screaming while being dragged off the plane) and then tweeted euphemistically, "I apologize for having to re-accommodate these customers." (The word *re-accommodate*, someone responded, "sounds like 'I'm going to re-accommodate your face with my fist.'"[5])

Following the episode, United's shares dropped as much as 4.3 percent, or $3.10 per share, losing more than $950 million in market cap. Less than a month after the incident, Munoz was hauled before Congress to explain himself. He accepted responsibility, calling the event an "epic mistake," and repeatedly expressed his regrets. Nevertheless, his belated apology didn't earn him any sympathy. United's brand remains one of the worst in the airline industry (a fact that its competitors are conveniently exploiting), and Congress pushed hard on Munoz and other airline industry executives to make things right for customers.

Why did United's employees act so callously? Why didn't they care about their customers? Why didn't they think about the epic disaster they were about to create for the brand? Why didn't they look for creative alternative ways to get their staff to Louisville—just a five-hour drive from Chicago? Why did they think such brute tactics were called for? Why didn't the pilot intervene? And why did the CEO think that what Jimmy Kimmel described as "sanitized, say-nothing, take-no-responsibility, corporate BS speak" would soothe an angry public?

The answer, in short, is a dysfunctional culture. In United's value structure, sound decision making, autonomy, and responsibility are clearly not a priority. United seems to have indoctrinated its employees to blindly follow rules and procedures rather than training them to think on their feet and deal with situations on their merits, or doing what seems best to help the team to win in alignment with ethical values. Even if customer care is not as high a value in United's culture as the company claims, I'm sure that financial performance is. The actions of United's employees were not just insensitive, they were also counterproductive. They destroyed a tremendous amount of brand value for no real reason—except covering their backsides by doing what they were told by their superiors or a rule book.

In Part 1, I said that the hardest problem of an organization is to align its members in pursuit of a common goal. This difficulty is explained by the clash between two economic theories. "Nonlinear optimization," as we economists call it, prescribes that employees must avoid attempts to improve their individual or team performance indicators (e.g., sales revenue, productivity, customer satisfaction, employee rotation, debt days outstanding, inventory turns, and so on) if those indicators clash with the organization's global performance indicators (such as profits, growth, and economic value added). To encourage them to "optimize the system," to use another economics term, their performance needs to be measured and incentivized based on these global indicators.

On the other hand, "optimal contract theory" proves that when self-interested employees know more than their managers about the conditions surrounding them, their capabilities, and their efforts, the only way to financially motivate them to work hard is to make them accountable by basing their compensation on their individual performance indicators. This, unfortunately, incentivizes employees to do the exact opposite of what nonlinear optimization theory prescribes.

For example, United employees are promised a reward (such as continued employment, a bonus, or a promotion) if they follow their managers' instructions, and a punishment (getting fired, losing their bonus, or getting demoted) if they don't. This incentivizes employees to do as they are told by their bosses. Such an arrangement is expeditious and works well in most circumstances. But this system encourages people not to apply their special knowledge to a given circumstance or think about the consequences that their actions might bring about for the company. When the United crew members saw the situation escalate badly with Dr. Dao, they might have considered that it would be best for the company if they left the poor fellow in his seat. But since their job was to do what they were told, they shut down any such doubts and received a starring role in an infamous viral video.

In the previous chapter, I explained how a leader could realign an individual's interest in the mission through appealing to an ethical purpose. In this chapter, I argue that an equally important tool for any leader is an effective culture. Culture acts as an emotional force field that aligns organizational members in the same way that a magnet aligns iron shavings. And it does so without requiring financial incentives based on individual performance indicators. This is because peers observe one another's environmental conditions, talent, and effort much more accurately than any manager. And cultural norms enforced through the threat of social sanctions such as embarrassment, exclusion, and isolation are much more effective than financial incentives to align an organization.

WHAT IS CULTURE?

"Culture might eat strategy for lunch," the great management guru Peter Drucker supposedly said.[6] Yet culture seems like an abstract concept, for most of us, difficult to grasp and impossible to design. But ignoring culture is an expensive mistake. When Ram Charan and Geoffrey Colvin asked why CEOs fail,[7] they found that it was because they were unable to fully execute their strategy. What these CEOs don't understand is that culture is the key to strategy execution.

I think of culture as a human-centered operating system, a set of basic instructions that guides the behavior of the members of the organization. Like an information systems platform, culture provides the essential capabilities required to run the business processes—most important, strategy execution. If the culture is not adequate, the strategy will not be fully executed, just as Microsoft Office for Windows won't run on a Mac. And when the strategy fails to execute, the CEO and the organization fail.

MIT professor Edgar Schein defined culture as a pattern of shared assumptions, beliefs, and expectations that guide members' interpretations and actions by defining appropriate behavior within the organization.[8] I prefer to simply define culture as the set of beliefs people hold about "what we value and how we do things around here." These values and norms set expectations about "what one has to think, say, and do in order to be one of us." On the other hand, culture includes also the set of beliefs about things that one *cannot* think, say, or do if one wants to be one of us—that is, the taboos. Culture exists in the minds of the people who live it. It's not what anyone says, but what everyone understands. It is a mostly subconscious map of how to proceed in alignment with the group's norms and remain as a member in good standing.

An effective culture addresses the hard organizational problems of disengagement, disorganization, disinformation, and disillusion. It engages employees around a noble purpose, ethical values, and meaningful goals. This elicits their internal commitment and provides a sense of individual and collective identity. It also coordinates employees' expectations and behavior. Most important, an effective culture does this without depending on formal control systems or reducing the autonomy required for excellent performance in complex, ambiguous, and constantly changing situations.

Formal "thou shalt" and "thou shalt not" rules never yield extraordinary performance. Requiring employees to follow formal procedures is like asking them to paint by the numbers. There's not a lot of originality, capability, or thinking involved. Formal rules standardize performance, but they are useful only in recurrent predictable situations such as a preflight inspection routine, and in high-safety organizations in arenas such as emergency response, deep-ocean oil drilling, or the military, where sticking to the rules can mean the difference between life and death.

• • •

To really enjoy our jobs, we need work that is varied and challenging, work that not only allows but also demands autonomy and discretion. In fact, one of the crucial attributes of the most effective organizations (as identified by Jeffrey Pfeffer in his book *The Human Equation*[9]) is that they rely on self-managed teams and decentralized decision making. That is, employees are given a lot of discretion and autonomy.

The less leaders direct employees, the more ownership they take and the better they perform. In 1983, for example, Toyota took over a failing General Motors assembly plant in California. Toyota didn't change the equipment or the workers. The only thing the company changed was the production system from one based on formal rules to one that gave workers much more autonomy. The result was a dramatic improvement in productivity and quality. Labor costs dropped almost 50 percent.

Unlike formal rules, culture empowers employees to think and act on their own, increasing their engagement and the bonds among them. Letting their colleagues down is much more of a concern than breaking rules. Thus, organizational members monitor not just their own behavior, but also the behavior of their colleagues against the organization's strategic objectives. This frees up their managers, who do not have to micromanage them and can instead focus on the really important work of leadership: engaging their employees in pursuit of the organization's goal.

Stories of Southwest Airlines' employee empowerment with regard to customers are the stuff of legend. Consider this one from 2011: A Los Angeles man's grandson was beaten into a coma by his daughter's boyfriend. The unfortunate child was near death. The man's wife called Southwest to arrange a last-minute flight to Denver so that he could say good-bye to the child. But getting to the L.A. airport was a nightmare, and getting through security was worse. Nobody at TSA gave a damn. Finally, the man made it to the gate twelve minutes after the plane was scheduled to depart—but he was shocked to find that the pilot had held the plane for him. The man thanked the pilot profusely, and the pilot said, "They can't go anywhere without me, and I wasn't going anywhere without you. Now relax. We'll get you there. I'm so sorry."[10] Compare that kind of treatment to what Dr. Dao received at the hands of United Airlines, and you can understand why customers would much rather fly with Southwest.

Companies like Southwest, Nordstrom, Zappos, and others that have a great reputation for outstanding service[11] all empower their employees to do what it takes for customers. Once these companies started operating, their strategies were obvious to everyone—and yet, nobody could copy them because their cultures grew stronger employee by employee, year after year. Such companies prove that culture is the ultimate source of competitive advantage because it takes years for any competitor to replicate. That's why it's such a strong barrier to competition.

THE FOUR PILLARS OF AN EFFECTIVE CULTURE

An effective culture is built on four pillars: *high consensus, high intensity, productive content,* and *high adaptability.*

Consensus is the degree to which members agree on values and norms. *Intensity* is the strength with which members hold values and norms. An effective culture needs both consensus and intensity. If intensity is high but consensus is low, an organization can break apart into "warring factions"[12] where one group (say, sales) battles another (say, product engineering). If consensus is high but intensity is low, the organization will wallow in mediocrity. (In such a disengaged culture, members agree on what's important, but nobody cares enough to put in their best effort to achieve it.)

Content consists of the specific attitudes and behaviors defined by the behavioral norms. A high-consensus/high-intensity culture that upholds counterproductive values and behaviors will handicap the organization. For example, consider a firm in which political gamesmanship is the way to achieve status and power. In such a place, people undermine each other, and a person's status is more important than what he or she does or says. In such a culture, the goal is to prove that one is right and others are wrong, and destructive criticism is the surest way to climb the corporate ladder. Such an organization may pay lip service to culture and espouse collaborative values, but these values never turn into action. Those are the organizations that attract egocentric, hypocritical, narcissistic leaders and followers.

There are two types of organizational content: platform and strategy. *Platform* norms are the foundation of every interaction among organizational members and their external stakeholders. (In the following chapters, I'll describe three platform norms that I consider essential for any organization: response-ability, collaboration, and integrity.) *Strategy* norms are the ones that focus employees' attention on the key variables required to fully execute the organization's strategy. They help negotiate priorities and make decisions for the sake of the common goal. An effective culture must support strategy execution; its norms must be strategically relevant. In fact, it is impossible to evaluate the effectiveness of a culture, without relating it to the organization's strategy.

Consider how Southwest supports its strategy with platform norms. The airline's simple strategy is to offer short, convenient flights at low cost. To do this, it flies just one kind of plane (Boeing 737) and eliminates first-class seats. Because its airplanes fly point-to-point without forcing passengers through hubs, its arrival times are carefully coordinated (and passengers don't have to face the hassle of transferring). It doesn't ask passengers to pay hidden fees, such as for checked bags. Because it keeps its promises to customers, it has a tremendous reputation for service.

Southwest Airlines' employee values are "a warrior spirit" (which the airline describes as fearlessness in giving workers everything they need to support customers); a "servant's heart" (treating others with respect, following the Golden Rule); and a "fun-luving attitude" (reflected in the word *luving*).[13] Employees at Southwest know they must "do what it takes to make the customer happy," including friendly, open joking on the public address systems (something like "Hi, I'm Captain Amanda Smith. Yes, I'm a female pilot and as a benefit, if we get lost on the way, I won't be afraid to stop and ask for directions").[14] They have room to maneuver around the rules in order to deliver on the brand promise. They understand the company's goals and the strategies to achieve them. And they care about what their coworkers will think of them if they don't uphold the values and norms of the culture.

Southwest has a team-based culture in which people support one another to execute the strategy of on-time departure and arrival. One *Forbes* writer, Carmine Gallo, described it this way: "Like a polished pit crew in auto racing, each member of the team feels responsible for the success of their colleagues." A pilot told Gallo that "We genuinely like each other. And when you like each other, you have each other's backs. We take one for the team." The founder and former CEO, Herb Kelleher, added this: "Attitude is very important and has to be weighed with experience and skills. Someone with a high IQ who is a backbiter is a disaster for your organization. Someone who is outgoing and altruistic and can work convivially will be a huge asset."[15]

When a trusting culture supports strategy this way, companies become industry leaders. Apparel retailers Nordstrom and Zappos, for instance, focus on a "customer service" strategy supported by people who are empowered to do whatever it takes to make the customer happy. Apple's strategy of innovation is supported by people encouraged to think creatively, and so on. In organizations with effective cultures like these, the strategy norms quickly and powerfully align people behind the most important success drivers.[16]

Adaptability is the ease with which norms can change to maintain the organization's viability in the face of environmental changes. As MIT's Edgar Schein argued, culture must address not only the need for internal integration but also the need for external adaptation.[17] An effective culture needs to have high adaptability to avoid the dangers of rigid conformity and to become flexible, innovative, and creative. Adaptability acts as a sort of antidote for traditionalism, encouraging divergent behaviors as a part of "what it means to be one of us." Adaptability gives social approval to exploratory, creative, and innovative activities that bring about change. Researchers have found that organizations with a high consensus, high intensity, and strategically relevant culture outperform the competition over the long run, provided they have norms and values that promote adaptability.[18]

While a high-consensus, high-intensity culture can improve performance in a static environment, it may worsen it in turbulent ones. Such a culture offers employee consensus, discipline, and willingness to pursue the organizational goals. But strong norms can induce organizational members to always take the status-quo position and chastise those who deviate from it. Cohesive groups tolerate less variation in members' behavior, so they can easily fall into groupthink. In turbulent environments, this constrains an organization's ability to respond to new challenges. For example, when Japanese carmakers entered the U.S. market in the 1970s, American companies dismissed them based on assumptions such as "Japanese don't know how to make cars," "Americans won't buy low-quality Japanese cars," "Americans won't buy small vehicles," "Fuel economy is not a significant factor in vehicle choice," and so on. They held on to these high-consensus high-intensity beliefs until it was too late to catch up with the Japanese companies. Today, Honda, Toyota, and Nissan build more cars in the United States than GM, Ford, and Chrysler.[19]

Thus, an effective culture must promote the freedom and support necessary for people to challenge assumptions, take risks, learn, and grow.[20] When people feel safe, they are much more likely to offer ideas, question the status quo, seek feedback, experiment, reflect on results, and discuss errors or unexpected outcomes openly. If you instill the perception that "taking intelligent risks,"[21] as we say at LinkedIn, is "the way we do things around here," people will be more willing to discuss problems, develop new ideas, and try new things.

HOW IBM CHANGED ITS CULTURE

In 2003, the year after Sam Palmisano took over as CEO of IBM from Lou Gerstner (who saved the iconic firm from near shipwreck during a massive market shift in the mid-1990s[22]), the company ran a seventy-two-hour experiment called Values Jam. The goal was for IBM's employee hive-mind to help update IBM's century-old corporate values (first written in 1914 by President Thomas Watson Sr. as "Basic Beliefs": "respect for the individual," "the best customer service," and "the pursuit of excellence"). Fifty thousand of the company's 750,000 employees engaged in a forum conducted over the company's intranet to answer the question, What does IBM stand for?

"Unfortunately, over the decades, Watson's Basic Beliefs became distorted and took on a life of their own," Palmisano told the *Harvard Business Review*.[23] " 'Respect for the individual' became entitlement: not fair work for all, not a chance to speak out, but a guaranteed job and culture-dictated promotions. 'The pursuit of excellence' became arrogance: We stopped listening to our markets, to our customers, to each other. We were so successful for so long that we could never see another point of view. And when the market shifted, we almost went out of business."

Palmisano printed out the two hundred thousand comments from the Values Jam, took them home, and read them over the weekend. People let off all kinds of steam, and there was vociferous criticism. "The electronic argument was hot and contentious and messy," Palmisano said. He received plenty of criticism himself, but he put his ego aside ("not easy for a CEO to do," he noted). For him, the Values Jam had produced invaluable insight into what needed to happen: "You could say, 'Oh my God, I've unleashed this incredible negative energy,'" he said. "Or you could say, 'Oh my God, I now have this incredible mandate to drive even more change in the company.'" The following Monday, Palmisano suggested that his executive team read every one of the comments. "If you think we've got this place plumbed correctly, think again," he told them.

After a long and messy process, the company agreed on three values that are now embedded in its strategy: (1) "dedication to every client's success," which means "having skin in the game of your client's success"; (2) "innovation that matters for our company and the world," which means inventing and building products that can make a positive difference in the world; and (3) "trust and personal responsibility in all relationships" (with employees, suppliers, investors, governments, communities).

These aren't just feel-good values; all strategic decisions are made in alignment with them. In line with its first value, "dedication to every client's success," IBM changed its management compensation scheme. Bonuses and raises for managing directors are based on client evaluations, and the longer horizon gives managers an additional incentive to satisfy the client over the long term.[24] "I think values inject balance in the company's culture and management system: balance between the short-term transaction and the long-term relationship, balance between the interests of shareholders, employees, and clients," Palmisano said. "In every case, you have to make a call. Values help you make those decisions, not on an ad hoc basis, but in a way that is consistent with your culture and brand, with who you are as a company."

For example, the values dictated a new pricing system, which not only spoke to the care-for-client issue but resolved internal alignment issues. Instead of having multiple units offer separate and confusing bids for hardware, software, services, and financing, IBM now offers a single price for each integrated offering. "To be honest, we'd been debating the pricing issue at the executive level for a long time. But we hadn't done anything about it," Palmisano noted. "The values initiative forced us to confront the issue, and it gave us the impetus to make the change."

Understanding that IBM stood for its second value, "innovation that matters for our company and the world," was crucial for all its smart people. IBM research has been making forays outside the computing realm and into areas such as health care. For example, the company codeveloped with Pfizer a system for Parkinson's sufferers that speeds up clinical trials. Off-the-shelf sensors and mobile devices work to define patients' digital signatures, see how they're feeling and responding to medication, and send their information in real time to researchers and doctors. Then an AI component looks for connections and clinical data such as medicine doses.[25]

"There is an unmistakable yearning for this to be a great company," Palmisano said of the conclusions from the Values Jam. "They [employees] want to be part of a progressive company that makes a difference in the world. They want to be in the kind of company that supports research that wins Nobel Prizes, that changes the way people think about business itself, that is willing to take firm positions on unpopular issues based on principle. We can't offer them the promise of instant wealth, which they may get at a start-up, or a job for life, as in the old days. But we can offer them something worth believing in and working toward."

Another thing IBM did was to allocate first-line managers a discretionary fund of up to $5,000 annually that could go toward generating business, developing and enhancing client relationships, or responding to an emergency. Trusting managers to make intelligent decisions about spending this walk-around money made the point that IBM lives by its third value, "trust and personal responsibility in all relationships."

"Instead of galvanizing people through fear of failure, you have to galvanize them through hope and aspiration," Palmisano said. "You lay out the opportunity to become a great company again—the greatest in the world, which is what IBM used to be. And you hope people feel the same need, the urgency you do, to get there. Well, I think IBMers today do feel that urgency. Maybe the jam's greatest contribution was to make that fact unambiguously clear to all of us, very visibly, in public."[26]

DEFINE THE STANDARD

Establishing culture norms is a four-step process that I call the "Four D's": define, demonstrate, demand, and delegate. *Define* means explicitly clarifying the standards for expected behavior (e.g., when and how to escalate a disagreement to higher-ups, as I discuss in Chapter 8). *Demonstrate* means comporting oneself according to the standard (e.g., escalating a disagreement collaboratively). *Demand* means confronting those who deviate from the standard (e.g., challenging anybody who escalates a disagreement unilaterally). And *delegate* means requiring that everyone on the team defines, demonstrates, and demands the standard for those who report to them (e.g., holding the same conversation about collaborative escalation with their teams). Beyond any standard, however, the ultimate norm of an effective culture is that everyone in the organization pursues its purpose ethically.

After establishing the values and the mission through stakeholder input, as IBM did through its Values Jam exercise, the next step is to have a conversation with your team in which everyone agrees on the ways to execute the organization's strategy, achieve its mission, and enact its values. Beyond that, the conversation should establish the ways of thinking and acting that you all want to model for everyone else in the organization. I have found that the best standard-setting conversations follow this pattern:

Propose: Explain why you think a given behavioral standard can help the group work more effectively and ethically. For example, I start my workshops with this proposal: "In order to better work together and respect people's need to concentrate on the material, I suggest that we all put our phones in silent mode, and that we do not use them within the room. If someone absolutely needs to answer a call or check messages, he or she can step outside the room to do it."

Check: Make sure that everybody agrees that the standard is workable, ethical, and truly improves effectiveness. For example, after making the proposal about phones, I add, "Does that seem like a good way to work together to you?" If people say yes, we move on. But this is not a perfunctory step. It's quite possible that someone might have a problem with the suggestion. In that case, a negotiation is in order.

For example, I've had more than one participant say, "Sorry, Fred. I'm expecting an important message that requires an urgent response. I'm happy to step out of the room to read it and reply to it, but it would be terribly cumbersome to stand up and leave every time my phone vibrates. I'd like to be able to quickly look and see if it's the important message. If it is, I'll step out. If it isn't, I'll wait till the break to read it. Would that be okay with you?"

Commit: At the end of the negotiation, ask people to make a commitment. Admonishments, ground rules, or agreements mean nothing if they don't turn into commitments. What binds people to behave in a certain way is their word, not mine. Asking for a promise is the crucial step I use to engage people's integrity. That's why the standard cannot be just a request or, even worse, an order. It needs to be a collective commitment. (More on this in Chapter 10, "Integrity.")

In my workshops, after the negotiation, I conclude by saying, "We have agreed that we will keep our phones silent. We might look at them to see who's calling or what message is arriving, but anything requiring more than a few seconds happens outside of the room. Can you all commit to that?" And then I don't continue until I get a yes from everyone present.

DEMONSTRATE THE STANDARDS

Just as children learn the culture of their family by observing their parents, new members learn the culture of an organization by observing their leaders. Anyone who wants to achieve a good standing will emulate the behaviors of those who reached the top. As a transcendent leader, you must behave according to the standards that you've set. After all, your behavior, and theirs, is the organization's brand.

As I've already pointed out in Chapter 5, nothing makes people in an organization more cynical than a leader who says one thing and does another, especially when demanding that people do as he or she says. Imagine the effect if, five minutes after people in my workshop and I all define a standard of behavior such as "We won't use our cell phones in this room," my phone rang and I took the call. It would be devastating. Such behavior on my part would convince everybody that my word is not to be trusted. Any contradictory behavior of a leader destroys trust. And without trust, organizational members can't coordinate actions effectively and deliver on their collective promises.

The problem is that even if a leader believes her behavior doesn't appear to contradict her declarations, other people can have a different view of how the standard works in a given situation. It is possible that you believe you are behaving in line with the standard—but someone else thinks you are not. This is why it's crucial to discuss the difference of opinion and take whatever actions are needed to dissolve the tension. The permission to question anybody who seems to break the standard, especially the leader, is a crucial norm in itself.

In my workshops, I encourage people to express any questions they might have about my behavior. I explain that my commitment is firm, but at times I may make a mistake or act unconsciously, and that I welcome people to challenge me. I'm always willing to discuss whether or not I am aligned with the promises I made. Any leader can recover from a mistake. But he or she cannot recover from a refusal to discuss the possible mistake without undermining the standard, his or her identity, and the organization's engagement.

You don't demonstrate your values only through personal, direct actions. You also express your values through the formal systems and processes you institute. Perhaps the most important of these processes is recruitment and selection. As bestselling author Jim Collins wrote, "You must get the right people on the bus, even before you know where the bus is going."[27]

Culturally naive leaders focus their recruitment efforts on the person-job fit, discounting the importance of person-culture fit. The unintended consequence of eschewing person-culture fit is that the organization's culture will grow haphazardly, like a weed, rather than like a cultivated plant. It will "eat strategy for lunch," making it impossible for the organization to execute.

Obviously, if a new hire is successful, he or she will grow into other jobs in the organization. These jobs may require different skills, but they will exist within the same organizational culture. So it is best to hire people who fit with the culture, even if they don't have all the skills necessary for their first job. People can learn new skills much more easily than they can incorporate new values and norms into their personality structure.

The online shoe and clothing shop Zappos, which is routinely voted one of *Fortune*'s "Best Companies to Work For,"[28] hires people who fit with the company's core values:

- Deliver WOW (customer delight) Through Service
- Embrace and Drive Change
- Create Fun and a Little Weirdness
- Be Adventurous, Creative, and Open-Minded
- Pursue Growth and Learning
- Build Open and Honest Relationships with Communication
- Build a Positive Team and Family Spirit
- Do More with Less
- Be Passionate and Determined
- Be Humble

The CEO, Tony Hsieh, also wants altruistic people to work for the company. "A lot of our candidates are from out of town, and we'll pick them up from the airport in a Zappos shuttle, give them a tour, and then they'll spend the rest of the day interviewing," Hsieh told a reporter. "At the end of the day of interviews, the recruiter will circle back to the shuttle driver and ask how he or she was treated. It doesn't matter how well the day of interviews went, if our shuttle driver wasn't treated well, then we won't hire that person."[29]

All new hires, regardless of their skills and experience, are expected to work in the customer call center for a month, an experience that immerses them into the culture. A week into this training, the new hires are offered $3,000 to leave the company, because if they aren't fitting in, Zappos would rather have them leave. If they take the money, they can't come back. Nearly 100 percent of the new hires refuse the offer.[30]

Culture is also set in employee recognition and promotion. Whom you reward and promote and what you reward them for sends a tremendously important message to everyone in the organization about the right way to behave. Your choice of whom to empower with formal authority to manage the people of your organization is one of your most fundamental leadership choices. The same holds true for those whom you reprimand, censure, sanction, deselect, and fire. If United's CEO had fired the flight attendants and pilot of Flight 3411 instead of praising them, he would have sent a powerful message that "we don't treat any customer this way."

At Zappos, new hires are carefully acculturated through socialization (meeting a variety of employees, working in the call center, and so on). Socialization is the process by which an individual comes to integrate the values, abilities, expected behaviors, and social knowledge that are essential for assuming a role as an organization member.[31] Key aspects of socialization include ensuring that employees acquire cultural knowledge and that they bond with one another.

At LinkedIn, new hires have a chance to reveal something that is not in their LinkedIn profile and to demonstrate a unique talent or special skill in our biweekly all-hands meeting, hosted by our CEO. People are invited to show a more personal side of themselves to their peers. This has the benefit of breaking the ice.

DEMAND THE STANDARDS

It's not enough to demonstrate the standards. As a leader, you must also confront people who appear to be deviating from them. If a participant took a call or started texting during my workshop and I didn't say anything about it, it would be as bad as if I had taken the call myself. Both actions would be equally harmful to the culture I'm trying to set for the workshop.

People can have different interpretations of what a given commitment might demand in a specific situation. One of the team members might believe he or she is behaving in line with the standard, while you believe that is not the case. It's imperative to clear that difference collaboratively; that is why I suggest that any challenge start with inquiry about the point of view of the person who seems to be transgressing the standard.

Demanding the standard is not without risks. Issues of self-esteem and public image can trip up even the most skillful efforts. I can't emphasize enough how softly a leader has to tread when he or she wants to raise a team's consciousness about acting impeccably. One of my saddest professional memories is precisely about my failure to do this effectively.

I called the room to attention. Everyone was back on time—except Max, the team leader. I asked the people in the room whether Max had let anyone know that he'd be late. The embarrassed silence meant that my secret prayer had not been answered.

This product marketing team had a reputation among its internal customers for being unreliable and untrustworthy. That's why Max had hired me to work with them. The topic of commitments was the centerpiece of the workshop. Right before the break, we had discussed the importance of honoring commitments. We agreed to make the workshop an experiment in creating a culture of trust. "In order to operate with efficiency and respect, I request that you come back from the break on time," I had said. "Can you commit to that?" They all nodded their heads.

"If for any reason you learn during the break that you need more time," I added, "please let someone know so he or she tells the rest of the group. Let's establish the standard that it's okay to come late if you let us know ahead of time, but it's a problem if you show up late without telling us. Is that acceptable to you?" Again, they all nodded their heads.

"Great," I said, "I take your head nods as a yes. We have defined a new cultural norm. Let's go to the break and demonstrate it when we return."

At the risk of appearing compulsive, I had put great emphasis on the impeccability of commitments, especially the ones that define group norms. I wanted the people in the room to feel the stress of having to keep track of time during the break, going to the bathroom before the last minute, perhaps cutting an interesting conversation short or not making that last phone call in order to return on time. Preparing for the worst, and not wanting to alienate anybody who made a mistake, I gave them an out: "If something important comes up," I explained, "you can honor your commitment even without fulfilling it. If you get stuck and can't find anybody to let us know, please apologize when you get back and just tell us that you needed to take care of something and couldn't find a way to inform us."

I felt sure that after such emphasis (overemphasis, some of their faces said) they'd all be back at the agreed time, or they would let someone know they'd be late, or at least they'd walk into the room apologizing. I didn't expect that someone would strike out, least of all Max himself. So I felt bewildered when I saw that Max didn't return on time and that he'd told no one he'd be late. I didn't know how this would end, but I dove into the next topic: holding people accountable for their commitments.

Fifteen minutes later, Max came in and quietly took a seat in the back of the room. I opened a pregnant pause to let Max apologize. My last bit of hope was that he'd say "Sorry" and explain that during the break something urgent had come up and he'd been unable to find a way to inform us. Owning up to the breakdown, explaining what happened, and reestablishing his commitment would have honored his word and preserved the trust of the group. It would have also made my workshop-leader life much, much easier.

No such luck. Max remained quiet. I don't believe he was testing me; he seemed oblivious to the fact that his late arrival called for an apology. To make matters worse, nobody seemed to expect anything different, or to note that there was any problem with Max's behavior. No wonder the team's reputation was abominable.

I took a deep breath. I wanted to be the wise and compassionate teacher, and to show Max and his team how to demand cultural norms as a show of support for the mission and values of the team. My fear, though, was that I would alienate the hell out of them by holding

Max accountable before his team. That was the rock. The hard place was that unless I brought up the issue, my own credibility would be undermined—at least in my eyes, if not in theirs. Since Max himself had hired me to raise his team's awareness around commitments, I'd be breaking my own word if I slid the issue under the rug.

"Max," I said with a little hesitation, "you're late."

"Oh, yeah, sorry. Something came up," he replied breezily.

"I understand," I said, "but I thought we had all agreed that if that happened, you would let someone know."

"Oh, right. Sorry," he acknowledged. "I was in my office."

I was debating whether to ask him if he couldn't have asked his assistant to contact us, or why he hadn't apologized when he came into the room, but one of the participants beat me to the punch. Or perhaps I should say, beat me *with* a punch.

"What point are you trying to make?" the participant questioned me. "Why are you being so disrespectful to Max?"

"Yeah, why are you picking on Max?" someone else added. "He was just a few minutes late."

This was going sideways fast.

"I don't mean to pick on Max," I said. "I'm trying to make a point about commitments and group norms that is at the core of this workshop."

One of the premises of the workshop, I explained, is that the way we manage any commitment is a pretty good indicator of the way we may manage every commitment. "I was called here because you want to improve your reliability and trustworthiness as a team," I said. "So we need to examine and change the behaviors that your internal customers are complaining about. I think that we can turn this breakdown into a breakthrough, if we take it as a learning experience."

The stern faces staring at me flashed red, but I was in too deep to backtrack, so I doubled down. "We agreed to return on time from the break. We further agreed that if that became inconvenient we'd let someone know. Max didn't do this. Moreover, he came into the room and sat down without apologizing. When I questioned him, his response seemed casually dismissive. Now you're all upset at me for pointing out this clear breakdown in commitment. If I were an external observer, I would not trust this team's commitments. Would you?"

"All's well that ends well," wrote Shakespeare, but this did not end well. We got through the rest of the workshop awkwardly, but that was my last interaction with Max's team. A few months later, I learned from someone else at the company that Max had left his job. I don't know if he quit or was removed, but I do know that it took a new leader to help this team regain its credibility.

Many years later, I met one of the participants of this fateful workshop, who remembered what had happened. Unfortunately, the lesson he drew from it was that I was such a hard-ass about people being late that I went toe-to-toe against the leader of his previous organization. I was disappointed, as this was definitely not the lesson that I wanted people to learn, or the way in which I wanted people to remember me. I realized that I hadn't earned the moral authority I needed to coach them in an area as thorny as the one of integrity and trust. I had overplayed my hand as a workshop leader and missed the chance help them grow.

DOUBLE-DEMAND THE STANDARDS

If you want to lead a healthy, functioning culture, you have to turn your standards into social norms. This means that every team member needs to feel personally responsible for upholding them—including demanding that others abide by them, too.

For example, when I work with a leadership team, I set a standard that requires everyone to listen respectfully to other team members without interrupting. During our time together, some team member invariably breaks the standard.

Here's how I handle such situations. Let's say "Rob" cuts off "Rachel" in midsentence. Instead of calling out the breach, I remain quiet. Almost always, everyone else does the same. When Rob finishes his statement, I ask: "Did anybody notice that Rob interrupted Rachel?" Of course, everybody notices; most of them nod uncomfortably. That's my cue to ask the crucial question, "Why didn't anybody challenge Rob?"

I then remind them that not interrupting is a standard that we had all set collaboratively; it was neither a rule that I imposed on them, nor a commitment that everyone made to me. Not interrupting is a commitment all of us made to everyone else. I clarify that I'm not just demanding that the team members follow the standard; I am demanding that they demand it of one another as well.

"I don't want to be the bad cop that keeps everybody in line," I add. "I hope that each one of us holds each other—including me—accountable for our commitment to listen respectfully to one another. Are you ready to share this responsibility with me?"

In a paper for the *California Management Review*, UC Berkeley professor Jennifer Chatham described, in third person, her experience of going to buy shoes at a Nordstrom store. A sales associate named Lance showed her nine pairs of shoes. None were the size or color or style that she was looking for. "As she was leaving," Chatham wrote, "another sales associate, Howard, approached and suggested that he could call a few other Nordstrom stores to find the shoes. Ten minutes later, Howard excitedly informed her that, though he had not found the shoes at another Nordstrom store, he did find them at a nearby Macy's (a primary Nordstrom competitor).

"Rather than sending her to Macy's, Howard had already arranged for the shoes to be overnight mailed to her home. 'Of course,' Howard informed her, 'Macy's will bill you for the shoes, but Nordstrom will pay for the overnight delivery charge.' Howard understood the importance of customer service and was willing to go above and beyond the call of duty to ensure that even Lance's customer was completely satisfied. Furthermore, while leaving Nordstrom, Chatham overheard an interaction that she was, clearly, not supposed to hear. Howard had gone back to Lance and said, 'I can't believe you didn't work harder to find those shoes for her. You really let us down.' Howard was not Lance's boss—they were peers—and yet, the norms encouraging customer service at Nordstrom are so strong that members are willing to sanction each other, regardless of status, for a failure to uphold those norms."[32]

DELEGATE THE STANDARDS

As a leader, in addition to demanding that each of your team members demonstrates the standards and that he or she demands the standards of every other team member, you must insist that they, in turn, demonstrate and demand the standards from their own team members and ask that they delegate the same thing to the next level down. Delegation makes the standards go viral. If this doesn't happen, the cultural norm never takes.

Many leadership teams I've helped come up with excellent standards in their off-sites. Most of them do a pretty good job of demonstrating and holding one another accountable for those standards. The most common failure I've experienced is this last step. Leaders fail to replicate their conversation with their teams and to cascade the standards all the way to the front lines. This creates a disruption in the fabric of the organization, since there's an "in" group that upholds the standards and an "out" group that doesn't know or understand why the senior people behave in some unusual ways in their off-site—including getting mad at them occasionally for things that used to be fine.

When an information system fails to produce its expected product, programmers first look at the program they executed to correct any bugs. If the program is sound, they need to go further upstream and debug the operating system, the presumption being that it's not providing the requisite process capabilities.

As a leader, you need to do the same thing when your organization fails to fully execute its strategy. Perhaps the strategy is flawed, but most often this is not the problem. The bug in the system comes from the inadequacy of the culture.

In the following chapters, I explain three essential process capabilities that are necessary parts of any effective culture.

Chapter 8
RESPONSE-ABILITY

TO BE PART OF THE SOLUTION, BE PART
OF THE PROBLEM

> The basic difference between an ordinary man and a warrior is that a warrior takes everything as a challenge, while an ordinary man takes everything as a blessing or a curse.
>
> —Don Juan, Mexican shaman

"Sorry I'm late. My other meeting ran over." How many times have you used this excuse?

Tacitly, you are saying, "Don't blame me. If my previous meeting had finished earlier, I would have been on time." Such a justification may be true, but it's disempowering. Why? Because to claim that being late isn't your fault, you have to claim that it was not in your power to be on time. The price of false innocence is impotence.

The fact that the other meeting ran over is just that, a fact. It didn't make you late; you made you late. You made either a deliberate or an unconscious choice to stay put rather than leave. You may not be responsible for the meeting running over, but you are accountable for your choice when it ran over.

"It's not my fault!" you might say. "I stayed at the previous meeting because it was more important to the company than the later one. Saying that the previous meeting ran over is just a polite way of saying that the second meeting was not as important to me as the previous one."

I am not saying that it's your fault. Nor am I saying that you made a bad choice or that you should have left the previous meeting to be on time. I can think of many circumstances in which I would rationally make the choice to be late. What I am saying is that it's a matter of choice, and if I want to establish a culture of accountability, I need to fully own my choice. As a leader, I need to be the example of what I want to see.

Moreover, I need to take responsibility to minimize the negative consequences for those who expected me to fulfill my commitment. In this case, I may have a reasonable justification for being late; for example, that I was in a crucial meeting with the CEO and the leadership team of the company. But it's much harder to find a reasonable justification for not sending a quick message to the people who are waiting for me in the following meeting. As we'll see in Chapter 10, sometimes you need to break a promise and make a mess, but you can always let people know immediately, apologize, and clean it up.

It's tempting to appear as a "victim" to duck from responsibility and avoid embarrassment, but the price of an excuse is high. If you want to be a transcendent leader, you need to accept full accountability for your actions in any circumstance, even in circumstances that are not of your doing. This means consciously choosing your response to events, rather than telling a self-justifying story in which events drive you. If you want your organization to control its destiny, you must lead from the front. Instead of seeing and presenting yourself as a victim of forces beyond your control, you must see and present yourself as a player responding to a challenge. Only then will you have the moral authority to demand that everyone else do the same.

Once, when I was climbing a mountain with Leslie, a colleague who's also an Outward Bound instructor, we found ourselves in a storm. I cursed the bad weather. Leslie laughed and shared her favorite saying: "There is no such thing as bad weather, only bad gear." The saying makes me think of other times I've complained about things that are beyond my control—and how fruitless that is. The storm doesn't care whether I am happy or sad, or whether I live or die. The storm is just a force of nature. It is what it is, exactly as it is, and perfectly so. It is up to me to dress appropriately and to deal with it. Since that day with Leslie, I've adopted a new practice. When I'm dealing with a "difficult person"—someone who poses a challenge to which I don't know how to adequately respond—I switch into "Outward Bound" mode. I see the person as a force of nature. He is who he is, exactly as he is, and perfectly so. It is up to me to act appropriately in dealing with him.

I've also realized that there are no such things as hard problems, only situations I am unable to resolve. If I can't lift a certain weight, it's not because it's heavy, but because my muscles are not strong enough to do it—at least not yet. There are certainly weights that are too heavy for anyone to lift—now or ever, but that doesn't contradict the point I'm trying to make. My argument is that it's always more empowering to tell the story of the player: when I fail, it's because I don't yet know how to effectively respond to the challenges I face. And the same is true for you—or it can be true if you are willing to eschew false innocence as the price you pay for power.

Response-ability is the foundation of transcendent leadership. Consider two ways in which the people in your organization can explain a delay: (a) "The project was too hard. There were too many difficulties, and nobody helped us." (b) "The project was challenging and we didn't know how to deal with those challenges effectively. We failed to ask people for help in a way that would elicit their commitment. And we were so focused on finishing on time that we didn't let people know of the delay with enough time to minimize the disruptions we caused."

In this chapter I will show that what I call absolute "response-ability" and accountability are an effective philosophy of leadership, business, and life. By exemplifying response-ability as a leader, and holding people accountable for their own response-abilities, you can turn defensive behaviors into creative ones, and negative feelings like resignation and resentment into genuine enthusiasm and commitment.

A BUMPY RIDE

On a bright November morning in 2010, Qantas Airways Flight 32 took off from Singapore en route to Sydney. Just before reaching eight thousand feet, passengers heard a loud boom and then a crashing sound.

One of the engines had caught fire. The ensuing explosion tore fragments through the underside of the plane. A red alarm flashed on the pilot's control panel. A siren shrieked in the cockpit. The plane started shaking. Suddenly everything started to fail—fuel pumps, electrical systems, hydraulics. Twenty-one of the plane's twenty-two major systems were damaged or completely disabled.

The pilot, Richard de Crespigny, turned the plane back to Singapore. On the emergency descent, the computer system sounded, "Stall! Stall! Stall!"; de Crespigny ignored the automated voice and stayed focused on his task.

The runway was just long enough for the plane to land—if the captain overshot the asphalt, the plane would crash into sand dunes. One hundred meters short of the dunes, the plane skidded to a stop. That's when de Crespigny turned on the PA system and said to the passengers, "Ladies and gentlemen, welcome to Singapore. The local time is five minutes to midday on Thursday, November 4, and I think you'll agree that was one of the nicest landings we have experienced for a while."

Investigators later said that Qantas Flight 32 was the most damaged Airbus A380 ever to land safely. De Crespigny was declared a hero.[1]

In my workshops, I ask people to imagine that they are flying with me in this same plane, and suddenly we hear the explosion and see pieces of the engine fall away. A minute later we see the pilot coming out of the cockpit and taking a seat in the cabin. Freaking out, we ask him what's going on. He responds that there's an uncontained failure in one of the engines. "Then what the hell are you doing here?" we ask him. "Why aren't you in the cockpit?" To our shock, he replies, "Because fixing this problem is not my job; this is a maintenance problem."

At that point I ask participants, "What would you tell him?" After some discussion, the group always concludes that it doesn't matter who or what caused the problem. What matters is the captain's absolute responsibility for the safety of the passengers and crew. Anything that happens on the captain's watch is his or her responsibility.

I've had to apply this hard lesson many times as the captain of my fifty-foot sailboat, *Satori*. Everything that happens during the sail is my responsibility. If a storm surprises me, I didn't look at the weather carefully enough. If something breaks, I didn't inspect it carefully enough. If one of my crew does something unsafe, I didn't train her well enough. If one of my passengers hurts himself, I didn't brief him thoroughly enough or check that he understood and was able to execute my instructions. Everything that happens on my boat is on me.

If you want to be the captain of your business and your life, you must accept full responsibility, accountability, and ownership for everything that happens in it. Rather than being a victim of external circumstances, you must be the master of your actions—the one who makes choices and produces consequences with ultimate response-ability.

In the play called "Your Business and Your Life," you are onstage as the central character. You are not a spectator; you are the writer-director-actor. You contribute to bring events about, and you contribute to shape the future—always. As a player, you are *in* the game; you affect the result. As a victim, you are out of the game; you are at the mercy of those to whom you have surrendered the field. What kind of leader do you want to be? More important, what kind of leader will you choose to be?

WHAT IS RESPONSE-ABILITY?

I define *response-ability* as the ability to choose one's response to a situation. It's about focusing on the aspects of reality that you can influence, instead of feeling victimized by circumstances that you cannot. It's about being the main character of your own life. Instead of asking, "Why is this happening to me?," a person who is response-able asks, "What can I do when this happens?" Response-ability means you don't take anything personally. It doesn't rain on you; it just rains, period. Instead of blaming the rain, you carry an umbrella to stay dry when it rains. And if you get wet, you know it's because you didn't bring an umbrella, because you were not prepared.

The same applies to your team and your organization. You and your colleagues have the ability to choose your response to any situation. You can focus on what you can do instead of on what is out of your control by asking, "How are we going to accomplish our mission in spite of this challenge?"

Many people confuse the ability to choose a response with the ability to choose an outcome. Response-ability does not mean success-ability. There is no guarantee that the actions you and your team take will yield the results that you want. The only guarantee is that you can respond to your circumstances in pursuit of your goals and in alignment with your values. That's the best we can do as human beings—and it's not a small thing. Our response-ability is a direct expression of our consciousness and free will. To be an effective leader, in fact to become fully human, you need to become fully response-able.

When you play cards, for example, you have no control over the hand you are dealt. If you spend all your time complaining and making excuses for your cards, you will feel disempowered and most likely lose the game. But if you see yourself as having a choice in playing your cards, your feelings will change. You'll have a sense of possibility. Even if you don't win a given hand, you can always do your best with the cards you've been dealt, play fair, and improve your odds of winning the overall game.

Responsibility is not about assuming guilt. You are not responsible *for* your circumstances; you are response-able *in the face* of your circumstances. To take an extreme example: You are not responsible for poverty. You didn't create it; it's not your fault; you're not to blame. Poverty exists independent of you. It was there before you were born and it will be there after you die. In a reasonable sense, poverty is not a problem of your doing. You are, however, able to respond to poverty. If you are born into poverty, you can work hard and look for avenues that will lead you out of poverty. If you care about the poverty you see around you in society, you can *make* it your problem. Poverty is a brutal fact—you can learn about it, study how to ameliorate it, donate time and money to the right causes and organizations, you can start your own organization or volunteer for the Peace Corps. You can, if you wish, devote your life to helping the poor.

We are not automatons. Rather, we are "autonoms"—self-guiding beings. External facts are information, not stimuli. We don't answer the phone *because* it rings. Rather, we choose to answer the phone *when* it rings, because we decide it is better to answer the call than not to. External circumstances and internal impulses influence our behavior but they don't determine it. They may tempt us, but they don't "make us do it." We are human; we are conscious; we are free.

Most people define *freedom* as the ability to do whatever they want. They want to be "free from" constraints. This kind of freedom depends on factors beyond their control. Freedom does not mean doing what you want without limitations or consequences. Such "freedom" is an impossible fantasy. True freedom is your capacity to respond to a situation by exercising your conscious will. This is your birthright. True freedom is a basic feature of human existence. You always have the power to respond to situations as you choose. You cannot make reality different than it is or choose whether your actions will be successful. But you can choose the response most consistent with your goals and values.

When you express this response-able freedom, you inspire others to be response-able as well—within your organization and beyond. A transcendent leader exemplifies the power of conscious choice in a way that empowers the whole organization to exercise it.

THE VICTIM[2]

In *Conscious Business*, I made a distinction between a "victim" and a "player." In the ten years since its publication, thousands of people have told me that the distinction brought clarity, power, and control to their lives. Effective, transcendent leaders are players. So I'd like to introduce a central concept of that book to you (or reintroduce it, if you've read my previous work). Although the distinction is very simple to grasp, it's quite difficult to apply—especially when it counts the most.

A victim pays attention exclusively to factors he cannot influence, seeing himself as passively suffering the consequences of external circumstances. The victim wants to avoid blame and claim innocence. Since he believes he has nothing to do with the problem, he doesn't acknowledge that he's contributed to it or can contribute to solving it. When things go wrong, the victim seeks to place blame on anybody or anything but himself. Consequently, since he is not part of the problem, he cannot be part of the solution.

For the victim, life is a spectator sport. His favorite place is on the sidelines, not the field. He loves to criticize those who are in the game. But his opinions crowd out his actions. This makes him feel safe because, although he can do nothing to help his team, he cannot be blamed when his team loses. He tends to blame the players, the coach, the referees, the opponents, the weather, bad luck, and everything else. Although his explanations may be technically correct, they are disempowering. What he blames, he empowers.

For example, one summer day as I was working on this chapter, I felt thirsty. My wife, who was working next to me, asked me if I wanted something to drink. "Yes," I told her, "some soda water, thank you." She said she'd bring it to me, "Right away, as soon as I send this e-mail." As I waited for her to get something for me to drink, I felt a deeper sense of thirst and a tinge of frustration. I realized that I was blaming her for my thirst; I was stuck in my chair, feeling sorry for myself. Then I thought, *If I'm thirsty and want water right at this moment, why don't I get up and get the water myself?* So I did. When I returned, my wife asked, "Why didn't you wait for me to finish?" I explained my victim mind-set—and my need to get myself out of it. I let her read this paragraph, and we both had a good chuckle.

Human beings seem predisposed toward victimhood, just as we are predisposed toward sugar. Both of them give us short-term pleasure at the expense of long-term pain. In their early years, my children would complain when "the toy broke." I never heard them say, "I broke the toy."

Just like little children, we choose to adopt the "it's not my fault" victim stance when we want to protect ourselves from blame. It is not uncommon in organizations to hear that "The project got delayed," or

"The customer was unreasonable," or "They started it." We want to look good, to project an image of success—or at least to avoid the blemish that comes with failure.[3] Victimhood is an attempt to cover up our failures so that we look more capable than we really are. Whether or not we like to admit it, many of us depend on other people's approval. Thus, we expend a great deal of energy building an "unblamable" public identity.

Besides disempowering us from acting appropriately in the face of reality, the victim story prevents us from learning. As long as our problems are not our fault, we tend to wait for others to change or solve them. As a leader and as a player, you need to ask yourself what you need to learn in order to better respond to the situation or to better avoid this situation in the future.

Victimhood is like a drug that simultaneously relaxes and excites us. It relaxes us because whatever has happened is not our fault. It excites us because we feel that we have the right to blame others. The righteous indignation of the innocent victim is as addictive as heroin. But it stops us from looking in the mirror and asking ourselves: *What do I need to do in order to stop cocreating this?*

Rather than asking, *Who screwed up? Who wronged me? What should they have done instead? Who should pay?*, ask yourself what you can do to solve the problem or prevent it from occurring again. Blame obscures who and what is contributing to cause the problem. When things go wrong between people, each individual owns a piece of the mess. But this is not how most of us assess things. As the saying goes, "Success has many parents, but failure is an orphan."

The truth is that each of us contributes to a bad situation. We are all response-able for finding a way to make things right. It will be much easier to address the situation if all those involved become players and acknowledge their contributions. I call this "200 percent responsibility."

THE PLAYER

Leaders are players. The player pays attention to the factors she can control. She doesn't deny that there are many things over which she has no power, but she chooses not to focus on these things, precisely because she cannot control them. Instead of feeling overwhelmed by external circumstances, she sees herself as someone who can respond to them. Her self-esteem is founded upon doing her best, expressing her values, and learning how to be ever more capable. If something beyond her control happens, her explanations focus on her own participation in the event, since she realizes that she is the defining factor in the outcome. "If you want to be a part of the solution," she reasons, "you have to see yourself as a part of the problem. Unless you recognize your contribution to a bad situation, you won't be able to change that situation." She chooses self-empowering explanations that put her in control.

For leaders and players, the world is full of challenges that call on them to respond as what the shaman Don Juan would call a "warrior." The player does not feel omnipotent, but she faces challenges squarely and realistically and manages her emotions with equanimity. The player always describes herself as a significant part of her problems. She is willing to take the hit of accountability because it puts her in the driver's seat.

Because players feel empowered, they carry themselves and speak with a moral authority that inspires confidence in others. And the choices they make—even when the outcome isn't perfect—pay off in one way or another down the road. By behaving in a response-able way, they bring an extra measure of goodness into their lives and the lives of those who follow their lead.

Taking the stance of the player is not without cost. Freedom and accountability are two sides of the same coin. But if you own your actions, you can be asked for your reasons for your decisions and held accountable for their consequences. The price of power is accountability.

EXTREME OWNERSHIP

"My mind was racing," SEAL commander Jocko Willink recalled in his account of the most important leadership lesson he ever learned, and the unbearable price he almost had to pay for it. "This was our first major operation in Ramadi, and it was total chaos."

Four separate SEAL units in various sectors of the city were working with U.S. Army and Iraqi forces to clear out an entire neighborhood of heavily armed insurgents, building by building. In total, about three hundred American and Iraqi troops—friendly forces—were operating in the same hotly contested area of the city. The fog of war "was thick with confusion, inaccurate information, broken communications, and mayhem."[4]

Willink's command post had received two calls for help, one from U.S. advisers embedded with the Iraqi army, the other from a SEAL sniper team. Both were involved in firefights against heavily armed insurgents. Willink decided to respond first to the Iraqi army position. When he arrived, a gunnery sergeant was coordinating an air strike to wipe out what was believed to be a group of hard-core mujahideen in a nearby building. "I'm working on getting some bombs dropped on 'em," the sergeant told him.

Willink had a bad feeling about this. Something didn't add up for him. They were very close to where the SEAL sniper team that had also asked for support was supposed to be. In addition, the Iraqi soldiers had entered the area before the SEALs had a chance to "deconflict" it—that is, to determine their exact location and to communicate it to all the other friendly units in the operation. Willink was not sure whether the firefight was with the actual enemy or with the SEAL sniper team.

"Hold what you got, Gunny," Willink ordered the sergeant. "I'm going to see who's in that building." He approached the door to the compound, which was slightly open. "With my M4 rifle at the ready, I kicked the door the rest of the way open only to find I was staring at one of my SEAL platoon chiefs. He stared back at me in wide-eyed surprise."

Willink and the SEALs in the building quickly figured out that they were in the midst of a "blue-on-blue," or friendly-fire situation. Willink was shocked. "I felt sick. One of my men was wounded. An Iraqi soldier was dead and others were wounded."

Blue-on-blue is the worst thing that can happen, according to Willink. "To be killed or wounded by the enemy in battle is bad enough," he noted. "But to be accidentally killed or wounded by friendly fire because someone screwed up is the most horrible fate."[5]

When the SEALs completed the last mission of the day, Willink went to the battalion tactical operations center where he had his field computer set up to receive e-mail from higher headquarters. "I dreaded opening and answering the inevitable inquiries about what had transpired," he remembered. "I wished I had died out on the battlefield. I felt that I deserved it."[6]

As he began gathering information for the ensuing official inquiry, Willink discovered serious mistakes made by many individuals, both during the planning phase and on the battlefield during execution: "Plans were altered but notifications weren't sent. The communication plan was ambiguous, and confusion about the specific timing of radio procedures contributed to critical failures. The Iraqi army had adjusted their plan but had not told us. Timelines were pushed without clarification. Locations of friendly forces had not been reported. The list went on and on."

Not all the errors came from the Iraqis. Willink's own SEAL troop made similar mistakes. "The specific location of the sniper team in question had not been passed on to other units. Positive identification of the assumed enemy combatant, who turned out to be an Iraqi soldier, had been insufficient. A thorough SITREP (situation report) had not been passed to me after the initial engagement took place."[7]

Willink put together a presentation summarizing his findings. The information was all there, but he felt something was still missing. He still hadn't identified the single point of failure that had led to the incident.

"Then it hit me. Despite all the failures of individuals, units, and leaders, and despite the myriad mistakes that had been made, there was only one person to blame for everything that had gone wrong on the operation: me. I hadn't been with our sniper team when they engaged the Iraqi soldiers. I hadn't been controlling the friendly Iraqis that entered the compound. But that didn't matter." The lesson Willink learned was that as the senior leader on the ground in charge of the mission, he had to become responsible for everything that happened and take complete ownership of what went wrong. "That is what a leader does—even if it means getting fired."[8]

Willink presented his conclusion to his commanding officers in a formal review, as is customary, attended by all his soldiers. Despite the tremendous blow to his reputation and his ego, he took full ownership of the situation and apologized to the wounded SEAL. Doing this not only preserved the trust of his officers and the respect of his troops, but it helped him keep his job. It also allowed everyone to learn valuable lessons to avoid repeating these mistakes. These lessons were later incorporated in the training drills for all SEALs.

"There are no bad units, only bad officers," wrote Willink later. "This is a difficult and humbling concept for any leader to accept. But it is an essential mind-set to building a high-performance, winning team." He concluded that on any team or in any organization, the ultimate responsibility for success and failure rests with the leader. "The leader must own everything in his or her world. There is no one else to blame. The leader must acknowledge mistakes and admit failures, take ownership of them, and develop a plan to win. The best leaders don't just take responsibility for their job. They take 'extreme ownership' of everything that impacts their mission."[9]

I agree with the spirit of Willink's conclusion. And I would like to make a different point. In addition to the leader taking total responsibility for anything that affects the performance of the unit, every team member needs to take total response-ability in the face of any circumstance that affects the mission. Each person is accountable for the way in which he or she prepares, responds, and learns from the challenges that he or she has to confront. There is no blame for events that depend on factors beyond one's control, but there must be full accountability for preparing and dealing with them with effectiveness and integrity.

ABSOLUTE RESPONSE-ABILITY

"We got screwed," complained Stu. "We announced this product as the hottest thing since sliced bread, but after we sold it to our best customers, the product and finance people realized that it was not as profitable as the earlier version. So they withdrew it from the market. Now I've got a lot of pissed-off clients who have lost their trust in us."

Stu is a sales executive at an enterprise software company I advise. Several months before, the company had launched a much-anticipated new version of their flagship product. The company had touted its upgraded system to its best customers while it prepared to launch a sales campaign to acquire new customers. The salespeople had worked hard to sell the new version to their existing customers, who had proved eager to adopt it.

But the product had proved significantly harder to use than anybody had expected. The heavy demands for training and technical support made it uneconomical. The support costs eroded margins to the point that the previous version was much more profitable. So the company decided to withdraw it. This decision was made without the participation of, and even without giving information till the last minute to, the sales organization. For Stu, this felt like a terrible double whammy. Not only did the salespeople look terrible to customers as representatives of the company, but they also looked stupid for being out of the loop of what was happening or, if they were in the loop, malicious for being unwilling to communicate the problem to their customers until the very last minute.

This is the kind of thing that salespeople, to say nothing of the customers, deeply resent. The resentment manifests as a loss of trust in the brand and in the people who represent it. In particular, salespeople can be bitterly angry toward the product development people, seeing it as a betrayal.

When I ran a workshop on "becoming a trusted adviser" for the sales executives of this software company, the participants took the position of victims. They felt justified in their feelings. They were mad as hell and felt miserable. "The product people screwed us. There was nothing we could do about it!" they complained.

They got mad at me when I interrupted their complaints. "I disagree," I challenged them. "There is always something you can do about it, and even more things that you could have done before it. But to see the things you could have done, you must give up your victim story and take the position of the player."

Here's an account of the dialogue that I had with Stu, the most vocal of the victims:

Stu: The product people screwed us. How can customers trust us anymore?

Fred: Obviously, unless we address this issue, calling a salesperson a customer's "trusted adviser" is dead on arrival. Do you have any ideas?

Stu: Sure! If a decision to pull something off the market is being considered, we should be involved in the discussions. And if the decision is made, we should have a strategy to announce this to customers with plenty of time to let them adjust with minimal consequences.

Fred: That all sounds good to me. Can you do it?

Stu: No. It's not up to me. This is something that Product should do. Right now, we sales executives have no say in these matters.

Fred: Your idea seems reasonable, but you can't implement it. So where does that leave you?

Stu: Up shit creek without a paddle.

Fred: Is that where you want to be?

Stu: Of course not.

Fred: So then why stick to that story? It gives you a justification, but it doesn't give you a solution.

Stu: What's the alternative?

Fred: Consider the situation as a challenge that you are facing, rather than as something someone is doing to you. Can you describe the essence of this challenge?

Stu: The challenge is that I'm trying to build a relationship with customers based on trust, where they believe that I have their interests at heart and that I will take care of them, while other parts of my organization are destroying this trust by discontinuing products that I sold to my customers.

Fred: Excellent. Now comes a really hard question. How have you contributed, by doing or by not doing, to create this situation?

Stu: What? Are you saying this is my fault?

Fred: No, Stu. I'm saying that you are part of the system, so you must have been involved in some way in cocreating this. If you want to be the solution, you have to place yourself as part of the problem. This is not about your faults but about your ability to influence things.

Stu: OK. I'll give it a try. If I was going to blame myself . . .

Fred (interrupting): Please don't blame yourself, Stu. I am asking you to empower yourself.

Stu (laughing sarcastically): If I were going to empower myself, I would say that I sold the product to the customers, making an implicit commitment that we would continue with it for some time. I never discussed this openly with them, but it's an obvious assumption that we all made. I didn't check this assumption with the product organization. In fact, if I were going to be really hard on myself, I'd have to admit that this is not the first time that something like this has happened. So in the back of my mind I was worried that this product would not make it. But I didn't say anything to my customers, or to the product people in my company . . . Shit, I feel terrible saying this.

Fred: I get it, Stu. It stings. But you're doing great. This is the price of power. You can do something about the problem and perhaps regain the customers' trust. The next question is, Could you have done something to prevent this from happening?

Stu: Clearly, yes. I could have negotiated with Product some conditions about maintaining the product for a certain time. Or if I couldn't do that, I could have told the customers that this product was in a testing period and that we couldn't guarantee that we would continue to support it. I could have negotiated some conditions with the customer—maybe they could test it with a discounted price, or be reimbursed if we discontinued the product, or something. I don't know if my boss would have let me do any of this, but I could have raised it.

Fred: Did you ask?

Stu: No. I guess I was too eager to sell the new product. And I was afraid that I'd get chastised for not being a team player.

Fred: Since we're practicing here, let's take it to the limit. Let's say Product doesn't budge and the company doesn't allow you to negotiate any conditions with the client. Is there anything you could do to preserve trust with your customer?

Stu: I have to answer yes to your question. Man, I'm embarrassed I didn't think of this before . . . If worse came to worst, I could have told the customer the truth. I could have discussed the potential for any new product to not become what we call "commercially viable" and being discontinued summarily. Once a product has been out for a year or so and it becomes part of our core, we are very careful about any changes in it, but until it proves its worth it's at risk. If a customer doesn't want to take that risk, I would advise them to not buy it, at least right away. Right now, that disclaimer is, literally, in the small print that nobody reads.

Fred: How would you feel about doing that?

Stu: Like I'm betraying my company.

Fred: It sounds to me like you're being responsible and acting with integrity. If the company is not willing to back the product, and even puts that caveat in small print in the contract, it's not a betrayal for you to be straight with your customers. You know that their assumptions about the continuity of the product are mistaken. Alerting them about the truth is what a trusted salesperson would do. My next question is: What can you do now?

Stu: I can talk to my customer and own up to the fact that we were not as transparent with them about the product as we should have been.

Fred: We?

Stu: Sorry, *I* wasn't as transparent as I should have been. But before I do that I need to speak with my manager and clear it. And I also want to ask my manager and my teammates to join our voices to discuss this matter with Product. And if we can't get satisfaction, then we can take the matter to the CEO.

Fred: What lesson do you take from the experience, and from this conversation?

Stu: It is much easier to be the victim in a situation like this. But the only way to solve it is to be a player.

A DEFECT IS A TREASURE

The Japanese proponents of total quality management say that "a defect is a treasure." In the same way that a fever alerts you that something is wrong with your body, a defect alerts you that something is wrong with your business—or the domain of your life in which the defect appears.

The defect is often buried under the surface. To find it, it's necessary to avoid the temptation to just fix the problem without looking for the root cause. If you lower the fever with medication, you'll suppress the symptom, but you'll never find the underlying infection. Treating symptoms instead of the cause can have serious consequences, the least of which is that the real cause of the problem continues to create trouble. To find a cure you have to diagnose the source of the fever and then prescribe a treatment for it.

The total quality recommendation is to "ask five times why." Under this scrutiny, the defect reveals its source. If you find and address this root cause, you will improve the system at a fundamental level. You will not only solve the specific problem that caught your attention, but many potential others that an out-of-control process could produce. For example, when LinkedIn users or customers report an error, our engineers don't just rush to fix it. They go "under the hood" to debug the system.

A defect, more generally, is any gap between what you desire and what you get, between your vision and your reality. The tension between these two poles is like that between the two poles of a battery. The difference in charge between positive and negative generates the electricity that can energize a circuit. Action springs from dissatisfaction. Dissatisfaction with the current state drives your effort to shape a different future.

Before you can prescribe, you need to diagnose. Before you take effective action, you need to find the root cause of the problem. When you get a result you want to change, first ask yourself why it happened. Too often our first impulse is to attribute causality to factors beyond our control. As I've argued, this may be part of the truth, but it's the truth of the victim. This explanation discharges the battery and makes us unable to improve anything.

FROM VICTIM TO PLAYER

An essential step in shifting from victim to player is to change your explanation of events. Instead of saying, "The meeting made me late," say, "I stayed late at the meeting." Here are some examples of player statements: "I didn't back up the file"; "I missed my deadline"; "I lost track of time and stayed too long"; "I could not find a way to reach our profit targets"; "I did not establish rapport with the client"; "I couldn't convince senior management to support the project."

Even when unexpected things happen, use the language of the player. Instead of focusing on the event, acknowledge that you did not anticipate the possibility. You can say, for example, "I did not prepare for such a traffic jam," "I did not foresee that the weather could turn nasty," "I didn't think that our suppliers wouldn't deliver on time," or "I underestimated the risk of the project."

The specific words are less crucial than the frame of mind. Consider the difference between the first and the second statements in the following pairs of sentences:

VICTIM	PLAYER
It's impossible.	*I haven't found a way yet.*
Someone should have done it.	*I didn't check on it.*
I couldn't do it.	*I chose not to do it.*
You shouldn't do that.	*I ask you to not do that.*
I'm being kicked out of the room.	*I need to free up the room.*

The victim sentence of every pair argues that "I'm not in charge." The player claims that "I'm making a choice."

In my workshops, I help people understand this shift from victim to player through the following exercise:

"Consider a bad experience you had, or are having right now: an ineffective meeting, a harsh conversation, a business or personal problem. Choose a situation you think was brought about by people or forces beyond your control. Now answer the following questions from a victim's perspective." The questions to elicit the story of the victim are:

1. What happened to you?
2. Who's to blame for it?
3. What should this person have done instead?
4. What should this person do now?
5. What punishment does this person deserve?

I do this exercise in small groups. While one group member complains, I encourage the others to "help" him by sympathizing with expressions such as "I can't believe they did that to you." "That is so unfair." "They shouldn't treat you like that." "Those people are so mean!" "You deserve better than this."

Once everybody has answered the questions, I ask people to look around the room. Everybody is beaming and laughing. The mood is boisterous. As I've said, victimhood is a drug.

Then I tell the people in the workshop the hard truth. "Validating the victim's helplessness is not friendly," I say. "Just as you don't really support an alcoholic by buying him another drink, you don't really support a victim by telling him that he has been treated unfairly. Alcohol and victim explanations may soothe the person who consumes them, but they are ultimately destructive. Your drug dealer is not your friend. A real friend offers you long-term wellness rather than immediate gratification. He blends a compassionate acknowledgment of your pain with a fierce challenge of your self-disempowering beliefs." At that point, people stop smiling and become quite serious.

In the workshop, I go on to the second round of questions. But let me put in a caveat before we continue here. In real life, if you are trying to help someone become a player, you can't just ask these next questions. You must first validate the negative impact that the situation has on your counterpart while at the same time not buying into their victim story. (The best way to do this is through empathetic listening and inquiry, which I will describe in the next chapter.) Being a player does not mean being Superman or Wonder Woman. Problems do upset us when they are caused by others' negligence or wrong behavior. Being a player doesn't mean that you deny these painful facts of life; rather, it means that you don't get stuck in them. Your feelings are the beginning of the story, not the end.

When someone has had a chance to express and release their grief and anger, you can invite him or her to answer the following questions from the player's perspective. It is vital that you *refer to the same situation*. The facts remain the same; what changes is the story. The purpose of the exercise is to see how the player's point of view illuminates opportunities for action and learning that were hidden before. The story of the player is not more truthful than the one of the victim, but it is more effective because it shifts the player from the passenger's to the driver's seat.

The questions to elicit the story of the player are:

1. What's the challenge?
2. How did you contribute (by doing or not doing) to create this situation?
3. What's really important to you?
4. What can you do now to accomplish that?
5. What can you learn from this experience?

These questions are as useful in personal as in professional situations. A manager can use them to help employees let go of the victim's story, a spouse can use them to help a husband or wife, and parents can use them to help their children deal with challenges. The important thing to remember is that when you present these questions as a loving challenge, love—in the form of empathy and compassion for the other's pain—comes first, and challenge—in the form of poignant inquiry to invite the other to own his power and accountability—comes second.

A CRIME STORY

Andrés, an Argentinean who attended one of my workshops, returned to his home in the outskirts of Buenos Aires. He arrived around 6 p.m. and parked his car on the street. As he stepped out, two armed robbers assaulted him.

The thieves pointed a gun at him and ordered him to open the door of his house. Andrés told them calmly, "Listen, guys, my wife and daughter are inside. If I come in with you, they'll freak out and start screaming. Nothing good can happen after that. You can take my car, my wallet, my phone, even my life, but you can't take my family. I will not open that door."

The thieves took all his valuables and ran away.

Andrés later told me what had happened. After expressing my sorrow and outrage, I asked him what he thought in that critical moment. He said, "I wasn't going to open that door. I made it clear to them that they'd have to shoot me if they wanted to get into the house. I'm glad that they just robbed me. But even if they had shot me, I'd still feel I had done the right thing.

"If they shot me in the street just because I didn't open the door," Andrés continued, "God knows what they would have done inside to my wife and daughter. And if they shot me, the noise would have alerted the neighbors who would have called the police. I might have died, but they would have run away, and so I would have saved my wife and my daughter." He laughed. "Not quite a happy ending, but not the unhappiest one, either."

Andrés was more than a player; he was a hero. He was clearly victimized by ruthless thugs. He was innocent. He didn't do anything wrong or bring this on himself. He faced a horrible threat with poise; he kept his cool and chose his response with courage and love—even though he had a gun to his head. He is a role model for me. Anytime you feel that you have no choice, I suggest you do what I do: remember Andrés's story and realize that even though you may not like your options or their consequences, you always, *always*, have a choice.

Chapter 9
COLLABORATION
ESCALATION IS NOT CONFRONTATION

If you want to go fast, go alone. If you want to go far, go together.

—African proverb

Before I came to work at LinkedIn, I was a leader at Axialent, the consulting firm I cofounded. Our operations center was located in Buenos Aires, where we ran administration, finance, marketing, executive assistance, and materials production. It was an arrangement that allowed us to serve our worldwide clients efficiently and at low cost.

In one of our one-on-ones, Skip, the manager of our Sydney-based Asia Pacific subsidiary, complained that he was not getting the service he needed from Buenos Aires. Due to the eleven-hour time difference, coordination was sloppy, materials were not ready on time, scheduling client appointments took forever, and communications in general were extremely cumbersome—squeezed to a one-hour window that was awkward on both ends. "I want to hire an administration person, but Charlie (the manager of the operations center) is blocking me," he said with some bitterness. I listened to Skip and told him that he had a good point, so I'd speak to Charlie—something I later regretted.

I called Charlie and told him about my conversation with Skip. His first comment was an untranslatable and irreproducible Argentinean

190

expression that refers to the genitalia of the female parakeet. That, and the fact that he referred to Skip as a backstabbing son of a bitch, made me guess that he was not happy at all that Skip had talked to me. Then Charlie proceeded to remind me that it was company policy to centralize operations in Buenos Aires, and that this policy was decided (by me, mainly) for many good reasons: it was cheaper, it was better for managing operations employees, it created a sense of community among them, and it allowed us to leverage them as they could shift from one region to the other when there was some peak in demand, and so on. I told him he had good points, so I'd speak to Skip again. (I ended up regretting this, too.)

After several individual conversations with Skip and Charlie without getting any closer to a solution, I realized that my managerial process was flawed. I was sick of the virtual shuttle diplomacy between Buenos Aires and Sydney, of the escalating conflict between Charlie and Skip, and I resented having to come up with a solution by myself. So I sat down to develop a conflict resolution process that would prevent all this. I called it "escalating collaboration." Before I describe this process, let me describe what happens when people have to work together under pressure.

COLLABORATION VERSUS HELP

A gasoline pipeline explodes in a drought-parched town. The fire department and ambulances rush to a nightmarish scene: thick flames licking through dry brush and trees, black smoke, houses and barns on fire, screaming animals and burn victims writhing on the ground. A first responder radios the local hospital's emergency room. "We have at least eighteen burn victims here. How many can you take?" "We don't have enough staff to deal with this," the emergency room coordinator replies. "You've got to triage."

In emergency rooms, disasters, and on battlefields, triage is the process of sorting victims based on their need for immediate treatment when medical resources are limited. To maximize the number of survivors, first responders and medical personnel divide the victims into three categories: (1) those who are likely to live, regardless of what care they receive; (2) those who are unlikely to live, regardless of what care they receive; and (3) those for whom immediate care might make the difference between living or not. Only people in the last group receive immediate medical attention.

On the face of it, triage may seem cruel because some people are left to suffer and others to die, but it is the only rational response to such a situation—the one that maximizes the number of survivors. Mistakes by first responders can result in avoidable deaths. There are three possible mistakes: (1) treating someone who will live, even without treatment; (2) treating someone who will die, even with treatment; and (3) not treating someone who could have lived with treatment but will die for lack of it. The first two errors are called "false positives" because the responder has accepted a patient who should have been rejected, thereby wasting precious resources. The third error is called a "false negative" because the responder rejects a patient who should have been accepted. As you can imagine, having to make fast, life-or-death decisions in an emergency situation puts terrific stress on first responders.[1]

Now, imagine that you and I are first responders treating two burn victims. Each of them has been assessed as worthy of medical attention—meaning that each can probably live with treatment but is likely to die without it. As we work side by side, your patient goes into cardiac arrest. You could surely use my assistance to save him. But as you are about to ask me for help, you look over and see that my patient is also in a dire state. Would you want me to stop what I'm doing in order to help you? Would you accuse me of lack of collaboration if I remain focused on saving my patient?

If you are committed to saving the maximum number of people, the answer to both questions is no. In this instance, team collaboration is not about trying to help each other "horizontally" as friends do, but about working together "triangularly" in the pursuit of a shared goal. Paradoxically, the best way to collaborate may not be for us to help each other, since what each of us is doing is more valuable for the goal. So we can work side by side, without any interaction, and still be collaborating.

While the logic of this argument is unassailable for someone like *Star Trek*'s Mr. Spock, in normal humans emotions can block rationality. We take it personally when others refuse our requests for help; we can feel that they are not being collaborative. I have heard people complain that someone is not being collaborative when what they really mean is "he refused to do what I needed."

Then there is the familiar problem of attribution bias. To paraphrase Matthew 7:5, we all tend to see the speck in our brothers' eyes and miss the log in our own. We use a totally different standard to define non-collaboration when someone refuses to help us ("She only cares about her needs!") than when we do the same to him ("I'm staying focused on what the organization needs most!"). When my coaching clients complain that someone hasn't collaborated with them, I ask them, "Do *you* believe you have to accept all requests for help from those around you?" They're often stumped.

I've shown earlier how disengagement, disorganization, disinformation, and disillusion can tear a company apart. Because individuals work to achieve their own KPIs (key performance indicators), they optimize their subsystems, disregarding the system. They consider those who contribute to their individual goals as collaborative, and those who don't as uncooperative. True collaboration disappears because nobody is willing to consider the best way to help the team win—regardless of whether doing so means pursuing their KPIs or deferring their own tasks to help someone else achieve a more important goal. And so it is that organizations stumble along, behaving inefficiently, incoherently, and self-destructively.

Recalling the analogy of the blind men and the elephant from Chapter 4, each of us holds specific information about our piece of the organization, but no person—not even the senior managers who only see the whole elephant's outline from afar—can calculate the best course of action. Even the most truly engaged people who are committed to accomplishing the organizational mission can disagree about strategic choices. They may be aligned around the goal but misaligned regarding the way to achieve it. That's why conflict is a fact of life, even in the best-led organizations.

Skip and Charlie were touching different parts of the elephant. Skip cared about serving the clients in his region in a time-efficient manner; Charlie cared about efficiency, flexibility, and keeping a lid on costs. Their interests led them to different recommendations. They both wanted the organization to succeed, but they disagreed vehemently on how it would happen. To make matters worse, they became so attached to their opinions that they saw each other as enemies—which led to personal strife, loss of cohesion, and poor decisions.

HOW NOT TO RESOLVE CONFLICTS

When people disagree with each other, their discussions typically turn into a tug-of-war in which one person tries to convince the other that he or she is right and the other is wrong. This zero-sum dynamic always ends up in a stalemate or an argument, with each person trying to prove his or her point and undermine the other's, making it impossible (a) for either of them to learn something new or (b) for the two of them to work together creatively to come up with better solutions.

When two parties fail to reach an agreement in a one-off interaction, they can just "agree to disagree" or "walk away from the deal." But when the parties are members of a team with a shared objective, that isn't possible. They have to figure out a way to work together in pursuit of the team goal. So when two parties fail to reach an agreement in organizational settings, each party resorts to a kind of lobbying I call "unilateral escalation"—the equivalent of siblings running to "tell on" the other to Mommy or Daddy. Each party goes to the manager (usually behind the other's back) to argue in favor of his or her position and against the other party's. Their common goal is to enlist the manager's help to overwhelm their opponent with superior force. This escalates the conflict and further erodes the relationship. The "loser" feels defeated and resentful, which is especially bad in a long-term work relationship.

This kind of contention also fosters a political atmosphere, creates a divide between winners and losers, and puts the manager in the role of choosing a favorite. Instead of reinforcing commitment to the goal, such arguments generate malicious compliance. The losing party may try to prove that he or she is right by sabotaging the decision while appearing to toe the line, just to prove a point. As a client once told me: "One of the greatest satisfactions in life is being able to say to those who made a bad decision, 'I told you so.'"

When managers need multiple conversations with each of the conflicting parties to find out what the different parts of the elephant are, everyone's time is wasted. There's no joint problem solving; there's no exploring of creative alternatives. Productivity goes out the window. In short, this kind of triangulation is a disaster. Unfortunately, such behavior is standard practice in most organizations.

HOW TO RESOLVE CONFLICTS

Escalating collaboration allows people to express and understand each other's needs and create new solutions. It addresses the It dimension of task through intelligent decision making, the We dimension of relationships through mutual respect, and the I dimension of self-worth through the consideration of everyone's needs and values. And it does all this in the context of the shared goal the team is pursuing.

In escalating collaboration, people focus on winning *with* the other rather than *against* the other. Collaborators understand that to create the most value, they need a working relationship, and that such a relationship can only be founded on respect for each party's interests. This approach reveals people's preferences and constraints and engages everyone in building solutions that go way beyond the original alternatives. It maximizes efficiency through cooperation.

In escalating collaboration, the disagreeing parties work together to prepare a shared narrative that integrates their arguments without hostility. If they can't come to an agreement after conducting an integrative negotiation, following the rules of escalating collaboration, they invite a senior person into the discussion as a facilitator-arbitrator. The senior person's job is to contextualize the information of both parties, bring in a more systemic perspective, and make a judgment call if necessary.

Escalating collaboration doesn't guarantee the right decision, but it produces a more intelligent process that strengthens relationships and helps everybody feel appreciated as valuable contributors. The objective is to use all available information and everyone's creative powers to reach a superior decision, a decision that everybody will buy into and commit to implement because they've participated in it. Escalating collaboration keeps everyone engaged in the pursuit of the organizational mission, without any sour feelings between apparent winners and losers.

THE SEVEN STEPS OF ESCALATING COLLABORATION

Escalating collaboration requires the attitudes and skills I explained in my earlier book *Conscious Business*.[2] I won't repeat those explanations here; instead I'll briefly summarize the specific instructions for this process. I encourage you to make this process one of the cultural norms of your organization and use it to define the way to resolve any conflicts among all your employees from day one.

When two people with different points of view enter into a discussion, the goal is not for either of them to "win" or to prove that one of them is right, but rather to figure out the best decision for the team. The rules are:

1. Those in conflict frame the issue collaboratively. Every conflict among organizational members is a disagreement about the best strategy to achieve a common goal. The difference of opinion about what to do arises in the context of a larger collaboration to achieve a mission they are both committed to accomplish.

2. In a dialogue with each other and in the absence of the manager, each person presents his or her point of view. The other listens appreciatively (as I describe below). To define their points of view, each speaker answers five questions put to them by their counterpart:

(a) What do you want?

(b) What do you plan to achieve with that?

(c) How will that further the organization's mission?

(d) What leads you to think so? (What facts and what logic?)

(e) What do you propose we do?

3. Each person inquires, trying to understand not only each other's point of view but also his or her reasoning and the larger context in which that point of view makes sense. They respectfully check each other on matters of fact and logic, clarifying assumptions, beliefs, and inferences.

4. The two parties use creative problem solving and integrative negotiation (see "How to Be Understood" below) to *dissolve* the conflict. That is, they work to find a way in which both parties get what they need while respecting the resource constraints. If they find it, then there is no more conflict and everyone commits to implementing the decision.

5. If the parties can't find a way for everyone to get what they need, they look for a compromise both can live with. If they find one, then there is no more conflict and everyone commits to implementing the decision. (If they can't compromise, it is essential that neither party surrenders in order to "not raise a fuss," "get on with the program," or, ironically, "be a team player." Both must hold their positions so that the organization can find the best new equilibrium through steps 6 and 7.)

6. If no compromise is acceptable to both parties because it appears to jeopardize one or the other person's ability to contribute to the organizational goal as they have committed, the participants explore how *relaxing* some constraints might dissolve the conflict or help them reach a compromise.

7. Then the parties jointly escalate the conflict to the next level of management. Together, they meet with the manager and ask for his or her help in creative problem solving, relaxing the constraints, or prioritizing the alternatives through a judgment call.

Escalating collaboration means that all the parties to a conflict engage their managers together rather than separately. It's out of bounds to ask a manager for an intervention or resolution without the other party being present. Nor can any manager intervene unilaterally in the conversation between conflicting parties—or, worse yet, discuss the issue with another of their managers.

APPRECIATIVE LISTENING

Admittedly, there are times when someone can be just plain wrong. But those times are much fewer than you believe, and even then it is best to first elicit the reasoning that brings the person to the wrong conclusion by seeking to understand his or her point of view. Then you can explain much more effectively why you believe that the person is in error.

Let's say that you and a colleague are touching different parts of the elephant, as Skip and Charlie were doing. To avoid triggering a conflict, consider that you and your counterpart hold your opinions because you have different points of view, different experiences, different beliefs, different assumptions, different needs, and different tactical goals. Against all your instincts, you must find out how your counterpart, the one who disagrees with you, is "right"—meaning his or her position makes sense given his or her information, beliefs, assumptions, goals, and values. Furthermore, you have to let him or her know that you really "get where he or she is coming from." That's what you do with appreciative listening.

"Seek to understand before you seek to be understood" is a wonderful recommendation. But most people have no idea of how to do it. In my many years of teaching people how to communicate, I haven't found a single client who, without intensive training, was able to do consistently the five things I describe below when under the slightest hint of emotional stress:

1. Listen quietly, without interrupting or completing the other person's sentences.
2. Let the other person know you are listening by focusing all your attention on him or her (instead of on your phone), maintaining eye contact, nodding, and saying, "mm-hmm." Occasionally encourage the other with short phrases such as "Go on, please," "Tell me more," or "How was that for you?" A particularly effective technique is to repeat the last few words of the other's statement in an inquisitive tone.
3. When the other person finishes an idea, summarize its essence and ask if you understood him or her correctly. Let the other modify or add to your understanding until he or she is are satisfied that you really "got" what he or she wanted to say.
4. Ask questions to understand the reasoning that leads your counterpart to his or her point of view. Use open questions as much as possible, and avoid confrontational questions (you can challenge the other's ideas later in the conversation). During the answers to these questions, continue to apply points 1, 2, and 3.
5. Validate that the other's perspective makes sense and seems reasonable (given his or her beliefs). If you disagree with something the other said, don't get into an argument about it; rather, acknowledge his or her point of view and wait for your turn to explain yourself to present any disagreement.[3]

There's a funny story that illustrates how radical these simple instructions can be. I was in Shanghai, teaching a workshop for executives of a financial services company. As usual, I gave them an assignment after teaching them the "seek to understand" process. "Go back home and, without saying anything about the workshop, ask someone in your family (or a friend), 'What's on your mind these days?' (or simply 'How was your day?'). Then just seek to understand without saying anything else for at least ten minutes."

Before I could say "good morning" the next day, one of the participants said he wanted to share something. He was so eager that I gave him the floor. He pulled out his phone and told us that he had called his wife (in Beijing, where they lived) and had a conversation, which he recorded. He proceeded to put the phone next to the mike and pressed the play button. I couldn't understand anything from the recording because it was in Chinese, but after about thirty seconds the whole room burst out in laughter. People were laughing so hard and speaking in such an animated tone that I was very curious. After the jokes died down, the owner of the phone translated for me. The conversation went more or less like this:

Husband: What's on your mind?

Wife: Why do you ask?

Husband: I'm interested in listening to you.

Wife: What's wrong?

Husband: Nothing is wrong, I just want to know what's on your mind.

Wife: Something's wrong. You never listen to me.

Husband: I want to listen to you today. Don't you like it?

Wife: No! It makes me wonder what's wrong.

I've since changed the instructions so workshop participants don't shock the people in their professional and personal lives by suddenly behaving strangely. "Most people are used to you not seeking to understand them," I tell the participants, "so you might raise their suspicions if suddenly you start behaving as I propose. I recommend you explain to them what you've learned and make an agreement to try it out as an exercise."

People might use appreciative inquiry deceptively, just as much as they can lie about any feelings or intentions. But appreciative inquiry is not a manipulation tool. It is an ethical tool for mutual learning that follows the rule "Seek to understand others as you wish to be understood."

HOW TO BE UNDERSTOOD

If you want to make it easier for a colleague or employee to understand you, you need to present your view as a personal perspective, rather than as "the exclusive truth." Instead of saying, "You're wrong and I'm right," your attitude should be, "You have valid reasons for holding your opinion, and so do I." Here's what I suggest.

1. Explain to your counterpart that you don't want to argue that you are right. Rather, you want to present to him or her what you consider is an argument worthy of consideration. You would like him or her to understand your point of view to compare it with the one he or she presented, correct it if it seems wrong, or integrate it if it seems useful.

2. Present your point of view in first person. Use "My opinion is," "I think," or "I believe." Avoid saying anything in second person, as it can be inflammatory. "You are wrong," "You should," "You don't know," and other such expressions will almost surely derail the conversation. Also avoid using third person. "This is the way it is" or "The fact of the matter is" are almost as bad as "You are wrong." Avoid using first person plural as well. "We need to," "We are supposed to," or "What we ought to do is" will sound to the other as "You should" and cause a reaction. There is no "we" without an alignment of the "I"s. Really, the only safe way to speak is in first person. (And no cheating. You can't say, "I think that you are wrong." "I think you are an idiot" is no better than "You are an idiot.")

3. Explain why you think what you think; share the evidence and reasoning that lead you to your conclusion. Illustrate your argument with examples and concrete stories. Tell your counterpart or team member what you believe are the implications for action of your reasoning and what you'd like to see happen. Include any proposals for next steps that you have.

4. Offer to clarify anything that the other person wishes to understand better. Invite him or her to ask any questions he or she has about your point of view.

5. Invite the other to state any questions about the accuracy or completeness of your evidence and reasoning.

6. Ask the other for his or her opinion of your point of view. This is the way you open the next phase of the conversation, where you try to integrate the arguments into a single narrative.

GETTING TO YES

If you have a disagreement with someone, the way to stimulate a constructive resolution is to frame the issue collaboratively, building a narrative that finds a mutually beneficial outcome for the conversation. This is obviously the case when people belong to the same organization, but even in apparently oppositional situations it is always possible to frame the issue collaboratively.

For example, instead of the buyer saying, "My goal is to buy the product for the lowest price," and the seller saying, "My goal is to sell the product for the highest price," both could say, "Our goal is to find a mutually beneficial transaction." Then you must acknowledge each other's interests, concerns, and needs and discuss the best way to take care of them for both of you.

In the classic book about negotiation called *Getting to Yes*, Roger Fisher and William Ury showed how individuals who disagree achieve a win-win outcome. They call their process "integrative bargaining." The key to integrative bargaining is to negotiate based on interests rather than positions. For example, after my wife suggests we go out for dinner, I might tell her: "I don't want to go out tonight." When I stake out my position in this manner, I am setting myself up for an impasse, since my wife will surely say, "Well, I do." If my goal is to resolve the situation, I might ask instead, "Why is eating out tonight important to you?" Suppose she answers, "I'm tired and I'd rather not deal with cooking or cleaning." (Our deal is that one cooks, the other cleans.)

Then I have several options. I could say, "I would like to watch tonight's game. Do you mind if we stay home for dinner but I take care of the cooking and clean up after the game?" Or "Do you mind if we order takeout?" or "Do you mind if we go to the sports bar in the mall?" Or we could explore several other options that would allow me to watch the game and her to avoid cooking or cleaning. By identifying the interests that motivate both of you, you can come up with creative solutions that integrate everyone's needs.

WHEN NOT TO LISTEN TO YOUR EMPLOYEES

The Golden Rule is the first requirement of any fair process. When Skip and Charlie escalated unilaterally to me as a manager, I should have asked them, "How would you feel if your counterpart came to me alone to advocate for a decision that favors him? What would you like me to do in that case?"

The obvious reply would be something like Charlie's colorful Spanish curse. Both wanted me to hear their side of the story. The only way to do that fairly is in a three-way conversation. (The exception is when an employee fears retribution, as in a whistle-blowing or harassment case. In such an event, the employee should speak to the manager privately.) I realized that by discussing the problem with only one of the parties to the conflict, I was rewarding their unilateral escalation and fostering the practice in the future. I was getting only biased, incomplete information, and putting myself in between two people who'd never learn to work through their differences together.

To nip this dynamic in the bud, transcendent leaders have to get a commitment from everyone in the organization to abide by the principles of escalating collaboration. Everyone has to understand that this is the way in which any conflict will be resolved, and that any deviations will be frowned upon. Of course, this doesn't prevent someone from sharing information with someone else, or asking for coaching from his or her manager; only unilateral escalations are discouraged. Sometimes this is a fuzzy boundary, but most often managers can tell whether the request for help, communication, or coaching is genuine, or if it's a subtle way to advocate for a position in violation of the established escalating collaboration process.

If one of your employees attempts to escalate a problem unilaterally to you, you must demonstrate the standard and hold him or her accountable to it. The first time someone tests the boundaries I tend to be soft, educating the person about the rules of the process. After that, I tend to be hard, confronting the person about breaking the commitment to only escalate collaboratively, not unilaterally.

Knowing what I know now, this is how I would have responded when Charlie came to me to lobby against Skip:

1. I'd ask Charlie, "Have you discussed this matter with Skip?" If he says no, I'd remind him of the commitment against unilateral escalations and ask him why he is bringing the matter to me without having discussed it first with his counterpart. I'd explain that I'm willing to help him and Skip if they can't find a solution by themselves, but that I'm only going to participate in a three-way conversation that has been properly prepared.

2. If Charlie answers yes, I'd ask him, "Have you invited Skip to come with you to see me?" If he says no, I'd remind him of the commitment against unilateral escalations and ask him why he is bringing the matter to me without having invited his counterpart. I'd explain that I'm willing to help him and Skip if they can't find a solution by themselves, but that I'm only going to participate in a three-way conversation.

3. If Charlie answers something along the lines of "Yes, but he said it wasn't worth it," I'd ask him, "Have you told Skip that you would come to see me alone?" If he says no, I'd ask him to tell this to Skip, because if he doesn't, Skip is likely to believe that Charlie went to see me "behind his back."

4. If Charlie answers yes, I'd thank him for bringing the matter to my attention and explain that I would like to discuss it with both parties present. Then I'd call Skip and ask him why he refuses to jointly escalate the matter to me. I'd explain to him that he does not

have a choice on this, as the agreement is that when people can't agree, they must escalate the issue collaboratively.

At LinkedIn, we established a ground rule called "Five-day alignment." It prescribes that if two people cannot agree on a decision within five days, then they automatically escalate jointly to their managers. We established that rule after some decisions that had been delayed for weeks and months were finally escalated to the leadership team, who were able to resolve the issue in less than an hour. It's understood throughout the organization that refusing to escalate jointly when two people have failed to reach alignment after five days goes counter to our cultural norms.

THE ROLE OF THE MANAGER

Escalating collaboration emulates the court system; managers in the hierarchy are analogous to appellate judges, with the senior leadership team being like the Supreme Court. After going through their initial negotiation without a mutually satisfactory resolution, both parties come together to the manager with a common narrative and a shared objective. No person can argue for his proposal on the basis that it will affect his individual or his team's performance. Such argument would be rejected as illegitimate. The goal is not to score a point for his subteam, but to win the game as a part of the organizational team.

Managers carry the decision authority because they represent the "property rights" of the organization's owners. They get to make decisions not because they are right, but because they have been empowered by the owners of the assets to do it on their behalf. The managers, in turn, have a fiduciary responsibility to act on behalf of the owners. If they make a mistake, the price will be paid by the owners—who in turn could lose trust in the management. So the managerial authority comes with responsibility and accountability. The managers make a decision because they have a wider perspective of the organization, because they can internalize costs and benefits that are externalities to the parties of the conflict, and because it's their head on the chopping block if they miss out. They put the owners' money where their mouth is and have to explain themselves if results are not what the owners expect.

It's important for everybody to understand that there are no winners or losers from the process. Managers don't make "the right decision." They make a decision that seems best to them, but they could be wrong. When managers rule in favor of one alternative to the detriment of the other, it's essential that they explain to all the parties in the conflict why they do so, in alignment with the organization's mission and values. The manager should also praise those who escalated collaboratively the conversation for allowing him or her to learn the necessary details of the situation in order to make an intelligent decision. It's essential that managers never chastise those who escalate collaboratively to them.

Once the issue is resolved, the "case" remains as a precedent that informs the members of the organization how the court (senior managers) is likely to rule (decide) in similar instances. If a manager believes that the issue is being improperly escalated, he or she can refuse to hear it and send it back to the "lower court."

Escalating collaboration allows managers to preserve cultural integrity because it takes triangulation and end runs out of the equation. By forcing the teammates to communicate respectfully *before* presenting their evidence and viewpoints to their supervisors, and to describe in detail what their concerns and interests are, management also underscores that strong interpersonal relationships and individual engagement are essential for the health of the organization.

After I thought long and hard about escalating collaboration at my consulting firm, Axialent, I decided that we had to demand it as a cultural norm. I explained to all the employees why this process would be a good way to address any conflict and discussed with them what they thought about it. What, if anything, would they recommend beyond my definitions to be able to commit to the process? At the end of that conversation, all of us agreed to the ground rules, including Skip and Charlie.

Because Skip and Charlie couldn't come to an agreement, the three of us agreed to meet by videoconference.

"Fred," Charlie started, "we need your help, because we can't decide by ourselves what would be the best course of action for the company."

After asking them to explain the trade-offs in more detail, I asked them what creative ideas they'd explored, even if they hadn't agreed on them.

"We talked about hiring someone in Buenos Aires but put them on a different schedule," Skip volunteered. "This person could come into the office at 5 p.m. Buenos Aires time, which is 6 a.m. in Sydney. They could spend an hour with the rest of the operations crew to coordinate things with them, and then stay till 1 a.m., which is 2 p.m. in Sydney. This would give them plenty of time to connect with the Asia Pacific employees and clients."

"The problem is that we can't leave the office open till 1 a.m. with a new person," Charlie added. "And it would be depressing for them to be alone in such a big space. In addition, the part of the city in which we have the office is not the safest at night. I wouldn't want one of our employees on the street after business hours."

Before I could speak, Skip took the words out of my mouth. "Wait a second. I don't really need this person to be physically at the office. They could just as easily work from home. If there are things the person we hire needs from the office, we could have them sent to their house, or maybe they can pick stuff up in the afternoon."

"Whoever we hire would still full-line report to you, Charlie," I added, "with a dotted line to Skip, but they'd work from home mostly focused on the needs of Asia Pacific. Would that work for you?"

"It could work," Charlie said tentatively, "but I don't have the budget to hire an additional person. Right now the regular crew manages Asia Pacific's requests during business hours. I don't have a dedicated person whom I could ask to switch schedules, and I don't feel like letting go of any of my staff as they are working well serving operations in America and Europe."

I turned to Skip and asked if he would be willing to fund this employee from his budget. "It would be much cheaper for you to hire someone in Argentinean pesos than in Australian dollars."

"I would," Skip replied, "but then I'd want them to be full line to me and dotted line to Charlie. If I fund that hire, I want to be able to assign work according to my priorities."

Before I could ask, Charlie said, "I can live with that."

In the end, we hired an Aussie woman who had moved to Buenos Aires after falling in love with an Argentinean. She worked out so well that we implemented a similar system for our European offices. Skip and Charlie ended the conversation on good terms, feeling that their needs had been met through a fair process, mostly led by them. (Indeed, they could have reached all but the last point of agreement—about budgets, over which I had final authority—without me.)

Just as triage rules are all about saving lives and making intelligent decisions in crisis situations, escalating collaboration offers leaders a crucial tool for building a cohesive, respectful, and high-achievement culture. It forces people away from their angry, self-righteous desire to be "right" and to show others they are "wrong." It answers the question "What is the real goal here?" with "The organizational mission." It sets a cultural norm of cooperation in the interest of the organizational purpose. It offers managers a way to harness the forces of conflict to propel the organization forward—very much like the tension in a battery can energize a circuit. If, as a leader, you are able to achieve this, your organization will gain a great competitive advantage.

Chapter 10
INTEGRITY
YOUR WORD IS YOUR BOND

Del dicho al hecho hay gran trecho. ("From said to fact there's great gap.")

—Spanish proverb

Five frogs are sitting on a log. Four decide to jump off. How many are left? Answer: Five. Why? Because there is a great gap between deciding and doing.

Decisions are worthless unless they turn into commitments, but commitments are worthless unless they are made, kept, and honored with integrity. Integrity is an essential condition for effective work. When people cannot count on each other to deliver on their commitments, it's impossible to execute plans and achieve goals. Besides the material losses, lack of integrity has a tremendous cost in human relationships and personal stress. It's very demoralizing to work in a community without integrity.

The impact of integrity (or lack thereof) is similar to the one of honesty. Imagine how destabilizing it would be to work in an organization where people are dishonest, in a place where you never know if the other person is telling the truth or lying. It would be impossible to accomplish anything. Worse yet, it would be impossible to relate to others on a level beyond pretense. Imagine how disengaged and despondent you'd quickly become.

Lying is straightforward: it's the opposite of telling the truth. But integrity is harder to define: we don't always clearly understand when we violate it. Although we do understand in the abstract that lack of integrity is bad, we consider transgressing against it a minor issue. But integrity is as critical as honesty for effective relationships, both in business and in life in general. We need a practical definition that lets us see when we transgress. And we need to understand that whatever short-term benefits we imagine lack of integrity can afford us, they are dwarfed by the extraordinary long-term costs in the It, We, and I dimensions.

I define *integrity* as honoring your word. A person with integrity keeps her promises whenever possible, and still honors them if she is unable to do so. You make a grounded promise by committing only to deliver what you believe you can deliver. You keep the promise by delivering it. And you can still honor the promise when you can't keep it by letting the person you are promising know of the situation, and taking care of the consequences.

Some commitments are explicit. For example, you promise to deliver your work product by April 9, or you promise to pay the mortgage by October 10. Other commitments are tacit: everybody expects you to abide by social rules of clothing, speech, action, and so on. Still other commitments are in the middle: when you enter into an employment relationship, you commit to abide by the company's policies and to hold a fiduciary responsibility to act in the best interests of the owners.

In an interview before a World Championship match, a journalist asked Mike Tyson's opponent what his plan was for the fight. The boxer gave a detailed description of how he was going to fight Tyson. Then the journalist turned to Tyson and asked, "What do you think about that, Mike?" Tyson's answer was so pithy it made headlines: "Everybody has a plan until they get punched in the mouth."[1]

Reality often punches us in the mouth. Things don't go as planned due to innumerable factors out of our control. Sometimes nature gets in our way in the form of a big storm. But most of the time, the disruptive factors spring from human nature. The problem is not that things get out of our control. What destroys an organization's ability to execute in the face of inevitable surprises is that people don't act with integrity. Worse than that, most people don't even know what integrity means.

In this chapter, I'll show you how to build and operate an integrity-based execution system. The goal is threefold: to deliver results (the It), to enhance trust (the We), and to conduct oneself with integrity (the I). You'll learn how to make commitments in a way that enhances trust and promotes efficiency. More important, you'll learn how to preserve integrity, trust, and efficiency when things change and you, or others, are unable to deliver on commitments.

AN EXPENSIVE MISTAKE

Jared, the CEO of SuperNuts, Inc. (not a real company but a stand-in for a real client of mine in a different industry), was furious. He had lost the biggest outsourcing contract in the company's history due to a blunder by Victor, his operations manager. Furthermore, Victor's blunder was an infringement of a company policy that Victor knew very well. Jared wanted to rake Victor over the coals, but he was worried that Victor would get so upset that he'd quit. Angry as he was, Jared wanted to keep Victor on because Victor was one of his oldest and most respected employees.

When Jared asked me for help, my first question was, "What happened?"

"Victor really screwed up," Jared said. "We signed a huge outsourcing agreement with Organic Food Stores to produce their almond butter. The contract specified that to avoid contamination from peanuts, the facilities that produced the almond butter could not handle any peanut products. I signed the contract without a second thought, since our company has the same policy.

"Last week, while we were setting up, Organic Food Stores sent a surprise audit team to the plant that would be making their almond

211

butter. They analyzed empty containers and found traces of peanuts.[2] They asked the workers at the plant if there were peanuts being processed somewhere in the facility, and they confirmed that in a different sector of the plant there was a line producing peanut butter.

"When the auditors reported their finding, Organic's outsourcing manager went ballistic. He referred the matter to their lawyers, who sent us notice that they were rescinding the contract due to our noncompliance. As if this wasn't fun enough, they informed us that they were considering suing us. What a mess!"

Jared told me that he'd discovered that several months earlier Victor tried to improve efficiency and utilization by producing both almond butter and peanut butter in different lines at the same plant. He and the plant manager devised a cleaning procedure for the containers that prevented contamination. Victor asked the plant manager to conduct exhaustive tests to check that the procedure was safe. They found it to be so, so Victor gave the order to launch the peanut butter line in the almond butter plant. The decontamination process worked—so well that there was not a single problem for several months. That's why nobody outside the plant knew that the company policy was being circumvented.

"In fact, the Organic auditors did not find any contamination; they only found minimal traces of the wrong molecule in some of the containers. Without the supersensitive equipment they were using they would have not found it, because the microscopic quantities were well below the detection limit in any product test. But find it they did, and all hell broke loose.

"This created not only a financial loss for us," Jared continued, "but it's also a public relations nightmare. Organic reported the reason for rescinding the contract to the trade media. Our industry is small, so everyone knows that we really messed up with one of the big players. Our reputation and credibility have taken a big hit, to say nothing of the personal embarrassment I'm feeling."

Jared wanted to have a constructive conversation with Victor, but he was so angry that he felt like he would blow it. So I proposed that Jared and I do a "Houdini," a special role-playing exercise I named for the great escape artist Harry Houdini. I play my counterpart and, in so doing, put myself into a conversational barrel. Then, like Houdini, I do my best to get out of the barrel before I plunge over a metaphorical Niagara Falls. The Houdini role play allows me to model constructive behaviors for my client (Jared), and for him to empathize with his counterpart (Victor). It also lets Jared experience how disarming it can be to interact with someone who uses a skillful conversational method.

In these scenarios, everything I say has to be aligned with the beliefs, emotions, and values of the person I'm working with. I have to play my client more authentically, more collaboratively, and with more integrity than they can even play themselves. This role playing is a real thrill for both parties, and it's very effective.[3]

In my Houdini dialogue with Jared, I told him I would play him and he would play Victor. Before we launched into the dialogue, I asked Jared what he wanted to achieve through the conversation. I inquired about his goals for the task, for the relationship with Victor, and for himself.

Here's what we said to each other:

Jared: I'd like to understand what happened and why Victor made the decision to bring the peanut butter production into the facility against the company policy, especially without telling me. I want to make it clear to him that this was a big mistake and make sure it will never happen again. I want Victor, and everybody else, to follow the rules.

Fred: Anything else?

Jared: I'd like to repair the three dimensions you mentioned—the It, the We, and the I. With regard to the task, I'd like to get Victor's help to own up to his mistake and apologize to Organic Food Stores, and ask them to reconsider their decision to rescind the contract. Since he made the decision, I want him to be in the room with me when I talk to Organic Food Stores's executives. Regarding the relationship, I'd like to reestablish trust. I feel betrayed, and my confidence in Victor has been shaken. He's been a solid contributor for many years, so I'd like to not lose him over this breach. As far

213

as my personal feelings and values go, I'd like to restore a sense of integrity. I would like Victor to apologize and to forgive him. I don't want to stay resentful, and I don't want him to carry a chip on his shoulder.

Fred: It looks to me like the problem is not just with Victor. There were a lot of people in the plant who should have known about the company policy of keeping peanut products separate. It concerns me that nobody raised a red flag when Victor gave the order to start the peanut butter line. The fact that nobody said anything tells me that the problem is much deeper than just one person making a bad decision.

Jared: You're right. This is not just a conversation with Victor. This is a cultural issue that Victor and I need to address with his staff.

Fred: Then let's also ask for Victor's help to reinforce the company standards.

Jared: Sounds good.

Fred: Let's start the role play. I'll play you, Jared, and you play Victor. I'll say some things that may surprise you, so you'll have to improvise. Just let your intuition guide you, and don't worry about trying to play Victor exactly. Don't make him nicer than he is, but don't make him nastier, either. Put yourself in his shoes and speak as you feel like doing. Let's set the stage in my (Jared's) office. I've called you (Victor) to discuss the problem of Organic Food Stores.

(Now the role play starts. I've marked the following role play with asterisks to distinguish it from the dialogue above.)

Victor* (played by Jared): I'm sorry, Jared. This surprise audit really screwed us. We had a very reliable process for decontamination, but these guys came looking for dirt. The traces of peanut butter they found would have never caused any problems.

Jared* (played by Fred): I understand, Victor, that the unexpected audit found a very small residue of peanut butter in the containers.

Victor*: Yes, it was barely detectable.

Jared*: Victor, I'd like to have a conversation with you about what happened. My goal is to understand what led you to take the decision to start a peanut butter line in the almond butter plant, and why you did that without discussing it with me first. I'd also like to find if there's a way to make things less terrible than they are, not just with Organic, but also within our own company. This is a breach of trust that we need to fix so we can work together as a team. Does that sound good to you?

Victor*: Yes. I feel very bad about what happened.

Jared*: What actually happened, Victor?

Victor*: The plant had excess capacity, and our other plant that produces peanut butter was not able to cope with the high demand. So I thought that if we could ensure that the two substances would never mix, it would be great to use our excess capacity in the almond butter plant to cover for the production deficit in the peanut butter plant. Otherwise we would have to outsource production while having some of our equipment standing idle. It would have been quite expensive. All our tests of the scrubbing procedure were satisfactory so a few months back we started the peanut butter line. And we never had a problem. Until last week.

Jared*: I realize that the scrubbing was quite effective. And I can't blame you for trying to save the company money through efficient utilization. In fact, I think that the second line is a good idea given that we can avoid contamination.

Victor*: I'm glad you see it that way! I thought you were upset with me.

Jared*: I am very upset, but not because you tried to improve our processes. I appreciate your commitment to try to do the right thing for the organization. You've been a great contributor for many years, Victor. That's why I chose you for my leadership team.

Victor*: Then why are you upset with me?

Jared*: I am upset with you because you and I had an agreement not to mix almond butter and peanut butter in the same plant. You broke that agreement. You changed your commitment unilaterally, without letting me know and renegotiating it with me.

Victor*: Agreement? Commitment? What are you talking about?

Jared*: There's a company policy that specifies that almond butter and peanut butter production will not take place in the same plant. You committed to implementing that policy. That's a promise you made to me.

Victor*: I never thought of the policy as a promise.

Jared*: What did you think it was?

Victor*: I don't know. I never thought about it this way. I assumed it was a safety rule, something that you wanted me to follow to avoid contamination. But since I found a way to avoid contamination, I thought I was respecting the spirit of the policy even if I didn't follow its letter.

Jared*: I see that. Perhaps I failed to explain to you that when you agreed to follow this policy I took that as a personal commitment from you to me. I counted on you abiding by it. That's why I signed the contract with Organic, which had a covenant saying we would not produce peanut products in any of the plants where we'd produce their almond butter. Since you never told me you were planning to do otherwise, I assumed that you were following our policy.

Victor*: So you think it was a mistake to repurpose our excess capacity?

Jared*: Not necessarily; I don't know if it was or it wasn't. What was surely a mistake was not discussing it with me first. That's what bothers me, Victor. You and I had an understanding that you'd follow the policy. You changed your mind, but you never checked with me. You didn't tell me. You didn't ask me. You didn't explain to me, or give me the chance to participate in, the decision. So I signed a contract with Organic that was in default before the ink on it was dry.

I was out of integrity, as I am ultimately accountable for everything that our company does.

Victor*: When you put it that way, I feel like I have let you down. I should have told you but, you know, I thought it would be better to ask for an apology than for permission.

Jared*: That is the big mistake, Victor. That's a get-out-of-jail-for-free card that you can use to break any promise. I can't believe you'd want others to argue like this when they break promises to you. That's the death of trust. If people can disown their promises because they'd rather ask for an apology than for permission, what value would anybody's word have?

Victor*: You're right, Jared. I totally screwed up by not discussing the matter with you. I'm very sorry.

Jared*: I accept your apology. I assume that this will never happen again.

Victor*: I learned a hard lesson, Jared. I will follow the policies religiously from now on.

Jared*: That's the wrong lesson, Victor. Policies are not dogma. I don't want you to follow them religiously. I want you to think out of the box and consider ways to improve our operations even if they challenge a policy. But what I want you to do then is to bring the matter up to me so that we can renegotiate our agreements. By the way, that's the same thing that I'd need to do with the board if I agree with you and want to change a policy I have established with them. The lesson is that there is absolutely no legitimate way to break a promise unilaterally. It is always better to ask for permission than for an apology.

Victor*: That makes perfect sense. But this isn't the way many people work. Lots of people in and outside our company don't deliver on their promises on time.

Jared*: In that case, we've got a business problem around execution, and a cultural problem around integrity, Victor. And my belief is that these are two sides of the same coin. I feel responsible, and I'd like your help in addressing it. But before we do that, I'd like to go with you to Organic and offer our apologies for the breach. I'd like you to explain what happened. If we can regain their trust, perhaps they'll reconsider their decision about the outsourcing deal.

Victor*: I was given specific instructions from our lawyers to avoid any contact with Organic.

Jared*: I'll speak with the lawyers. There's an issue of integrity here. We made a mistake and we must own up to it. Organic has been very reasonable in the negotiations. I trust that if we come clean with them, they will not use that against us—and they may even forgive us just like I'm forgiving you. On the other hand, if our apology ends up hurting us, we'll take that as the price we must pay for our default. I'm willing to escalate this up to the board if our chief counsel of legal doesn't approve of it.

Victor*: It's kind of embarrassing. I'd rather not rub salt in our own wounds.

Jared*: It stings, for sure. But what's the option? To hide and pretend nothing happened? What message would we be sending to our own people? I want this to be a culture-setting event, Victor. My first goal is that people understand that policies are not imposed upon them. They are proposed, and people agree to abide by them. This agreement is a commitment that puts their personal integrity, as well as their trustworthiness, at stake. I want everybody to be clear that asking for permission is not just the best way to deal with the need to renegotiate an agreement; it is the only way.

The real Jared stepped out of his role and remarked, "You make it look so natural! You said exactly what I wish I had said in our earlier role plays as myself. Why can't I do it?"

"Don't be so hard on yourself, Jared," I replied. "This is as 'natural' as a great golf swing. It takes practice. So let's start practicing. Let's re-play this conversation, but you'll be you (Jared) and I'll be Victor. I'll play a very easy Victor, first. And once you are able to engage me constructively, I'll ramp up the level of challenge progressively to see how you handle it."

We did that, and after a couple of repetitions Jared was ready to have the real conversation with Victor. He was so excited that he called Victor into his office right then, taking advantage of the fact that I was there. Victor looked forlorn and apprehensive, no doubt because he knew he had screwed up royally and that his head was on the chopping block. But he behaved very well. He acknowledged his mistake and asked Jared to forgive him. Jared did a fantastic job and accomplished all his goals. It was the easiest facilitation I've ever done. I didn't have to open my mouth at all during the meeting.

HOW TO MAKE A COMMITMENT

The preferable path to integrity is to keep your promises; that is, to do what you committed to do. You deliver the work product by April 9; you pay your mortgage by October 10. When you make a commitment, you incur a debt; when you deliver, you pay that debt. Therefore, you must make only promises that you intend to keep. Borrow only the money you intend to repay.

Here are the conditions for integrity when you make a promise:

1. *Promise only what you believe you can deliver.* If you don't think you can keep your commitment or have significant doubts about it, don't make a promise until you clear them. Since the promise is about the future, there's always a risk that you may not be able to deliver. But this shouldn't stop you from promising. A promise made with integrity that turns out to be beyond your reach is like a statement you make with honesty that turns out to be false. Just as an error is legitimate while a lie is not, a promise based on an erroneous assessment of capability has integrity, while one done with the knowledge of incapability does not.
2. *Make a plan.* To assess your ability to deliver, you need a robust plan that counts on skills and resources that you have or can

reliably acquire. The plan must include foreseeable contingencies and strategies to deal with them. If you know of contingencies that could derail the plan, you have to let your creditor know at the time that you make the commitment—which is now conditional upon the contingency. Too often people make promises without any idea of how they will deliver. This is the source of endless breakdowns and breaches of integrity.

3. *Have a tracking mechanism.* You must assess whether the plan is on track. If you detect a significant deviation, you need to consider that your commitment is in jeopardy and let your creditor know right away.

4. *Have a communication protocol.* In this way, you can inform your creditor of any problems in a timely manner. For example, my assistant has instructions to include the telephone number and e-mail address of any person with whom I've scheduled an appointment, so that I can reach him or her if something goes wrong. My assistant also gives my counterparts my phone number and e-mail address in case any of them needs to reach me.

5. *Promise only what you really intend to deliver.* Be careful about the temptation to be "nice" and please others—especially those in authority. Before you promise, check in with yourself and consider whether you truly intend to do what you are about to promise. I often feel inclined to make commitments that I know I will later regret. But after many cases of "morning after" stress and disappointment in myself for committing to do things that I knew I shouldn't have committed to do, I've realized that it is best to avoid the "night before" promise, even if that frustrates the other person.

HOW TO ASK FOR A COMMITMENT

There's a world of difference between an order and a requested promise. The order relies on the authority of the person who issues it, but a promise relies on the integrity of the one who accepts the request. An order is typical of a boss, and it's all about eliciting compliance. A request is typical of a leader, and it's all about eliciting commitment. Coercion and threats will, at most, get you obedience but never discretionary effort.

When someone fails to execute an order, the boss's complaint is usually "You didn't do what I ordered you to do." When someone fails to deliver on a promise, the leader's confrontation is usually "You didn't do what you promised to do." Which one would hold more sway over you?

For a commitment to hold properly, it's important that the promisor feels his or her integrity is at stake. A commitment, after all, is a contract, so the promisor has to understand the request and freely accept it. (Think of this as "informed consent.") If you are going to get someone's commitment rather than their compliance, they must feel they're "signing on the dotted line" willingly, because they believe your request is productive, reasonable, and fair.

I can't count the number of times I've heard employees allege that they can't say no to their bosses' requests. Targets, goals, budgets, and plans are often imposed on employees without asking for their commitment. In the employees' minds, this means that their integrity is not at stake, because they didn't *really* say that they could do what they were asked to do. If you want to be a transcendent leader, your authority must be moral rather than formal. You have to allow your reports to respond to your requests with something different than an obedient "yes, sir" or "yes, ma'am"—because a person who can't say no can't really say yes, either.

That doesn't mean that your reports can just say no without further discussion. The basic employment contract specifies that they will do their best to honor your requests within the limits of their skills, resources, and values. As a leader, you will have explained to your reports that everything you and they do together is to help the team to win, and to play by the rules (i.e., in alignment with the organization's mission and values). So if they decline a request, it behooves them to explain to you why, in a way that can allow a collaborative negotiation.

For example, my own employees have often declined my requests because their plate was full. They explained to me then what they were doing and the dates by which their existing commitments (mostly to me) were due. I was nearly always able to reprioritize their tasks in a way that fit their schedules, and that was compatible with the urgency of my need.

The commitment is the result of an interaction between someone who requests (the requester) and someone who receives that request (the receiver). I use the following guidelines to structure clear requests:

1. *Explain.* Describe the gap between what's going on and what you'd like to achieve. Present the request as a way to bridge this gap with the help of the receiver.

2. *Ask.* Be explicit with your ask. Use the direct form of the verb ("I ask you to . . ." "I request that you . . ." "I beg you to . . ." "I invite you to . . ." and so on). Specifically define the conditions for satisfaction of the request, including deadlines.

3. *Inquire.* Give the receivers a chance to respond. Are they ready to make a promise? Do they want to decline your request, or do they need something more from you before responding?

A formula that integrates these three steps is: "In order to move from A to B, I ask you to deliver C by D. Can you commit to that?" or "I need your help to accomplish B. My request is that you do C by D. Can you do it?" (where A is the current state, B is the desired state, C is what you are asking, and D is the time by which you are asking for it).

HOW TO GET A COMMITMENT

It's essential that after making a clear request, you don't accept a less than full commitment. People often try to hedge, so they don't say no directly but instead give you a murky pseudo-commitment like "Let me see what I can do," "No worries," "Someone will take care of it," "We'll do our best," or "I'll try." In the famous words of Master Yoda, "Do or do not. There is no try." The only answer that is a commitment is this one: "Yes, I promise," or "Yes, I commit." No "trying," no "seeing," no "someone," no "we"—nothing but "I promise" is acceptable.

The best way to challenge "weasel" answers (and even to double-check the ones that seem clear) is to rephrase them as well-formulated promises, along the lines of "I understand you are promising to deliver *C* by *D*. Did I get that correctly?" I bet that most of the time you'll get some hesitation from the other person, signifying that he or she was not really making a promise. And often you'll get a clear "No," signifying that your counterpart was reluctant to decline but unwilling to commit.

In my years of teaching this material, I have found only three acceptable answers (the last one with four subanswers) to a request. These answers clearly define who commits (or not) to deliver what by when:

1. *"Yes, I promise,"* or "Yes, I commit."
2. *"No, I decline."* It's much better to know that the other person is unable or unwilling to make the commitment than to believe that they're promising to do something that they're really not committed to delivering.
3. *"I'm not ready to commit yet because . . ."* The receiver may not understand how your request helps you with your need, or how it meets the objective of the organization. Perhaps there is some conflict between your request and the receiver's preexisting commitments, some policy of the organization, or something else.

When you hold formal authority over others, you must establish very clearly that they always have the right to say "I'm not ready to commit." You are *not* giving people the right to decline your requests, but you are giving them the right to explain why it may be problematic to accept them. It's perfectly legitimate for them to do this for any one of these five reasons: (1) they don't understand what you're asking them to do, or by when; (2) they don't believe they have the skills or resources to deliver; (3) their ability to deliver depends on factors out of their control that may derail their plan; (4) they think that what you're asking them to do would go against helping the team to win, or against a company value, standard, or policy; or (5) fulfilling your request would conflict with a prior commitment they've made to you or others.

If the receiver says, "I need clarification," it means he or she needs to better understand your need or the conditions of satisfaction of your request. (By the way, this is an extremely useful answer when you receive a poorly formulated request.) If the receiver does fully understand what you are asking, they may say, "I can commit to give you C by D if you give me X by Y (or if X takes place before Y)." This is a conditional commitment that depends on some condition being fulfilled by you, or by reality.

Alternatively, they may say, "I can't commit to do C by D, but I could do X by Y. Would that work for you?" This is a counteroffer that, should you accept it, becomes a commitment.

"I commit to respond to you by Y" is an appropriate response when the receiver needs to check his or her resources before making a definite (or conditional) commitment (or declines, or counteroffers). Notice that the commitment is to give you an answer at a specific date.

When leaders give followers permission not to accept requests, they are giving them permission to do what's right for the team. Along these lines, I remember a story I heard in first grade about General José de San Martín, the Argentinean equivalent of George Washington.

Before one of the battles, San Martín went to the munitions depot to check on supplies. He was about to walk in when a soldier blocked his path. (In the Argentinean army, it is unthinkable for a plain soldier to even speak to an awe-inspiring general, let alone stand in his way.) When the soldier stepped in front of him, San Martín ordered him to let him through. The soldier said respectfully, "With your permission, my general, you gave us specific orders to not let anyone with spurs on his boots into the munitions depot." Whereas a lesser commander would have reprimanded the soldier for insubordination, San Martín congratulated the soldier and made him an example of integrity. He had vowed to enforce San Martín's order, and he did—even upon San Martín himself.

HOW TO RENEGOTIATE A COMMITMENT

No matter how robust your plans are, you will not always be able to keep your promises. That is a manageable problem, though, since you can still honor your word. To maintain integrity, you must inform all parties involved as soon as you know that you may not be able to keep your promise. And you need to take care of the negative consequences that your failure to deliver will produce for them.

Even if you are holding yourself to the highest possible standards when making your promise, there will be times when you simply can't deliver by the due date. You want to ship, but the plant did not finish production. You want to pay your debt, but someone did not pay you. Life is unpredictable; sometimes you might find yourself unable to follow through on your commitment—or maybe delivering is so onerous that it doesn't make sense to do it. In these circumstances, it is all the more important to maintain effectiveness, trust, and integrity.

When you can't, won't, or think you shouldn't fulfill a promise you've made, the secondary path to integrity is to "honor" it. That means that you do your best to take care of your creditor (the recipient and holder of your promise) to maintain trust in the relationship, and to reinforce a culture of integrity.

Doing this involves the following steps:

Announce. Let your creditor know that your delivery is at risk as soon as you consider that this risk is material. Don't wait until the last moment—or, worse yet, past the due date—to inform your creditor that you won't be able to fulfill your promise. Too often, people try desperately to avoid the awkward moment of informing their creditors of a possible breakdown, missing the chance to minimize its consequences. They work until the last minute and then default, surprising their unsuspecting creditor. (And then they resent it when the creditor gets upset.) If your creditor asks you, "Why didn't you tell me earlier?," the only honorable answer is "Because I didn't know."

The earlier you issue the warning, the better, as long as it's a real warning of a material risk. The rule of thumb I use is to put myself in my creditor's shoes and ask myself whether I'd want to know that there's a problem.

Apologize. Tell your creditor that you recognize your commitment and that you would like to renegotiate it in a way that minimizes the negative consequences, maintains trust between you, and honors your word.

Explain. Let your creditor know what unforeseeable circumstances are preventing you from fulfilling your promise. Don't use this as a justification or an excuse. Make it clear that you are fully responsible and accountable for your commitment and are telling your creditor what has happened so that he or she understands that the breakdown wasn't due to your negligence (or if it was, to own up to your mistake). This is why it's so important to announce the problem as soon as it becomes material.

Inquire. Ask your creditor what consequences are likely to ensue from your inability to deliver. Focus on the practical costs that your creditor and others will have to bear due to your unfulfilled promise. Then ask what your creditor would like you to do to minimize these consequences, and to make it up to him or her with some compensation for the unmitigated losses. What you can't resolve, you can restitute. The goal is to take care of your creditor and others who will suffer consequences.

Negotiate. See if you can offer something even better than what your creditor asked for in the first place. Taking into account your creditor's concerns and costs as well as your own resources, try to come up with a recovery plan that takes care of the situation as best as possible given the constraints. If you can't do what your creditor requests, explain why and engage in a collaborative negotiation (i.e., put in practice what you learned in the previous chapter).

Recommit. Make a new commitment to deliver what you and your creditor negotiated. Make sure you specify what you will deliver and by when.

Check and learn. Ask your creditor whether he or she is satisfied with the process, or if there's anything more to clear up. Make sure that trust has been reestablished and integrity maintained. Also, take notice of the cause of the breakdown and remember it as a risk next time you make a similar commitment.

In my workshops, I ask people if they would like others to fulfill these conditions when making commitments, and I always hear a unanimous "yes." Then I ask them, "When was the last time that anyone renegotiated a commitment with you following these principles?" The silence is deafening, but it gets even louder when I ask about the last time they renegotiated a commitment in this way.

Paradoxically, it is possible to increase trust when you can't keep your word, if you honor your word. People know that, sooner or later, circumstances beyond your control will prevent you from fulfilling one of your promises. But as long as you deliver, they won't know how you will behave—and whether they can trust you—when you can't. When that does happen, if you take care of them with integrity, they will redouble their confidence in you.

MY APOLOGIES

My daughter Sophie's birthday is on August twenty-sixth. I was in the United Kingdom the week before her fourteenth birthday, facilitating a very important executive meeting for a client. The meeting was scheduled to finish on Friday night. I was going to fly back to the United States the following day and be at Sophie's birthday party on Sunday, as I'd promised.

Someone once told me, "If you want to make God laugh, tell him your plans." God must have had a good chuckle, because the team did not reach a decision on Friday and decided to finish the meeting on Monday. The leader of the team asked me to stay and help them the following week. I wanted to do this, but if I stayed, I would break my promise to my daughter. I told the team leader that I would get back to him by 9 p.m.

I went to my hotel, called Sophie, and explained the situation to her. "Sophie," I said, "if you want me to return as I promised, I will do it. I still have my ticket for tomorrow morning. But before you say you do, let me ask you a question. Is there anything that I could do with you to celebrate your birthday the following weekend that would be better than having me at your party this Sunday?"

Without a moment's hesitation Sophie replied, "Skydiving! Oh, Daddy, I've always wanted to do that! It would be even better than having you at my party." I told her that I would do some research and get back to her in an hour.

I googled "Skydiving" in our city and found that there was a flight club that offered tandem jumps, but it turned out that Sophie had to be at least eighteen years old to do such a jump. So I called Sophie and explained that she wasn't old enough to jump, but that the flight club offered what was described to me as "very exciting glider flights." After a brief negotiation, we agreed on a two-part deal. I could stay in London and, in exchange, I would take her on the glider flight the following Sunday and on a tandem jump when she turned eighteen.

And so it was settled. I stayed, helped the team complete their discussions successfully, then flew back to Sophie and took her on a glider ride the following Sunday . . . which delighted Sophie and made me sicker than her favorite roller-coaster ride did.

Early in my career, I consulted two companies (let's call them "A" and "B"). Company A had engaged me to do a three-day workshop on a specific date and agreed to pay me X dollars.

A month before the date of the workshop, Company B asked me if I would be a keynote speaker and facilitator for an all-day conference with their top five hundred leaders. This conference was on the middle day of the three-day workshop I had committed to do for Company A. For this keynote and facilitation I would get paid $2X$ dollars.

I definitely wanted to do both engagements (and make 3X dollars). But if I couldn't do that, then I'd rather do Company B's keynote, since it demanded one-third of the time for double the money. But I had already given my promise to Company A, so I was afraid that I would have to decline the engagement with Company B.

I called the learning and development manager at Company A and told her, "Mary, I've been asked to do a keynote on a day that conflicts with our upcoming workshop. I know that you have already invited the executives and that several of them have confirmed their attendance. I realize that changing the date at this stage would be costly for you. So I have the following proposition: If you'd like me to do the workshop as planned, then I will do it. But if you are willing to reschedule it, I will do it at a later date for free. I'll waive my fee. You'd only pay for the travel and accommodation. What do you think?"

Mary didn't need to think too much. "Deal!" she replied immediately. "Our budget is quite stretched, so it would be a welcome relief to save the money. I'll deal with the change of date. If anybody complains, I'll explain to them why we're doing it."

At the end, we rescheduled the workshop for the following week. I was able to do both jobs, and got 2X dollars for them, which was a good deal for me. In addition, my reputation as a supportive, flexible, and trustworthy consultant grew significantly. I worked with both these companies for many more years.

HOW TO HOLD OTHERS TO ACCOUNT

Let's say that, like Jared in the almond-butter story presented earlier, you've been let down. Somebody made a promise to you that he or she didn't fulfill. You are upset and want satisfaction. Execution is suffering, trust has eroded, and integrity is in question. You feel bad, and you want to make your defaulting counterpart feel bad, too. My advice: Don't. If you go with your impulse, you will make everything worse.

Resentment calls for revenge, but that's a terrible way to deal with the problem. Like a sugary soda that tastes good but doesn't really quench your thirst and compromises your health, self-righteous indignation doesn't really solve the problem. And it can leave your relationship in tatters.

On the other hand, if you want to execute with efficiency, preserve trust, and maintain integrity, you can't stay quiet if there's a breakdown. Silence is consent, so if you say nothing, you will be endorsing the behavior. You need to make a productive complaint.

When you complain productively, you seek to restore effectiveness, trust, and integrity. You confront only once, and you follow through to resolution. At best, you end up with a new agreement that closes the matter. At worst, you realize that your counterpart is not trustworthy, and you can responsibly decide what you want to do about it.

There are seven steps for a productive complaint.

1. *SET YOUR INTENTION.*

Review your purpose for complaining and ensure that it is productive. You want to have a mutual learning conversation to repair the breakdown and lay the groundwork for better future interactions.

2. *ESTABLISH A COLLABORATIVE GOAL.*

Share your intention with your counterpart as an invitation. For the conversation to succeed, both of you should want to improve your working relationship, not to accuse each other and defend yourselves. Your shared goal should be to address a breakdown that is affecting your work, your relationship, and your well-being. Again, your mantra should be "Repair and prepare."

3. *VERIFY THE COMMITMENT.*

Many problems result from miscommunication at the time of commitment. You think you requested X; your counterpart thinks she promised Y. If this is the case, have a new conversation about the commitment and then discuss how to avoid repeating this misunderstanding in the future.

4. *VERIFY THE BREAKDOWN.*

Check that your counterpart agrees that he or she did not fulfill the commitment. Your counterpart will probably give you a justification. Don't engage in a discussion about it. At this point you are just trying to establish the facts.

5. *ASK WHAT HAPPENED.*

Besides helping you understand the other person's perspective, inquiry shows respect. It helps you evaluate whether the causes for the default arose after the promise was made and were unforeseeable. It also helps you separate the practical issues from the trust and integrity ones. The practical issues are related to keeping one's word; trust and integrity issues are about honoring it.

For example, if one of my colleagues missed a meeting without letting me know in advance that he or she wouldn't attend, I would ask them what happened. If they tell me that our CEO had demanded an urgent meeting, I would say this: "I can certainly understand that the CEO's request has priority over mine. If he called me, I would have canceled the meeting with you, too. What I don't understand is why you didn't let me know right away that you couldn't make it. It would have taken you just thirty seconds to call or send me a text message to apologize and explain what happened."

6. *NEGOTIATE A RECOMMITMENT.*

To repair the breakdown, you may need your counterpart to recommit to the original promise, or you may require some additional conditions. The key is to clearly ask for what *you* need to close the issue, restore trust, and feel at peace. If you do get satisfaction, drop the issue, forgive, and forget. Don't keep the matter as a "resentment trump card" to play in future conversations with this person.

7. CHECK AND LEARN.

Ask your counterpart if he or she is satisfied with the process. Make sure that trust has been reestablished and integrity maintained. Also, take notice of the cause of the breakdown and consider it as something you can both foresee the next time you make a similar agreement.

INTEGRITY, PROSPERITY, AND EVOLUTION

The evolution of humankind owes more to the division of labor than to the invention of the wheel. Many civilizations, such as the early Egyptian, thrived without the wheel, but no societies thrived without specialization. With increasing specialization, however, any society needs to develop methods of integration. Otherwise, the parts will break apart and the original whole will dissolve. When differentiation leads to fracture and independence rather than to relation and interdependence, the system collapses. And when this happens in the economic sphere, prosperity, well-being, and development go backward.

The market economy is the best integration mechanism for humans. It promotes social cooperation with maximal freedom and minimal conflict. It has evolved through thousands of years of social experimentation. Mutually voluntary transactions between buyers and sellers of goods and services within the institutional framework of property rights and the rule of law have allowed for the biggest demographic explosion, the biggest increase in the standard of living, and the biggest extension of life expectancy in the history of the world. Each one of the transactions in the market or in an organization is mediated by a prior agreement and by the trust that commitments will be fulfilled.

Whether we are coordinating our actions as buyers and sellers or we are working together as fellow organizational members, our ability to produce results depends on the integrity with which we exchange requests and promises. Integrity is the glue that allows us to reintegrate the specialization that underpins modern society. Integrity and trust are essential factors of production. As the political economist and author Francis Fukuyama has noted, "Economic life depends on ... trust. This is the unspoken, unwritten bond between fellow citizens that facilitates transactions, empowers individual creativity, and justifies collective action. . . . The social capital represented by trust is as important as physical capital."[4]

But it is not only economic well-being that depends on our integrity. The social bonds of trust strengthen or weaken with it as well. When you promise frivolously or default carelessly, you harm your relationships. That's why, if you want to be a transcendent leader, you need to be impeccable about your commitments. Your word must absolutely be your bond. And you must demand that everyone else operate with the same level of integrity.

PART 3
SELF-TRANSCENDENCE

Chapter 11
GET OVER YOURSELF
TO LEAD EVERYBODY, BE NOBODY

The wicked leader is he who the people despise. The good leader is he who the people revere. The great leader is he who the people say, "We did it ourselves."

—Lao Tzu

Before Jeff Weiner became CEO at LinkedIn, I coached him while he was an executive at Yahoo. One evening over a nice meal and a few pints of Belgian beer, Jeff shared with me his personal mission: "To expand the world's collective wisdom."

"That reminds me of a Buddhist teaching," I said. "'Wisdom without compassion is ruthless; compassion without wisdom is foolish.'"

"Hmm," Jeff replied. "Maybe I should modify the mission. How about 'to expand the world's collective wisdom and compassion'?"

"Yes! If that's your quest, count on me as your ally." We sealed the pact with a toast.

A few years later, after Jeff became the CEO of LinkedIn, he invited me in as a consultant and then asked me to join the company as a vice president. I was flattered but had reservations. I'd been my own boss ever since I'd left MIT in 1996 to start a consulting company. I'd spent nearly twenty years partnering with many clients. The prospect of committing to a single one of them gave me cold feet. I felt like a jungle animal being lured into a very nice zoo; I'd have all my needs met but would no longer be able to roam free. How would I transition from being an entrepreneur owner to an employee without feeling disempowered? Would I still respect myself in the morning?

I told Jeff that his offer was very appealing, but something was still holding me back. "What's your concern?" he asked.

I confessed that I was worried about surrendering some of my autonomy and freedom. "I join your company, I work for you," I explained, "that's my code. The problem is that I'm not sure I can work for you wholeheartedly as an employee."

"Don't work for me, Fred. Work for *our* mission," Jeff responded. "If you are serious about expanding the world's collective wisdom and compassion, let's do it together at LinkedIn."

"What do you mean?"

"Help us become an example of compassionate and wise management, and then let us use what we learn to help professionals and organizations all over the world. We play a key role in how companies hire and develop their talent and how people find jobs. Where else could you have this kind of impact?"

"Hmm," I replied, "I think I should modify my code to: 'I join the company, I commit to the mission.'"

"Welcome to LinkedIn." Jeff smiled.

In a race, the runners seem to be following the leader, but that is an illusion. The truth is that each of them is racing to the goal. The leader is simply the one closest to it. A true leader is the closest to the mission, its first follower. It may seem that the others are following him or her, but they are all pursuing the mission.

A meditation teacher once told me, "If you want to teach, you must love the truth more than you love yourself." In leadership terms this translates to "If you want to lead, you must love the mission more than you love yourself." Becoming a mission-driven leader requires a redefinition of who you take yourself to be. Instead of constantly trying to prove that you are worthy of admiration, praise, obedience, and awe, you have to get your ego out of the way. To address the hard problems of disengagement, disorganization, disinformation, and disillusion, you must inspire people to follow not you but a meaningful mission.

THE EGO TRAP

I once heard a story about a Russian woman who dreamed of becoming a ballerina. She practiced hard and eventually wound up taking workshops with renowned masters. During one such workshop, she asked a Russian teacher for his assessment. He told her bluntly that she didn't have what it took to make it to stardom.

The news crushed her. She gave up her dream and became a choreographer instead. Many years later she crossed paths with the Russian teacher and told him that she had given up dancing because of what he had said to her. "Oh," he said nonchalantly, "I say that to everyone. The dancers that have what it takes don't pay attention to me."

Like the ballerina, your ego stands between you and what it takes to become a transcendent leader. This brittle, self-doubting and always-ready-to-quit part of yourself cannot withstand anything less than perfection. It would rather be great at mediocrity than to strive for greatness.

In their book *Ego Free Leadership*: *Ending the Unconscious Habits That Hijack Your Business*, Shayne Hughes (of the leadership development firm Learning as Leadership) and Brandon Black (the former CEO of Encore Capital) define ego as the part of your psyche that is constantly preoccupied with self-worth and status. (I find it helpful to think of Ego metaphorically—as a person with a strong, dominant personality who likes to boss you around.)

Imagine that Ego is like a character in a play about your life. Ego adopts defensive or aggressive behaviors when its value is in question. Ego endlessly asks, "Do I look competent, smart, attractive, powerful, right, good, in control? Am I respected, admired, liked, appreciated, envied, revered?" When the answer is yes, it feels pride and peace; when the answer is no, it feels shame and anxiety.[1]

Ego wants endless acknowledgment, recognition, and success. Under its spell, each of us yearns to be the best, the smart one, the hero. We want others to need us, to look up to us, to follow us. When we know the answer or deliver the impossible, we feel worthy, powerful, superior; we glow with pride. Our brain is on fire with dopamine flooding our pleasure centers, just like a drug. The problem is that Ego's insatiable need for acknowledgment causes us at times to knock others down. Too many leaders crave power over people and groups because Ego tells them that they'll be worthy only if they are on top.

Ego focuses on our personal success as the measure of value. The lust for success and the fear of failure drives it. It creates constant performance anxiety because the rush of success is short-lived and the chance of failure is ever present. Even the slightest underperformance activates its fear of not being good enough. No amount of praise satisfies ego's endless hunger for reassurance.

Ego is competitive. It's always comparing us to those around, trying to increase our status by making us overvalue ourselves and undervalue others. It considers colleagues as potential threats—if they look better, we fear we look worse in comparison. Consequently, it prioritizes our individual success over the team's mission—especially when measured by individual performance indicators.

But if you lead from Ego, you will never engage your employees or your colleagues or your customers. Ego is so concerned with itself that it doesn't leave room for anything or anyone else. It's impossible to truly understand and support your employees and your customers if you're self-absorbed. Unfortunately, unless you do your personal development work, Ego will remain in control.

We develop automatic routines to deal with our anxiety about self-worth at the outset of our life. As children, these defensive routines protect us from painful feelings of hurt, fear, embarrassment, and guilt. If we touch a hot stove, our pain quickly teaches us not to do it again. The same goes for emotional pain; when we experience it, we draw conclusions about what caused it and how to avoid it in the future.

We keep reenacting these defensive routines because they provide us with what psychologists call "secondary gains." Even though these defensive routines harm our deep aspirations and sever our authentic connections with others, they soothe our egos. For example, by avoiding a difficult conversation with a low-performing employee, we make it impossible to address the root of the problem; we also accumulate resentment toward him that generally ends in a blowup. But because we fear being disliked and judged as a mean boss, we save our ego from the anxiety of confronting him.

The problem is that our experience of ego-pain is always ambiguous; its lessons are never clear. One of my favorite Aesop's fables is about a donkey that was walking along a path carrying heavy sacks of salt and fell in a river. The salt dissolved in the water and the donkey came out feeling light as a feather. The next time it traveled the path, the donkey jumped into the river to lighten its load. But this time the sacks were full of sponges and the donkey drowned. Like the donkey, our egos learn the wrong lessons early in life and draw self-limiting conclusions.

For example, I learned to link approval and love with academic performance, so I spent my life trying to prove I was lovable—all the way to an MIT professorship and a divorce. (When I was teaching at MIT, I read a *Boston Globe* letter to the editor that made me feel like I was in good company. It was from George Wald, a Nobel laureate in biology. "The truth is what one really needs is not Nobel laureates but love," he wrote. "How do you think one gets to be a Nobel laureate? Wanting love, that's how. Wanting it so bad one works all the time and ends up a Nobel laureate. It's a consolation prize. What matters is love."[2])

Any time you know what you should do but you can't bring yourself to do it, it is a sign that your ego is trying to defend itself. If you feel like a victim of circumstances or people beyond your control, your ego is in control. I'm sure that at a conscious level, you know that pursuing ambitious goals and growing or creating authentic relationships is more important than not failing, looking good, or avoiding rejection. But it's much harder to feel it in your bones. That's why, in spite of our best judgment and intentions, unless we work on it, we keep repeating ego-driven reactive patterns that falsely protect and limit us.

DISRUPT THE PATTERN

Because ego-defensive routines are stored as unconscious memories in the parts of your brain that develop earliest, trying to use your adult willpower to change them is like trying to convince yourself to touch a hot stove. No matter how much you tell yourself that you should have that conversation with the low-performing employee or listen quietly to someone who disagrees with you, doing so feels dangerous.

Hughes and Black argue that while you can't become completely ego-free, you can become more conscious and realize that you can choose either to give in to your egotistical impulses or to break free of them.[3] The moment of choice is when you feel what they call an "emotional pinch"—your body literally reacts to the perceived threat by tightening your muscles, frowning, hastening your breathing, and so on, and the ego starts engaging your old defensive routines.

When pinched, we become ineffective, even destructive. Our egos might drive us to become perfectionistic, oppositional, and critical of others. (When I'm under stress, for example, I tend to become hyper-rational, ice cold, razor sharp, and overly critical. My ego finds and magnifies flaws in others, seeking to prove that I'm right and they are wrong.) It could make you become competitive, controlling, and demanding. It could make you sarcastic, contemptuous, or condescending. You could procrastinate or become avoidant, withdrawing, and aloof. Each of us has his or her favorite reactive behaviors, which we use to assuage our ego's anxiety about not being good enough.

The key to defusing such a reaction is to look deeply at whatever primal and childish interpretation is driving the fear of potential failure, judgment, embarrassment, or rejection. For example, when I looked for the root of my performance anxiety, I remembered an episode when I was five years old, the night before I was due to start first grade. I had a meltdown in bed. My parents heard me crying, so they came to check on me. When they asked me why I was crying, I told them that I was afraid that they would get mad at me if I didn't do well at school. "Don't worry," they said, "you will do very well." Needless to say, what I was really hoping for was "We'll always love you, regardless of how you do in school." Like Aesop's donkey, my child-self absorbed the wrong lesson: If I'm successful, I'll be loved.

This deep dive into the root cause of ego triggers is never easy, but it does get easier with practice. "The goal is not to avoid having pinches," Hughes and Black point out, "but rather to notice and welcome them as opportunities to learn and grow."[4] They suggest that the way to dispel the illusory danger to your ego is to shift from a reactive defensive-aggressive pattern to a creative constructive orientation. Here are five steps that take you from here to there:

1. Notice the moments in your life when you experience a pinch. This might be an event or something someone says or does.
2. Instead of reacting to something external that pinches, search for what is triggered in you. If someone pushes your buttons, don't focus on him or her but on your buttons. What is that visceral discomfort you're trying to numb or blame others for? How do you feel your sense of self-worth is being threatened?
3. When you notice other people hiding behind defensive veneers of bravado, aggression, or indifference, consider the vulnerabilities that may be driving them, and empathize with their deeper fear.
4. Focus on your own highest goals and values. What do you really want for yourself? What would you like to convey to the other person? What do you care about the most? What example would you like to set through your own behavior and leadership? Connect with the deeper intention that motivates you to break your defensive patterns.
5. In talking with another, take the risk of sharing how you yourself feel vulnerable. Share your feelings about the perceived threat, not your mental chatter. Model a context of safety for mutual disclosure and connection.[5]

For example, I notice that when one of my colleagues presents a brilliant idea, my ego feels a pinch of envy and the desire to find a flaw in their thinking. Instead of surrendering to it, or pushing against my feelings, I become curious about them. When I look deeper, I discover that I feel vulnerable about not being the smartest person in the room. I have invested so much of my self-esteem in being admired for my intelligence that any time someone appears to be as smart as or smarter than I am, I feel under threat. My first instinct is to try to knock him or her down with some even more brilliant criticism—delivered with just the right touch of sarcasm.

When I see this tendency in myself, I stop myself immediately. That is not the way I want to relate to others. What I care about more than being admired for my brainpower is supporting those around me, so that they can shine as brightly as possible. I take delight in their brilliance and success. I allow myself to relax and appreciate their light; if there's an opportunity to help the person polish his or her idea even more, I offer my opinion respectfully, as a building block rather than as a missile. I try to be the transcendent leader I see myself as.

To get beyond an emotional pinch, I try to connect to a higher purpose and to the values that I espouse and that sustain me, through self-inquiry questions such as:

- How is this an opportunity for me and for others to grow?
- What will most help all of us take advantage of this occasion?
- What kind of relationship do I want to develop with this person?
- What is my intention for him or her?
- What matters more to me than my own success?
- What matters more to me than being liked?
- How do I want to show up in this situation?
- What values and behaviors do I want to exemplify?

I've found that accepting my feelings with understanding and empathy, and then reconnecting to my deepest goals and best intentions for the company, the team, and the individuals under me, brings me back to a more creative and effective state of mind.

• • •

If you want to become a transcendent leader and create a healthy culture in your organization, this kind of self-contemplation is not just part of your personal growth; it is an absolute requirement.[6] If you're defensive, territorial, competitive, aggressive, avoidant, and so on, you'll produce similarly dysfunctional behaviors in your followers. As I've said, transcendent leaders need not only to define the standards of the organization, but, most important, demonstrate them—especially when under stress.

THE EGO VS. THE SOUL

To lead is to inspire others to give their best to the mission. This "best" comes from what Mihaly Csikszentmihalyi, the renowned author of *Flow,* calls "the soul." "We attribute soul," Csikszentmihalyi wrote, "to those entities that use some portion of their energy not only for their own sake, but to make contact with other beings and care for them."[7] The energy freed up from the self-preoccupation and self-absorption of the ego becomes available for connecting with others.[8]

While the ego asks, "Am I the best, the most admired, the most valued?," the soul asks, "Am I contributing to others and helping them grow and develop? Am I connecting authentically to them? Am I making a difference in the world, living my values and purpose?" When the answer is yes, we feel happy, confident that we are on a meaningful path. There's no performance anxiety in these questions, for external factors can influence only success or failure, not integrity or peace of mind.

When the soul is in charge, I believe we experience a kind of unconditional power, knowing that we are capable of pursuing our noble purpose and demonstrating our ethical values in the company of those who share them. We might not be able to win the game, but we can always do our best and play honorably.

• • •

Nobody wants to just make a living. We all want to make a life, to contribute something important to others and the world. If you want to lead a soulful organization, you must look in the mirror and ask, "What is the point of what we are doing? Why does it matter? What am I, and the people I lead, really trying to accomplish here? What's our unique value to the world? How is our product or service enhancing our customers' lives? Why would the best people want to invest their life energy with us to achieve our mission?"

Your customers and employees can energize your organization only if they think that your product or service is truly life promoting, and that the conditions in which you produce it are worthy of admiration and emulation. This requires engaging their souls in a meaningful, ethical, transcendent project. These souls are sovereign; they don't surrender to someone else's authority. No person can have authority over another's soul. Soul is what you cannot extract by any extrinsic means. You can only *receive* it as a gift, because of the other's intrinsic motivation.

To get employees engaged in your organization, or to get customers to buy your products, you have to look hard at the purpose of other people's lives. You have to give them something that they find more valuable than alternative uses of their time, attention, and resources. Otherwise, they'll decline your offer, or accept it grudgingly. Value is in the eye of the beholder; a valuable opportunity is one that furthers your employees' or customers' life's purpose. The moment you lose sight of that, your culture and your business will suffer. This isn't just a moral matter; it's Economics 101.

That's why you need to reflect on how the service you are offering allows your customers to take care of their own concerns, and how the work you are offering allows employees to take care of theirs. When you address these questions, customers will become brand advocates and employees will become missionaries.

You must disrupt your ego's defenses and move to a *soul orientation* in order to foster a positive culture. When people feel supported and respected, they more easily lower their own ego defenses and face challenges constructively. On the other hand, if people feel unsafe due to fears or threats, they will act to protect themselves first, do their jobs (the ones on which they are evaluated) second, and contribute to the organization's mission last.

This soul-work is difficult and demanding. But there is no other alternative.

As I approached my forties, I hired a physical trainer to help me get in better shape. "I want to run a marathon," I told him.

"The question is not whether you want to run a marathon," he replied, "but whether you are willing to train for it."

When you get attached to an outcome without committing to the process, you fail. To genuinely commit to a goal, you have to be willing to do what it takes to achieve it. My coach's comment helped me through the many hours of training. As it turned out, the race was the easy part. The hard part was getting ready for it. During the long practice runs, I repeated a phrase I got from a book about the U.S. Special Forces, "Train hard; fight easy."

The transcendent leader is like a flag. People don't fight for the flag itself, but for what it symbolizes. Great leaders understand that they are not managing human resources, but conferring value and meaning to human beings.

A transcendent leader has no followers; he or she must self-efface to let people connect directly to the mission and the values. The leader's job is to "get out of the way."

INVESTORS RATHER THAN FOLLOWERS

Each one of us has precious capital, our soul energy. As such, we must invest it wisely to energize an organization that pursues a noble purpose, one that we're proud of, in community with people who share our values. That is one of the secrets of personal happiness, passionate engagement, and organizational success.

While I was contemplating whether to join LinkedIn, I had dinner with Reid Hoffman, its cofounder and chairman at the time. Over some of the best sushi I've ever eaten, I asked Reid why he hired Jeff as CEO of his company. He replied, "Because I trust him to manage LinkedIn in a way that realizes my vision better than I can manage it myself." In fact, Reid doesn't refer to Jeff as an employee but as a late-stage cofounder.

I feel the same way. I am the founder and chairman of myself. When LinkedIn hired me, I simultaneously "hired" Jeff as my CEO and late-stage cofounder. I hired him because I trust his commitment to our shared mission, and his ability to manage me to realize it—an ability I believe exceeds my own. It is true that I work for Jeff, since I give him the authority to allocate my efforts in service of LinkedIn's mission according to his best judgment. But Jeff also works for me, just as he works for Reid, managing my most significant asset (myself) to achieve my life's mission, which is to help people reconnect with their true nature. Just as Jeff selected me to work at LinkedIn to help accomplish the company's mission, I selected Jeff as the person to best manage my energy and commitment to bring wisdom and compassion to the business world. So just as I work for LinkedIn as vice president, LinkedIn works for me as the platform that enables me to pursue my purpose far better than I could on my own.

An example of this happened a year after I joined LinkedIn, when I finished producing and piloting a fifteen-module, seventy-video program of my *Conscious Business* book for LinkedIn employee development. When I proposed to publish this on LinkedIn's open platform so that the whole world could share in it, I was met with some resistance. The video programs had been an intensive, and expensive, effort. Why would we simply give this unique content away? Best to keep it as a unique professional development opportunity for our employees, some of my colleagues argued, to give LinkedIn something special to offer our people. I proposed that publicizing the material would attract even more potential candidates. My counterparts and I followed all the principles of collaboration I described in Chapter 9, but we still couldn't reach a consensus.

So we jointly escalated our debate to Jeff. He listened to the arguments, and after he understood and acknowledged all of us he said, "Both arguments are reasonable, so I'd like to decide this on the basis of our mission. How do you believe that we are more likely to connect the world's professionals to make them more productive and successful?"

"If we're serious about expanding the world's collective wisdom and compassion," I said, recalling my original conversation with Jeff when I joined LinkedIn, "we should share this knowledge freely." Looking around the room, Jeff asked, "Does anybody have an objection to this beyond what we've discussed?" Nobody did, so we decided to post the program at www.conscious.LinkedIn.com, where it is freely available.

By making the decision to publish the videos online, we kept our commitment to our members. And Jeff kept his commitment to our shared mission. This was a return on the life energy I invested in LinkedIn.

One way to think of followers is as investors. The leader is the entrepreneur, the first followers are the "angel" and "series A" investors, the following ones are the "series B" and "C" if necessary, all the way until the company becomes "public." One by one, individuals "hire" the leadership of the company to manage their personal capital, their life energy, and put it in service of a mission.

In 2010, an entrepreneur named Derek Sivers opened his TED talk ("How to Start a Movement") with a short video of a scene from an outdoor summer rock concert. A young man stands up and starts dancing to the beat, waving his arms in the air, doing somersaults, and generally looking like an escaped monkey. He looks ridiculous. But then another man stands up and joins the leader. The follower is the leader's equal; as they dance, the first follower calls his friends to join in. Then someone else gets into the act, and another and another. "If you nurture the other dancers and you make it easy to follow," the narrator says, "you can start a movement."[9] Sivers makes the point that without the first follower, and the second, and the third, there would be no collective effort at all. "Being a first follower is an underappreciated form of leadership."

One of the first followers at LinkedIn is Mike Gamson, senior vice president of sales. When I asked him why he "hired" Jeff as a leader, he told me, "I follow Jeff because he's worthy of it; what he's aspiring to bring us to (our mission) is worthy of it. The mission demands leaders of my caliber in subordinate roles in order to make it happen. Jeff needs leaders like me following him in order to accomplish our mission."[10] Ego-free mission-driven leaders attract ego-free mission-driven followers.

Not long ago, I gave a talk on this topic for a group of government officials, corporate officers, and international consultants in Riyadh, Saudi Arabia. When the time for questions arrived, a portly gentleman with a thick beard and dressed in the traditional Saudi attire raised his hand. "Why didn't you give the leadership example of the Prophet (Mohammad)?" he said in what sounded to me like a harsh voice.

I took a deep breath and said, "Because my knowledge of the Muslim faith is far below that of anyone in the audience. I'm a guest here, so I'd like to respectfully ask if you could tell me the leadership example of the Prophet."

"The word in Arabic to describe the followers of the Prophet is 'saheb,'" he quickly replied. "But the word does not mean 'follower'; it means 'friend.' The Prophet had no followers; he had spiritual friends who followed Allah."

As I thanked the gentleman (who turned out to be a university professor), I felt the collective sigh of relief from my LinkedIn colleagues who had organized the conference. At the end, the man came onstage and gave me one of the warmest hugs I've ever received after a talk. It was both embarrassing and invigorating to feel my worries about my lack of cultural understanding melt under this man's embrace.

A PASSIONATE FOLLOWER

A few years ago, I received a great gift from LinkedIn: the opportunity to work in Dubai, a dazzling, cosmopolitan port city and one of the United Arab Emirates (UAE). I'd admired Dubai for its economic progress and legal infrastructure for many years, and I found it hard to believe that the place had been a dusty Bedouin outpost only fifty years before.

Full of gigantic, wildly architected buildings situated along a beautiful stretch of coastline, Dubai is a dream to live and work in for the world's professionals. In fact, nine out of ten members of the Dubai workforce are expats who choose to invest their life energy there every day. Dubai has branded itself as a city with the highest quality of life, able to attract global talent. In the last several years, it has become the top city in the world for Middle Eastern professionals. While an expat can save double the money working in other places, the foreigners who work there prefer to stay in Dubai for its lifestyle, its cleanliness, its safety, its great health care, education, and culture.

In 2015, I had a chance to experience directly the economic and social miracle that the people of Dubai have been able to cultivate in the desert. When I asked, "To what do you attribute Dubai's success?," invariably the answer was "Leadership," referring to Sheikh Mohammed bin Rashid Al Maktoum, the constitutional ruler.

"Leadership," Mohammed Al Gergawi, the government's minister of cabinet affairs, told me, "is the ultimate resource to unleash passion. Some people drill for oil, we drill for leadership." Here's the story that he told me directly that illustrates how leadership trickles down in Dubai.[11]

Gergawi had been a midlevel functionary working as director of business registration for Dubai, but he was not a typical bureaucrat, and he never saw himself as the boss. For him, all people were important. Gergawi didn't work in a back office while other people helped the customers. Instead, he put his desk in the waiting area. He wanted to see how customers were treated, and he tried to find ways to help them.

One day, an old local man came in, looking confused. Gergawi saw him and offered to help; he gave the old man some coffee and sat with him while the old man waited for his turn. Then he accompanied the man to the service counter when he was called, to make sure everything went smoothly. When the man finished his business, he thanked him and left. Gergawi never gave him a second thought.

A couple of years later, Gergawi received an employment offer from a private company tripling his wage, so he resigned. Then Sheikh Mohammed himself sent Gergawi a letter giving him a big promotion—something extremely unusual, since Gergawi was fairly low on the totem pole. This was an offer he couldn't refuse.

Gergawi was torn between his duty to thank the sheikh and his nervousness about coming before the country's ruler. "Part of our culture is to say 'thank you' in person, but I was reluctant to talk to Sheikh Mohammed because he is such an awesome person," he told me. "My mother kept pushing me to do it, so after two months I went to Sheikh Mohammed's Majlis." (The Majlis is a council during which ordinary people can take an empty seat next to the sheikh and talk to him one-on-one.) "At one point the chair was empty, so I gathered my courage and took the seat to thank him," Gergawi remembers. "I told him who I was, said 'thanks,' and stood up to leave in a hurry. But he put his hand on mine and held me down. He said, 'I know you. I have been watching you.' I was frozen in my seat."

One of the ways people get demoted or promoted in the UAE government is when a "mystery shopper"—someone who shows up incognito at various government departments to see how things are going—reports them. As it turned out, the old man who had visited Gergawi's department was such a mystery shopper. After his experience, he had told the sheikh about the kindness with which Gergawi had treated him. Without Gergawi's knowledge, the sheikh had put him in a high potential list and followed his progress ever since.

BURN, BABY, BURN

During a ceremony in the Mexican desert, I was sitting with a shaman watching a fire. The shaman handed me a log and asked me to meditate on what part of my ego I was ready to let go of. Then he told me to imagine that I had transferred that energy to the log, and he instructed me to put the log on the fire and watch it burn with full attention.

While watching the log burn, I had a flash of insight regarding my life that a voice inside me expressed in words: *I, too, am a log, and I am already burning. Every cell in my body is using oxygen to produce energy, just like this fire in front of me. And when my fuel runs out, I will die, just like this fire will die out. I am being consumed by the sacred fire of life.*

I have no choice about that. But I do have a choice about the altar on which I place myself. To what will I offer myself? I have put myself on the altar of such unimportant material and egocentric things. It is time to make a deliberate choice and start burning on the altar of meaning, love, and freedom.

It was the moment in which I began to write this book. I committed to my personal mission of "helping people remember their true nature, and express it consciously in business and beyond."

You, too, are burning. On which altar are you placing yourself?

Chapter 12
DIE BEFORE YOU DIE

FIND YOUR TRUE NATURE

And so long as you haven't experienced this,
to die and so to grow,
you are only a troubled guest
on the dark earth.

—Goethe

In a celebrated address to the Stanford graduating class of 2005, Steve Jobs said: "I have looked in the mirror every morning and asked myself: 'If today were the last day of my life, would I want to do what I am about to do today?' And whenever the answer has been 'No' for too many days in a row, I know I need to change something." The message was particularly poignant because Jobs had been diagnosed with pancreatic cancer a year earlier.

His reflection on death, however, was not a consequence of his illness. Jobs shared how an awareness of death had served him as a valuable coach throughout his life. He recalled that at age seventeen he had read a quote that reminded him to live each day as if it was his last, "because someday you'll most certainly be right." Understanding that he might die soon, Jobs said, was "the most important tool I've ever encountered to help me make the big choices in life, because almost everything—all external expectations, all pride, all fear of embarrassment or failure—these things just fall away in the face of death, leaving only what is truly important." He noted that "death is very likely the single best invention of life. It is life's change agent. It clears out the old to make way for the new."[1]

Jobs exemplified the Zen saying "Die before you die, so you can truly live." The first "die" means "confront the fact of your mortality"; the second, to die literally. Dying before you die means coming to terms with the finite nature of your existence in order to fully comprehend life's richness and possibility. If you leave thinking about your death until you are about to die, you will miss death's wise counsel. Paradoxically, dying before you die is the answer to the Jewish prayer, "Let me not die while I am still alive."

It's easy for anyone, even transcendent leaders, to conduct too much of life on autopilot, constantly distracted by everyday busyness. We can sleepwalk through life, focusing our attention on the trivial and frivolous. We indulge in too many activities that leave us empty and unfulfilled. But instead of filling this emptiness with a disciplined pursuit of meaning, we soothe our anxious nerve cells with more empty busyness and trivial pursuits.

Imagine that you have only three minutes to live, and you want to make one final phone call to someone. Whom would you call? What would you tell that person? And what are you waiting for? When you have just three minutes to live, you may not even be able to make that call. After I ask people in my workshops these questions, I see them calling loved ones during the break.

Once we understand that the clock is ticking and there's no time to waste, we want to elevate our sights, pursue something worthwhile, make every day count. The prospect of death directs us to focus on what truly matters: truth, happiness, meaning, love, friendship, gratitude, awe, compassion, peace, fullness, and freedom. And this responsibility is even more true if you aspire to be a transcendent leader, helping others fulfill their most meaningful purposes in the organization and in their personal lives.

A BRUSH WITH DEATH

In 2008, the management consulting firm Grant Thornton surveyed 250 CEOs of companies with revenue of $50 million or more. Twenty-two percent said they had had an experience when they believed they would die and, of those, 61 percent said it changed their long-term perspective on life or career. Forty-one percent said it made them more compassionate leaders.[2]

One senior manager who experienced a close encounter with death was Rand Leeb-du Toit. In February 2014, Leeb-du Toit worked as a research director at Gartner, the world's leading research and advisory firm in IT. He loved his job as one of the leaders of a brain trust advising a mix of Fortune 500 and high-growth businesses. Despite the pressures of his job, he took excellent care of himself. He ate healthy food, meditated, and enjoyed running, surfing, and stand-up paddling. He'd get out on the water and really push himself.

One Sunday morning, when it was still pitch black, he went for a stand-up paddle session on Narrabeen Lake, close to his home in suburban Sydney. After an hour on the water, he felt that something wasn't quite right. "I felt a bit more drained than usual, but then again I hadn't had breakfast and thought it was simply low blood sugar level," he recalled. He went to the office and worked all day, but that night felt worse. He tried to get to the bathroom and became disoriented.

"Then, I collapsed and died."

When the ambulance arrived, the paramedics discovered that his heart rate was running at 200 beats per minute. He was undergoing sudden cardiac arrest, which involves the electrical circuitry of the heart rather than the plumbing. Only 5 percent of people survive such an event, typically through resuscitation. He was in a state of heightened ventricular tachycardia—arrhythmia—and yet he was conscious (something that almost never happens).

Leeb-du Toit felt extremely grateful to be in the small percentage of people who survive such an experience. "That gratitude has made me feel I have a responsibility to make more of a difference in the world," he says. "I've been given this incredibly rare second life—what, though, am I going to do with it?"

For Leeb-du Toit, sudden cardiac arrest was the trigger for transformation. "The experience altered my perception of time completely," he wrote in an essay.[3] "I no longer feel the same sense of urgency to be busy and to track myself against a linear, progressive timeline. Instead, the past and future are compressed and I see me only living in the now."

The encounter with death taught him to focus less on things that satisfy his ego—making money, focusing on his career, building a business, and so on—and more on listening to his inner voice, his soul, and the things that resonate with him most deeply. Breaking through societal constructs and personal constraints helped him truly come alive and find joy. He quit his job and started a consulting company, coaching leaders to become more connected and empathetic, more transcendent. "Being more empathetic with others can not only create deeper connections and stronger leaders," he noted. "It also acts as a forcing function for solving many of the big issues in our world: hunger, poverty, suffering, and war."

Leeb-du Toit has achieved a greater understanding of purpose because of his brush with death. He's thinking bigger—much, much bigger. His example, like those of others, is permeating the wider corporate consciousness, like welcome rain into an exhausted soil.

Leeb-du Toit's rare opportunity for a second life compelled him to ask, "What am I going to do with it?" Is your life any less rare? Why not ask now, with equal gratitude, "What am I going to do with the remainder of this precious life?"

THE WORM AT THE CORE

According to the philosopher and psychologist William James, the "worm at the core" of the human condition is the gnawing, usually subconscious, awareness of our own impending death. Death is at the core of the symbolic fruit of the Tree of Knowledge. After eating this apple, Adam and Eve were forced from ignorant bliss in paradise into the harsh reality of mortality: "For you are dust. And to dust you shall return."

In *The Denial of Death*, the anthropologist Ernest Becker observed that the central driver of human behavior is our effort to deny and transcend the fact of our own death.[4] The notion that most of human individual and cultural activity arises as a response to death might sound far-fetched, but Becker made a compelling (and Pulitzer Prize–winning) argument that all civilizations arise from death awareness. He argued that all our religious, social, military, political, and economic institutions, as well as the traditions, rituals, and taboos that support the social order, are fundamentally defense mechanisms against our mortality.

"Although like all life-forms, humans have a biological predisposition toward self-preservation in the service of reproduction," Becker explained, "we are unique in our capacity for symbolic thought. This allows us to reflect on the past and imagine the future, realizing that death is inevitable and can occur at any time. We then need to manage this terrifying awareness by constructing shared beliefs about reality that minimize existential dread by conferring meaning and value. All cultures provide a sense that life is meaningful by offering an account of the origin of the universe, prescriptions for appropriate behavior, and assurance of immortality for those who behave in accordance with cultural dictates."[5]

As we become aware of our mortality, we become anxious; to manage this anxiety we try to create or become part of something that we believe will last beyond our physical death—art, music, literature, religion, political movements, institutions, nations, and empires. This is the ultimate motivating force behind many human endeavors. More specifically, it is the motivating force behind every organization.

The people who found, lead, and staff organizations expect to be remembered because of what they have done. They want to achieve the kind of notoriety that will last beyond their lives. It is the same psychological force that causes us to carve our initials in the bark of a tree, or to leave our name on a brick in Fenway Park, or on the wing of a hospital or university if we have enough money. If we feel that we have done something worthwhile and enduring, our fear of death lessens. If we are revered, honored, or even simply remembered, our anxiety subsides.

We try to protect ourselves against mortal anxiety through two psychological maneuvers. First, we try to shore up our "I" self—our self-esteem—through our accomplishments. We try to "look good," decorating our bodies and our homes and accumulating all kinds of toys. We also build our identity by making a difference, having impact, and claiming ownership of memorable feats. "Unlike the baboon who gluts himself only on food," wrote Becker, "man nourishes himself mostly on self-esteem."

Second, we shore up our "we" self by aligning ourselves with groups that share our worldviews—our religions, our languages, our nations, our politicians, our favorite sports teams, and so on. We defend ourselves against death anxiety through culture—by which Becker means all our religious, social, and organizational institutions and the traditions, rituals, and taboos that support the social order. The closer our death anxiety bubbles to the surface, the more tightly we bind to the groups that we identify with.

The drives for I-based self-esteem and we-based cultural belonging are double-edged. If we are lucky and have positive self-esteem, we enhance it by doing good work in the world—working to cure cancer, contributing to our communities, becoming admired leaders, and so on—and the more tolerant we tend to be toward others with alternative worldviews. If we have poor self-esteem, we shore it up by bragging, belittling others, and engaging in risky behaviors, and the more likely we are to demean or attack those who don't share our worldviews. (Fascinatingly, the greater your fear of death, the lower your self-esteem—and vice versa.)

Becker claimed that human beings have two selves, a "physical" self and a "symbolic" self. Our physical selves attend to our day-to-day problems. Our symbolic selves yearn to be part of something greater than ourselves. We are able to transcend the problem of our physical mortality through acts of small and large heroism, which allow the symbolic self to endure beyond the physical one. Anything we do that involves community—whether it's going to church, temple, or mosque; serving in soup kitchens; working for positive change on a community or governmental level; and going to the office when we feel engaged—touches on an "immortality project," that is, a belief system that lets the symbolic self transcend physical reality. Through such projects, we come to feel that we are part of something bigger and more eternal than our all too brief existences. This, in turn, confers meaning on our lives, the feeling that our lives are significant in the grand scheme of things.

From the cave dwellers who left their artwork on stone walls to the programmers who leave theirs in bits, human beings are always trying to leave their fingerprints (or "soul-prints") on history. We all want to say, "I lived and it mattered; see me, know me, remember me." We all want to feel that we have been "persons of value in a world of meaning," as Becker put it.

William James observed that "the greatest use of a life is to spend it on something that will outlast it."[6] A big part of it is being remembered. Every person wants to create or be part of something that can last beyond his or her physical existence. Very few of us can quench this thirst for transcendence on our own. Some of us satisfy our search for meaning through our families and children. But most of us need something more, an immortality project or mission that will make a difference to others in our community and the world.[7]

Unfortunately, immortality projects can be both good and bad. Besides being drivers of meaning, they are also drivers of war, genocide, bigotry, and racism. When one immortality project—say, a religion or a nation—collides with another, conflict arises as a test of whose way of life is right and whose is wrong. Such tribalism triggers aggressive and defensive behaviors, since both parties want to prove that their belief system is superior by eliminating the other. Much of human strife springs from the incompatibility of immortality projects that have generally been eliminative and unethical—eliminative because such a project seeks the obliteration of the rival, and unethical because it does so through aggression and violence.

DEATH AWARENESS AT WORK

The worm at the core has long gnawed on Wharton professor and best-selling author Adam Grant. As a child, he suffered an active imagination that became a kind of curse (he used to worry about the sun burning out, for example) and later turned into frequent existential musings.

In 2009, Grant and a coauthor published a paper that laid out how reminders of death affect people's behavior at work. They found that when people's reactions to reminders of death are "hot" (i.e., anxious and panicked), they tend to withdraw into their own beliefs and become more arrogant, judgmental, and bigoted. But when the reminders of death produce "cool" responses (i.e., reflective ones, as those in helping professions like medicine and firefighting do), people are more likely to think about the meaning of life and their potential contributions.[8]

Grant and his colleagues also found that when people think about death with equanimity, they are more "generative" (i.e., more engaged, productive, and helpful) if their jobs feel meaningful. But if their jobs feel meaningless, they are likely to quit and try to find a job that allows them to be more generative. Moreover, people who feel a "calling" at work are more motivated to leave behind a meaningful contribution, and to craft their jobs in order to make them more meaningful (e.g., by taking on helping initiatives like mentoring). By contrast, people who feel like they are merely job oriented (doing tasks to collect a paycheck) are less motivated to do so.

Grant's research reveals how much we suffer when we don't feel that we are persons of value in a world of meaning at work. We become anxious, disconnected, and disengaged. Moreover, these feelings are highly contagious and spread like a disease through a group, destroying its cohesion and effectiveness. Furthermore, organizations, just like human beings, can die of the disease of disengagement. In dead organizations, nobody cares. Everyone's just there to exchange minimum effort for a salary.

If you are the average working person in a dead organization, you lie under a double curse—the inescapable fact of your individual mortality, and the deadly social atmosphere of the organization you work for. This double attack undermines the individual and cultural pillars of your strategy for overcoming anxiety.

By contrast, transcendent leaders offer employees a chance to engage in an immortality project. They understand that all human beings feel haunted by the prospect of their own insignificance. To help them through this fear, such leaders offer followers, in exchange for their passionate commitment to the mission, the chance to manage their anxiety through meaningful work and membership in a noble, ethical, and successful community. As Mihaly Csikszentmihalyi wrote, "When a leader demonstrates that his purpose is noble and that the work will enable people to connect with something larger—more permanent than their material existence—[then] people will give the best of themselves to the enterprise."[9]

The question of a manager is "How do you . . . ?" (do something, fix something, etc.), but the question of a transcendent leader is "Who are you?" (as a conscious being). The latter question cannot be put to people in a dispassionate, arm's-length way. The leader needs to be "on fire" herself in order to "light up" and inspire her followers. That's why looking to death for advice is necessary. A transcendent leader understands that a noble purpose overcomes the limitations of physical life, projecting those who pursue it into a kind of symbolic immortality. By offering people this awesome possibility, the transcendent leader becomes someone who can guide her followers through the most fearsome prospect of all.

A transcendent leader proposes a mission through which individuals can achieve symbolic immortality. They can reduce their death anxiety, replacing it for feelings of significance, self-esteem, and belonging to a meaningful community. The transcendent leader elicits passionate commitment to a collective, noble purpose—which is the only way to manage disengagement, disorganization, disinformation, and disillusion. When this occurs, people really care and give their best. They look beyond their silos and their small decision-making issues. They align their best efforts in ways that no financial incentives or other management system can. Organizations that offer workers symbolic immortality through moral projects, in solidarity with peers, with opportunities to learn and grow autonomously, outcompete those that don't, reaping tremendous economic rewards as they become the dominant form in the meme pool.

Consider the difference between rowing and surfing. A boat moved by muscle is no match for natural forces. A board propelled by the waves flows in harmony with these forces. An organization moved by managerial authority is like a rowboat plowing against the current. One propelled by transcendent leadership is like a surfboard on a big wave.

DEATH AS A TEACHER

Dying before you die means coolly confronting your own mortality and integrating the awareness of it into how you lead. Dying before you die is the hardest and most important work that you can do if you want to truly live and truly lead. It does not require that you face death in a literal sense, but it does mean that you have to look deeply at your own life and its inevitable end and realize that everyone around you is on the same lifeboat. Once you come to terms with mortality, you can begin to elicit and inspire the internal commitment of those you are leading. You can fulfill their hunger for meaning through a collective mission because you are much more aware and empathetic. Dying before you die makes you the kind of inspiring leader people want to follow.

As a leadership coach, my job is to wake leaders up to what is most essential in them (which is, paradoxically, universal and far beyond "them") so that they can truly engage others at the deepest level. The most powerful leadership development process I've discovered is the "cool" consideration of one's death.

Nobody likes to think, much less talk, about the prospect of death. Perhaps baby boomers, now in their late fifties, sixties, and early seventies, privately wonder how much longer they have to live as their aches and pains kick in. But besides some boomer senior executives, many of the leaders I help are fairly young—between the ages of thirty and forty-five. Most are in pretty good health. Few have given the topic of their own death much thought at all. The subject has certainly never been covered in their business school curricula.

With that existential perspective in mind, I invite my workshop participants to "die before they die" in a reflective or, to use Grant's term, "cool" way. I first propose an exercise based on a notion that produces a vicarious near-death experience. It goes like this:

"Imagine that you are at the end of a long and rich life. You've accomplished everything you wanted, behaving honorably and building meaningful connections with your family, friends, and colleagues. You are proud of yourself for leaving a great legacy, and for having led an organization that brought great value to the world. You've done your work here, and you feel ready to go. So when you learn that your days are numbered, you take the news in stride. A lot of people who appreciate and admire you want to pay their respects, so they organize a 'living funeral.' (A living funeral is a celebration in which a living person with a life-limiting illness listens to the eulogies, praises, and farewells of family, friends, neighbors, and colleagues.) In the ceremony, a dear friend will stand in front of the audience and read a eulogy. Write the eulogy that you would like your friend to give."

For this exercise, I ask the participants not to be humble; the more ambitious and grandiose they can be, the better. That way, they set the highest standards for themselves. "This kind of eulogy can become a true north star for your life," I tell them. "It can help you discover who you want to be and how you want to act in order to leave the legacy you want to leave and feel proud of yourself."

As I ask people to read their eulogies to one another in small groups, everyone is touched by the beautiful aspirations they hear.

Next, I ask them to do a "gap analysis" in which they consider the difference between their current lives and the things they would have to do in the future to justify such a beautiful eulogy. What changes would they have to make? And then I challenge them by asking, "Are you ready to make these changes?" (The relevant commitment is not to the outcome but to the process. Analogously, the question is not whether you want to lose weight but whether you are willing to stick to the diet that gets you to your goal.)

Following those exercises, I then invite them into a "darker" one. I ask them to imagine that they have just died and have not had the time to change anything in their lives. I ask them to answer the following questions in the third person, as if they were their own "devil's advocate," substituting their own names for the "X":

- What dreams did X not pursue?
- What fears did X not overcome?
- What loves did X not express?
- What resentments did X not resolve?
- What apologies did X not make?
- What gifts did X not give?

When they're finished, I ask them to share some of their answers with the group. Some typical statements are:

"He didn't start his business."

"She never volunteered for the nonprofit."

"He died without making the trip."

"She never learned to play the piano."

"He was always afraid of not having enough."

"She couldn't overcome her fear of speaking in public."

"He didn't tell his wife how much he loved her."

"She never told her employees how important they were to her."

"He failed to make peace with his son."

"She didn't forgive herself."

"He wishes he had apologized to his partner."

"He should have spent more time playing and less time worrying."

"Her great idea died with her."

Many of the workshop participants return home with an existential bucket list. They feel more committed to pursuing their dreams, overcoming their fears, forgiving those who hurt them, apologizing to those whom they've hurt, and giving their gifts to the world. Months later, they send me messages and pictures as they cross off their bucket list items and flower into their true selves.

Try an experiment. Ask yourself the questions I listed above and see what comes up. Even this short brush with the prospect of your own mortality can heighten the intensity of your life. Facing the reality of your own death can be profoundly frightening, so it demands great courage. But it will also open you up in a way that nothing else can, setting you on fire with purpose and enabling you to inspire others. As Steve Jobs told the Stanford students, "Remembering that you are going to die is the best way I know to avoid the trap of thinking you have something to lose. You are already naked. There is no reason not to follow your heart."

CAN YOU DIE WITH THAT?

"Can you live with that?" is a typical question that people use to evaluate an option. I'd like to propose "Can you die with that?" as a complement. The idea is that when you're deliberating about a significant decision, you imagine that what you're about to do may well be the last gesture of your life. Then ask yourself whether you'd be at peace with your action, and if so, how you would do it.

Like a corrosive acid, death awareness dissolves the superficial, leaving only the essential, which is why it makes an excellent leadership counselor. For example, imagine sitting in a meeting. There is a seat in the corner where dark-hooded, skull-faced Death sits watching, and everyone is keenly aware of its presence. You can ask yourself how you would behave if you knew that you'd never have another meeting with the people in the room. The meeting is a final and unique opportunity to express your authentic values in action. Every utterance, every exchange, every decision, would be "death-proof," meaning that you could "die with that."

I actually do take a few minutes (or at least a deep breath) to meditate on this idea before I enter a coaching conversation, teach a workshop, or engage in an important dialogue. I prepare myself like this to always give my best parting gift, moment by moment, opening my heart and not holding back, as there's nothing to protect when I'm at the end of my life.

WHAT PSILOCYBIN TAUGHT ME

In a 2015 study about the use of psychedelics to reduce the fear of death, researchers found that cancer patients receiving just a single dose of psilocybin experienced immediate and dramatic reductions in anxiety and depression, and that these effects were still holding six months later.[10] They felt that the experience with psilocybin was among the most meaningful of their lives. They described feelings of unity, sacredness, ineffability, peace, and joy, "as well as the impression of having transcended space and time and the 'noetic sense' that the experience has disclosed some objective truth about reality." These feelings were every bit as real to them as any other experience.

Subjects overcame their fear of death by vicariously experiencing it. "A high-dose psychedelic experience is a death practice," said Katherine MacLean, a John Hopkins University psychologist. "You're losing everything you know to be real, letting go of your ego and your body. That process can feel like dying."[11]

It certainly felt like that to me

Shamanic journeys have fascinated me ever since I read Carlos Castaneda's stories about Don Juan.[12] Castaneda's experiences in nonordinary states of consciousness left an indelible impression on my young mind. For many years I dreamed of going to Mexico to find a shaman who could guide me into nonordinary realities.[13]

In 1998, a friend told me about the ceremonies a shaman held in the desert using sacred plants. I immediately applied. Eventually, I ended up in the desert of my fantasies with a shaman and a group of fellow psychonauts. I sat at the center of the circle and held the pipe that the shaman had ceremoniously loaded with a white powder. Since I didn't smoke, my main concern was that I'd embarrass myself by coughing and exhaling the smoke that I was supposed to hold in my lungs as long as possible. I closed my eyes and cleared my mind, taking three deep breaths. I brought the pipe to my lips and inhaled as the shaman lit its contents. Immediately, I felt my mind on fire. My throat itched and my lungs ached, but I didn't cough. Invisible hands helped me lie down. That was the last seminormal feeling I had for the next hour.

I had entered into an extraordinary realm, not because anything changed outside but because something inside me finally relaxed and dissolved into waves of bliss. The feelings were like intense light and heat, like spiced honey running through my veins. (As I write this, the expression makes no sense, but my memory of the experience is as clear as the feeling of my fingers on the keyboard.)

The waves grew stronger. I began to feel an ecstatic sort of pain. After a while, I started feeling as if I were burning from the inside. I felt an uncontainable, unbearable bliss that "exploded me out" of myself. Awareness was there, but it wasn't mine. I was there, but I wasn't the ordinary "me." I felt as if there was light dissolving me from the inside and, simultaneously, light dissolving me from the outside, penetrating through every pore of my skin.

The light outside wants to merge with the light inside, I just knew. *It is the false belief in the separateness that prevents this beautiful act of love. For the first time, I (as an ego) am unable to block the light. The light is going through me, appearing as me, becoming me, being me. I am the ocean of light appearing as the wave of Fred.*

I felt myself letting go of my fear of death. I felt completely safe— not because there was no risk, but because what was at risk was not really "I." I was laughing and crying, tears of joy and relief streaming down my face. I rolled with the ecstatic waves of pleasure-pain. *You die the way you live,* an inner voice said. *If you live in darkness, you are right to fear death. If you live in the light, there's nothing to fear.*

The author and neuroscientist Sam Harris has explained the shift in awareness produced by nonordinary states of consciousness better than anyone else I know. In *Waking Up*, he describes how his sense of the human mind's potential shifted profoundly through his experience with Ecstasy (MDMA).

> My sense of the human mind's potential shifted profoundly. (. . .) My capacity for envy, for instance—the sense of being diminished by the happiness or success of another person—seemed like a symptom of mental illness that had vanished without a trace. (. . .) It would not be too strong to say that I felt sane for the first time in my life. (. . .) I had ceased to be concerned about myself. I was no longer anxious, self-critical, guarded by irony, in competition, avoiding embarrassment, ruminating about the past and future, or making any other gesture of thought or attention that separated me from another.[14]

"The feeling that we call 'I' is an illusion," claims Harris. "There is no discrete ego living like a Minotaur in the labyrinth of the brain. And the feeling that there is—the sense of being perched somewhere behind your eyes, looking out at a world that is separate from yourself—can be altered or entirely extinguished."

When the illusion of the ego disappears, what is left is a stance of transcendent connection in *agape*. *Agape* is a very healthy platform for an organization to build upon as they unite in a mission and an expression of values.

In my personal journey, I saw that the feeling that I call "I" is a mirage. My ordinary state of consciousness—the one in which I experience myself as an ego having perceptions, thoughts, and feelings, making decisions, and taking action from about five inches behind my eyes—is a delusion. Although I'd had previous glimpses of this awareness through meditation practice, the noetic quality of the experience with the shamanic journey convinced me, in a way that I cannot doubt, that I am not who I used to think I was.

Beyond the scientific accounts I have read, I now know in a direct, undeniable way that my "ego," my sense of being a unified subject, is an illusion. Like blue skies, multicolored rainbows, and turquoise waters, the ego is not what it appears to be. In fact, it is nothing but an optical illusion of consciousness. I still have the strong impression that "I" am the owner of my experience, the one who perceives, thinks, feels, and wills from somewhere behind my face, but that "I" now vanishes every time I look at it closely in meditation. It is no more real than the desert oasis that appears in the distance but disappears as I get closer to it.

Such psychedelic experience can alter the fear of death very profoundly, and at the same time bring sanity to ordinary life. "Existential distress at the end of life bears many similarities with mental illness, including excessive self-reflection and an inability to jump the deepening grooves of negative thought," writes Michael Pollan. "The ego, faced with the prospect of its own dissolution, becomes hyper-vigilant, withdrawing its investment in the world and other people. It is striking that a single psychedelic experience should have the power to alter these patterns in a lasting way."[15]

We are all dying. We know it but we hide it from ourselves. Until we face up to it, our existential distress will always be there in the background, as a low-grade mental illness. We become self-absorbed, unable to connect with others or the world. We lose our souls. We become hypervigilant, hypercritical, hyperanxious. For most of us, shamanic substances are not safe. How can we then wake up from the bad ego trip in which we live? I believe that we can do so through meditation, and participation in a community of purpose, engaged to a transcendent project, led by a hero who has taken a journey to the underside and came back to share her or his gift of awareness with us.

"OH, WOW"

In his Stanford commencement speech, Steve Jobs said that death was "very likely the single best invention of my life." Death is the ultimate wake-up call. Death is a reminder of the preciousness of your human life, and of your limited time to experience and manifest it.

"I suppose it's not quite accurate to call the death of someone who lived with cancer for years unexpected," Steve Jobs's sister wrote in her eulogy for him, "but Steve's death was unexpected for us. What I learned from my brother's death was that character is essential: What he was, was how he died."

"The work of dying had to be done," she wrote. "Even now, he had a stern, still handsome profile, the profile of an absolutist, a romantic. His breath indicated an arduous journey, some steep path, altitude. He seemed to be climbing. But with that will, that work ethic, that strength, there was also sweet Steve's capacity for wonderment, the artist's belief in the ideal, the still more beautiful later."

And his final words were a mysterious, beautiful observation, repeated like a mantra, three times: "Oh, wow. Oh, wow. Oh, wow."[16]

Chapter 13
BE A HERO

TAKE THE JOURNEY

> Please call me by my true names,
> So I can hear all my cries and laughter at once.
> So I can see that my joy and pain are one.
> Please call me by my true names so I can wake up.
> And the door of my heart can be left open.
> The door of compassion.
>
> —Thich Nhat Hanh

Since the beginning of time, human beings have thrilled to archetypal stories of everyday mortals who are transformed through a confrontation with death. These stories follow cyclic patterns that begin and end in the hero's ordinary world.

The plot is always the same: The hero is called to a daunting quest that forces her out of her home and into an unfamiliar, strange, and dangerous world. Along the way she receives help from some kind of messenger or ally. She faces all kinds of challenges on the way—she may have to solve impossible riddles, escape from a trap, avoid a seducer, slay a monster, or all of the above. Then she must face an enormous challenge that ends in crisis, typically a near-death experience. The journey is frightening and terrible, and the hero undergoes loneliness, pain, exhaustion, illness, and despair. If she survives, she wins a gift (including that of greater self-knowledge) and returns home to bestow the gift and her wisdom on others. In the process, the hero is transformed from a mere mortal into a wiser and more transcendent being.

These stories are so timeless and universal that the great American mythologist Joseph Campbell called them by a single name: the "monomyth." Whether a religious figure (Jesus, Moses, Osiris), a literary or historical figure (Odysseus, Joan of Arc, William Wallace, Henry V), or a movie character (Luke Skywalker in *Star Wars*, Dorothy in *The Wizard of Oz*, Maximus from *Gladiator*, Katniss Everdeen from *The Hunger Games*, George Bailey in *It's a Wonderful Life*, and innumerable Disney movies), the hero is always cut from the same basic cloth because, after all, his or hers is the story of our own lives writ larger.

Heroism is necessary for transcendent leadership. The hero earns the moral authority to lead others by going first. She has to prove her values in the face of challenges in order to become a guide. Upon her return she can be trusted to lead wisely and compassionately, since she wouldn't have survived without those qualities.

All of us are capable of becoming heroes, but not all of us muster the courage to undertake the quest by ourselves. The journey requires digging deep, going into unfamiliar and threatening territory, and overcoming enormous challenges. It requires further that you discover the truth about your self, which reveals to you the truth about every self: we all long to connect to something larger than ourselves, to join it, to contribute to it meaningfully in our own unique way, to uphold what's true, good, and just.

The journey is daunting. Joseph Campbell points out that in most stories, the hero rejects "the call to adventure." Most of us are sucked into the journey by forces beyond our control, kicking and screaming. We don't have a choice, but we *can* choose how we walk the path. As the Scottish hero William Wallace says in the movie *Braveheart*, "Every man dies; not every man lives."

To fully live, we need an immortality project. We need a heroic quest to make our lives meaningful. The need for significance is the energy that propels extraordinary enterprises. To elicit the internal commitment of your followers for such an effort, you have to become a hero. And you can't become a hero until you face down your own demons.

MY JOURNEY

"No German in this house!" my mother snapped at my grandmother, who had said something in Yiddish. Her sharp tone is one of my earliest memories. Many years later, I realized that although they didn't experience violence directly, my parents shared the siege mentality of the Jews who lived during the Holocaust.

My grandparents fled Russia with their parents in the late 1800s, following a rising wave of anti-Semitism and a pogrom in which my mother's grandfather was killed. For them, Argentina must have felt like a new planet. They were terribly poor; for a time, my mother lived in an orphanage because her parents couldn't afford to keep her.

As children during World War II, my parents learned about Hitler.[1] After the war ended, they discovered the horror of the concentration camps. Despite the ten-thousand-mile gulf between themselves and Europe, they were deeply shocked, not least by the fact that even the countries fighting against Hitler, Britain and the United States, had rejected Jewish refugees who'd managed to escape, returning them to Europe's gas chambers and crematories.

I learned the story of the Holocaust in school. I saw the pictures of my people with the Stars of David sewn on their jackets, being loaded onto trains. I saw the horrifying pictures of starving and dead prisoners. I was full of judgment. I could not believe that "good Germans" stood by while their Jewish neighbors were swept into ghettos. How could they just watch and do nothing while something so terrible was taking place?

The siege mentality became less abstract to me when I was fifteen. In 1976, a military coup took place in Argentina. Everyone I knew felt relieved when the generals took over the government because they promised peace, stability, and a reprieve from left- and right-wing terrorism. Something had to be done; control had to be restored. Thus began the Argentinean "Dirty War."[2]

Life under the junta was both orderly and frightening. Everyone was nervous; the regime had imposed a state of martial law. My parents constantly warned me to be cautious and to stay away from signs of trouble. It was dangerous to go out at night. Everyone was being watched. We kept our eyes open and our mouths closed. I was careful to always carry my *cédula de identidad* ("identity card"), ready for the armed soldiers to board the bus and ask the dreaded "Papers, please." More than once, the military police searched bags and backpacks, taking those who didn't carry the right identification or who carried the wrong books.

In 1979, while I was at college, I worked the night shift at a computer center. As I exited the train station at the Plaza De Mayo every Thursday, I saw a gathering of women who carried a big banner and wore white kerchiefs marked with the initials of their own children and grandchildren who had disappeared without a trace. The "Mothers of Plaza De Mayo" demanded to know what had happened to their loved ones. They were nearly always surrounded by large numbers of police; sometimes there were arrests. Occasionally I saw the women and other protesters who had joined them seeking sanctuary in the huge cathedral of Buenos Aires, mistakenly believing that the priests would protect them.

As more and more people disappeared and the economy began to crater, the regime lost support. To gin itself up in public opinion, the generals decided to invade the Falkland Islands—Islas Malvinas, as Argentineans call them—starting a war with Britain. It was a swift, unmitigated disaster that shamed the military and returned Argentina to democracy.

Shortly after the Falklands War, when the grip of the military eased and their censorship started to crack, I got ahold of a mind-bending book called *Las Locas de Plaza de Mayo* (*The Crazies of Plaza de Mayo*) that described what had happened to the children of those mothers I passed every Thursday in the Plaza. I began reading the book one evening at eight and finished it at six the next morning. I wept all night. The children of the mothers I saw on the Plaza had been tortured to death. They had been drugged, put on planes, and dumped into the sea. They were shot and buried in unmarked mass graves. They were made to disappear; that's why they are called "los desaparecidos." The junta stole their victims' babies and gave them to families friendly to the regime. Between twenty thousand and thirty thousand people vanished. Fewer than six hundred have been found and identified since then.[3]

I felt terrible shame, horror, and rage at what the regime had done under my nose. Looking in the mirror, I realized that I was one of the millions duped in 1978, when we all took to the streets of Buenos Aires to celebrate Argentina's first place in the soccer World Cup. While human rights organizations boycotted the championship, decrying the military government's horrific record of abuses, the propaganda campaign inside the country blared nonstop: *"Los Argentinos somos derechos y humanos"* ("We Argentineans are right and human"). We all wanted to believe, as the government asserted categorically, that the international campaign was being waged against us as Argentineans, and not against the military regime's indiscriminate savagery.

Upon reading that book, I felt like someone who had just been released from an insane asylum. I realized that I had been sleepwalking past those mothers and grandmothers. It was a classic case of what psychologists call "disassociation"—the kind of thing that trauma victims experience. When you are in the nightmare or undergoing the trauma, the dream makes sense; but when you wake up, you realize that you've been suffocating beneath a thick carpet of propaganda, enforced from the top and supported by all the individual carpet fibers that are your relatives, friends, and neighbors. I was angry at everyone—not just at the terrible junta and the media but also at the "silent majority" that stood by, doing nothing while the killings were going on. I didn't see so clearly then that I was a member of this latter group.

Disgusted, I left Argentina as soon as I got my university degree. I didn't want to live there anymore. I went to UC Berkeley and then got a job at MIT. In between, through psychotherapy, meditation, and many personal development workshops, I tried to heal the pain of my country's collusion in murder—and my part as a not-so-innocent bystander. I became a teacher of conscious business, helping executives work and live more mindfully. My work became a bridge between the world of hard-core economics and business theory on the one hand, and one of philosophy, ethics, and spiritual wisdom on the other.

As I tried to come to terms with my anger and shame, I read *Shivitti*,[4] the autobiographical account of a Holocaust survivor who used LSD therapy to recover from his trauma.[5] Guided by the therapist and under the influence of the drug, the author remembered being in a truck in which he and others were being killed by noxious fumes. He recalled seeing a German guard smoking a cigarette outside. Then, in the therapeutic situation, he "became" the guard he had observed. He stood outside the truck, smoking a cigarette on a cold day, thinking nothing. He bore no hatred or malice toward the people he was killing; he just felt cold and wished for the war to be over.

In that moment, the patient realized that he was now "out" of the scene. That he could experience the situation simultaneously as both the guard and the prisoner—which meant he was neither. He was able to separate his identity from his traumatized self and adopt a transpersonal perspective. This LSD-driven inner psychodrama helped him heal. I longed to experience that kind of healing.

Each step I took in my hero's journey toward healing opened new doors, but the deepest truth didn't dawn on me until years later, during a coaching workshop in Germany. A man in the workshop stood up and shared that his father had been a concentration camp guard, a fact that burdened him with terrible guilt and shame. I felt great compassion for his suffering. I invited him to come onstage to have a conversation. As I listened to him, something clicked in me. Tears started streaming down my face. I explained to him that I was Jewish but that I felt my own shame as deeply as he did his, for he hadn't done anything, he was merely the son of someone who did something terrible. I, on the other hand, blamed myself for standing by like a "good Argentinean" during the Dirty War. I saw the mothers in the Plaza but hurried past them. I saw people pulled forcefully into the feared green Ford Falcons of the intelligence services, but looked the other way. I knew something evil was going on, but didn't want to know.

That was my "Shivitti" moment. All of a sudden, I realized most of the "good Germans" I had so abhorred must have been scared to death, just as I had been. I saw myself in the place of the Germans watching the Jews being taken. I felt like I was at once the German, the Jew, and the Argentinean boy who had walked past the distraught women in the Plaza. I was the "desaparecido" and the torturer, the kidnapped baby who grew up with the people who killed my parents, and the military officer who adopted this baby to raise him as his own. It was a profound experience. My heart opened; my judgments dissolved. I felt like I was looking at a diamond with infinite facets. The man and I wept and hugged. I was overcome with compassion. The terrible feelings of guilt and shame both he and I had felt for so many years dissipated. It was a life-altering experience for us both.

I experienced a vast openness at the center of myself, a space of serenity and peace that was much bigger than the "I" that I had believed myself to be. For a brief moment I felt that there was no "other," no sense of separation. Identification with my small self ceased, and my sense of I-ness extended to encompass everything human—and, beyond that, all sentient beings. It forever changed the meaning of the biblical dictum "Love thy brother as thyself" because I experienced my brother *as* myself.

A few years later, I fell in love with a German woman and lived with her in Germany for several years. Together, we visited many Holocaust memorials; I felt that our love was the best response to the evil that plagued our unique national histories. Though the relationship didn't work out in the end, I feel blessed for having experienced the goodness of the German people through her, her family, and her friends. Even my mother came to love this woman, who shattered all her stereotypes, and to whom she occasionally spoke in Yiddish.[6]

CRUCIBLES OF LEADERSHIP

Crises can eventually lead to awakening, provided the leader is open to learning from the painful experience. When facing terrible circumstances, the hero undergoes an ego death. He must lose himself to realize that what was lost was not his true self. To live fearlessly, he has to learn the hard way that what doesn't kill him (and even what does) makes him stronger.[7]

Before Jeff Weiner came to LinkedIn, he worked at Yahoo, where he had been a fast-rising young executive. But when a big project he was managing didn't go as well as he had hoped, he had to take a hard look at himself.

Jeff had delivered consistently great results, so he was asked to take on a very difficult project—stepping in to oversee a team that had been tasked with rebuilding a legacy advertising platform to compete with Google's. He knew that pulling off the project would be immensely difficult, but he accepted the challenge because he thought it was important for Yahoo.

The team worked day and night. Although they accomplished some things that had seemed impossible, they still didn't meet the ambitious expectations set by the company. Despite all the team's hard work, the project was deemed a failure. Because Jeff had in part defined himself by his previous successes, his self-esteem took a hit. In one of our coaching conversations, he told me that he was afraid he'd "lost his mojo."[8] He started to question some of his previous accomplishments. "I wonder whether my prior successes have been specific and situational, and not related to my ability or contributions," he told me. He also worried about what implications that would have for his career.

"You will emerge from this journey far stronger that you've ever been," I predicted.

"It's your job to tell me that," he replied skeptically.

"My job is to tell you the truth."

As I interviewed Jeff for this book, he shared with me that the confidence I had in him is the one he took into his heart, the one that allowed him to withstand the heat of his crucible, and the one that he now shares with those whom he coaches. "What did you see in me that allowed you to make that statement?" he asked me.

"Your hero's journey."

The problem, I told Jeff, was not that he wasn't good at his work.

The problem was that he had had too little experience with failure; he hadn't learned yet how to fail gracefully. He lacked resilience because he hadn't yet realized that he could turn failure into a source of wisdom and meaning. Having given everything he had to the project, he allowed it to define who he was, despite the fact that the chances of success were slim from the beginning.

"The faster you realize that you are not defined by your results, the faster you'll realize that you can derive your sense of self from things that are under your control; from your purpose, your values, your drive, your commitment, your intelligence, your care," I suggested. "When you get that, not only will you not regret this failure, but you'll appreciate it, because it will teach you this great lesson. In the long term, you'll see that you can achieve much more by having gone through this." Jeff drew from that a first principle, a life-affirming lesson that he now offers as advice to the many people he mentors: "Don't give your power away to things you can't control."

Jeff proved me right. Not only did he walk through the valley of the shadow of failure unscathed, he finished his hero's journey gaining an unshakable confidence and returning to his community with great gifts. He ended up becoming the admired CEO of LinkedIn, and sharing this transformative episode widely.

Resilience in the face of adversity is an absolutely fundamental requirement for leadership. In 2002, Robert J. Thomas and management guru Warren Bennis published their findings that one of the most reliable indicators and predictors of true leadership is an individual's ability to find meaning in negative events and to learn from even the most trying circumstances. In a *Harvard Business Review* article entitled "Crucibles of Leadership," they noted that certain people "seem to naturally inspire confidence, loyalty, and hard work, while others (who may have just as much vision and smarts) stumble, again and again." What makes the difference? "It's a timeless question, and there's no simple answer," they wrote. But we have come to believe it has something to do with the different ways that people deal with adversity." Put another way, the skills required to conquer adversity, and emerge stronger and more committed than ever, are the same skills that make for exceptional leadership.[9]

Thomas and Bennis found that the extraordinary leaders they studied all had one thing in common: they could point to "intense, often traumatic, always unplanned experiences" (or crucibles) that turned into a source of strength. Some experiences brushed with death, like Leeb-du Toit's. Others were huge moments of self-doubt, like Jeff's. For others, the crucible came in working with a challenging mentor.

All the leaders that Thomas and Bennis profiled had four essential skills: (1) the ability to engage others in shared meaning; (2) a distinctive and compelling voice—the ability to use language to deal intelligently with a difficult situation; (3) integrity and a strong set of values; and (4) "adaptive capacity" or "applied creativity"—an almost magical ability to transcend adversity, with all its attendant stresses, and to emerge stronger than before. Adaptive capacity, the authors suggested, is a combination of the ability to weigh a number of factors and put them into a context understood by all. Someone who combines all four of these skills has the qualities of a transcendent leader.

SHERYL SANDBERG'S CRUCIBLE

Sheryl Sandberg embodies the skills that Thomas and Bennis identified. She earned her stripes as an economist for the World Bank and as chief of staff for the U.S. Treasury Department. She then proved herself at Google, where she built and led the online sales and operations team. Today, she's not only the chief operating officer at Facebook, but she's also a well-known and passionate advocate for women in the workplace. (Her bestseller, *Lean In*, has sold more than 1.5 million copies and has sparked a movement.) The organization she founded, LeanIn .org, has launched more than 33,000 "circles"—communities focused on women's empowerment—that include hundreds of thousands of men and women in more than fifty countries. Through her work, she has become an inspiration to millions.[10]

Sheryl has faced many challenges in her life, but the toughest one was dealing with the death of her beloved husband, Dave, who died suddenly in 2015 at the age of forty-seven, leaving her a single mom of two young children. Here's a bit of what she posted in Facebook following a month of mourning:[11]

A childhood friend of mine who is now a rabbi recently told me that the most powerful one-line prayer he has ever read is: "Let me not die while I am still alive." I would have never understood that prayer before losing Dave. Now I do.

I think when tragedy occurs, it presents a choice. You can give in to the void, the emptiness that fills your heart, your lungs, constricts your ability to think or even breathe. Or you can try to find meaning. These past thirty days, I have spent many of my moments lost in that void. And I know that many future moments will be consumed by the vast emptiness as well.

But when I can, I want to choose life and meaning. [. . .] So I am sharing what I have learned in the hope that it helps someone else. In the hope that there can be some meaning from this tragedy.

I have lived thirty years in these thirty days. I am thirty years sadder. I feel like I am thirty years wiser.

I have gained a more profound understanding of what it is to be a mother, both through the depth of the agony I feel when my children scream and cry and from the connection my mother has to my pain. [. . .]

I have learned that I never really knew what to say to others in need. I think I got this all wrong before; I tried to assure people that it would be okay, thinking that hope was the most comforting thing I could offer. A friend of mine with late-stage cancer told me that the worst thing people could say to him was "It is going to be okay." That voice in his head would scream, "How do you know it is going to be okay? Do you not understand that I might die?" I learned this past month what he was trying to teach me. Real empathy is sometimes not insisting that it will be okay but acknowledging that it is not. [. . .]

I have learned how ephemeral everything can feel—and maybe everything is. That whatever rug you are standing on can be pulled right out from under you with absolutely no warning. [. . .]

I have learned to ask for help—and I have learned how much help I need. Until now, I have been the older sister, the COO, the doer and the planner. I did not plan this, and when it happened, I was not capable of doing much of anything. Those closest to me took over. [. . .]

I have learned that resilience can be learned. [. . .]

I realized that to restore that closeness with my colleagues [. . .] I needed to let them in. And that meant being more open and vulnerable than I ever wanted to be. [. . .]

I have learned gratitude. Real gratitude for the things I took for granted before—like life. As heartbroken as I am, I look at my children each day and rejoice that they are alive. I appreciate every smile, every hug. I no longer take each day for granted. [. . .]

Before Dave died, Sheryl told me, she rarely thought about mortality. Now she thinks about it all the time, and it spurs her feelings of the importance of focusing on making the world a better place. In actively choosing meaning, gratitude, and resilience, she became even more of an inspirational leader than she was before her loss.

I asked Sheryl how she herself wanted to be remembered. "Before Dave died," she told me, "I would have said, 'She was a good friend, wife, mother . . .' personal stuff. But now, in addition to that, I want to be remembered as fighting for equality for women, for helping more people understand why we need equality and more people embrace ambition for women. And finally, to help people overcome adversity. No one looks for opportunities to grow this way, but this happens and we do. . . . We owe it to ourselves and each other to embrace each other and find ways to help build each other's resilience."[12]

After freeing herself from ego, facing death, and finding her true self, the archetypal hero/leader returns to her community with the gift of her personal growth. Her example and way of living inspires others to undertake their own journeys and achieve symbolic immortality.

In *Lean In* (written before Dave's death), Sheryl's message is this: "Bring your whole self to work." Her battle cry challenged both men and women to understand that work isn't all about It, but also is about the I with all its needs and emotional messiness, and the We of community, teamwork, and friendship. After Sheryl Sandberg lost her husband and dove into unfathomable grief, she came back to work and discovered the deeper purpose of what she was working for. Eventually, Sheryl brought her gift back to her community through her blog posts and her second book, *Option B*, written with Adam Grant, which is a deep dive into resilience. The "Oprah of corporate America," as *Bloomberg Businessweek* called her, has been leading by example.[13] She's sharing her journey and encouraging other people to open up, be vulnerable, welcome the unknown, and face setbacks in a way that only she can do. Every day, she has changed Facebook's culture to be more open and for its people to be more emotionally aware in fulfilling Facebook's mission "to make the world more open and connected."

Sheryl's leadership goes well beyond her professional role. She inspires a very large number of people, including me, to work for a better world, a world that is more just, connected, open, inclusive, and supportive. She has gone through the fire of her transformation, earning the right to inspire those of us who admire her to step into the fire of our own heroic journeys.

SERVANT LEADERSHIP

Exemplary leadership is like a seed that falls on the followers' fertile hearts. It requires care and cultivation. It means learning how to listen and communicate in a way that keeps people aligned with the transcendent purpose of service; learning to negotiate differences on behalf of the immortality project; learning to coordinate and execute through impeccable commitments; and going beyond giving feedback to create a continuous improvement alliance that can withstand the fire of criticism for the sake of the mission.[14] These are the behaviors of a true "servant leader."

The expression "servant leadership" comes from Robert K. Greenleaf. "A servant-leader focuses primarily on the growth and well-being of people and the communities to which they belong," Greenleaf wrote. "While traditional leadership generally involves the accumulation and exercise of power by one at the 'top of the pyramid,' servant leadership is different. The servant-leader shares power, puts the needs of others first and helps people develop and perform as highly as possible."[15]

Transcendent leadership differs from servant leadership. A transcendent leader is the servant of an inspiring mission. She offers an immortality project that allows her people to embark on their own heroic journeys. A transcendent leader serves her followers in the sense that she enables them to infuse their lives with meaning, but she doesn't necessarily serve their individual needs.

Think of a military commander who's willing to put his own life, as well as the lives of his soldiers, on the line. He would go a long way to protect his soldiers, but he would also be willing to put himself and them at risk for the sake of the mission.

This kind of transcendent leadership is best exemplified by one of the most celebrated monologues in the English language—the "St. Crispin's Day" speech from Shakespeare's *Henry V*. On the feast day of St. Crispin, young King Henry is about to lead his wet, miserable, sick, exhausted troops into a great battle against the French, who outnumber them five to one. It's obvious to all of them that their chances of survival are very slim. But King Henry rallies his men by appealing to their desire for honor ("The fewer the men, the greater the share of honor," he claims). He tells them that their names will become as "Familiar . . . as household words." But he doesn't stop there. He also promises that his troops will rise in status to become his equals in heroism:

> And Crispin Crispian shall ne'er go by,
> From this day to the ending of the world,
> But we in it shall be remember'd;

We few, we happy few, we band of brothers;
For he to-day that sheds his blood with me
Shall be my brother; be he ne'er so vile,
This day shall gentle his condition;
And gentlemen in England now a-bed
Shall think themselves accurs'd they were not here,
And hold their manhoods cheap whiles any speaks
That fought with us upon Saint Crispin's day.[16]

Henry acknowledges that he could die along with his followers. He never promises victory; instead, he offers honor, integrity, fellowship, and history-making heroism. Henry and his men can achieve these nonmaterial goods unconditionally. As opposed to the external victory in battle, which depends on many factors out of their control, the internal victory in spirit is within their grasp. As Henry tells his followers: "All things are ready, if our minds be so."

Against all odds, Henry and his men win the battle. Shakespeare suggests that Henry's stirring speech is at least partly responsible for instilling the men with such an overwhelming sense of purpose and courage that they prevail in the end. (General Stanley McChrystal once told me that for hundreds of years this speech has been read to troops about to go to battle, and that it's still used today to inspire soldiers about to put themselves in harm's way for a noble purpose.)

YOUR HEROIC JOURNEY

Think of a time when you learned something very significant about yourself, others, and the world—a scary, painful, angering, or shocking situation that changed your life, your attitude, your approach to things. How did you feel as you entered this experience?

I've asked this question of thousands of participants in my workshops. Typical answers are "Scared," "Apprehensive," "Full of self-doubt," "Surprised," "Terrified," "Confused," "Shattered," "Betrayed," "Upset," "Angry," "Ashamed," "Hurt," and so on.

After they ponder this question for a while, I then ask participants how many of them would, at that moment, choose that experience again. Most reply that they would go to great lengths to avoid it.

That kind of response is what Joseph Campbell describes as the "refusal of the call to adventure." When he finds the gate to the underworld opens, the hero runs in the opposite direction. "Why me?" asks Moses when God commands him to speak to the Pharaoh. "I'm a stutterer!"

I point out that we rarely feel good when we're about to learn something of utmost significance. Such lessons are quite expensive.

I then ask them to break into small groups. The rules are as follows: Each person shares his or her story memory of the shocking experience, concluding with a consideration about what he or she learned and what impact that experience had on his or her life. Everyone agrees to listen quietly and respectfully to everyone else; the only expression allowed is one of appreciation for the storyteller's gift. No one must give advice or try to coach the person who shared the story. The only valid responses are "Thanks," "Oh wow!," and "Oh, wow. Thanks."

I then ask people how they felt at the end of the learning experience, once they were able to integrate into their life their new hard-earned knowledge. Typical answers are "At peace," "Joyful," "Proud," "Complete," "Loving," "Compassionate," "Appreciative," "Grateful," "Fulfilled," "Satisfied," "Happy."

"How many of you would be willing, at the moment you experienced that shock," I ask, "to embrace your experience as the price you had to pay for the knowledge you received?" Most of them raise their hands. "I would not choose to go through what I went through," a typical participant will comment, "but given that I had no choice, I feel it was powerful to give it meaning and learn something important . . ." And then with a smile he'll add ". . . which I surely don't ever want to have to relearn."

I then invite them to consider that many significant learning experiences start with a difficult challenge and involve some sort of crisis. It seems that the crisis process is necessary to replace a belief we hold dear for another one that is deeper, truer, wiser.

I then ask each participant to reimagine the experience to emerge victorious. I encourage them to look for both their inner resources (such as their values, virtues, beliefs, and so on) and their outer ones (such as family, friends, and mentors).

Finally, I ask them to remember a scary, painful, angering, or shocking situation that they are experiencing in their lives at this current moment, and see that experience as the beginning of a meaningful lesson that could enrich their lives. I propose they apply their inner and outer resources to the current situation and think of what they imagine they could learn from it now, what value would such understanding bring to them, and how would they feel when they emerge with that gift of new knowledge.

When we come back together, the energy in the room feels more settled, more solid. People's faces have an almost luminous expression, as if they have vicariously experienced the hero's journey and come back with a gift. The heat and pressure of the ordeal has turned their coal into a diamond.

This same exercise can be beneficial for a group experiencing a crisis situation, only writ larger. For example, when a regional telecom company was bought by a multinational corporation, the employees of the smaller firm, who had felt protective of their culture, were both frightened and in shock, and the combined new leadership team had to manage the transition. I asked the team members to write a letter from the future—What would being a part of the new, bigger company offer to teach them? The team emerged from the workshop with a great desire to make the new combination work.

I've found that once a team goes through the hero's journey in this kind of way, each member has earned the moral right to lead the rest of the company in an alliance.

Transcendent leadership requires a deep and strong interior life that aligns a leader with a transcendent purpose. I believe every leader needs to tune him- or herself up like a musical instrument, in order to make music that connects people with a noble purpose. In addition to the technical tools that can be learned in a classroom, the leader needs psychological and spiritual tools that can be attained only through personal transformation. The most powerful tool for eliciting others' commitment to the mission you want to accomplish is to extend your *agape* to them by supporting their growth and well-being and offering them ways to make their lives meaningful, noble, and worthy. To do so, leaders must stop identifying with and giving in to their power-hungry ego. They must experience what I call "ego death," in order to achieve leadership rebirth.

The journey of the heroic leader is fraught with trials that test us and reveal and sharpen our spirit. There's a natural pattern to human growth, a trajectory from unconsciousness to consciousness to super-consciousness. This process forces the would-be transcendent leader to take a hard look at herself, face her biggest fears, find her strengths with the help of allies, and win the battle to become herself, create her destiny, and become the master of her life. Only after you have walked the path of the hero and vanquished your shadows can you bring your gift of wisdom to your community. Only when you have found your deepest truth can you become a model for others and inspire trust rather than cynicism.

By working to enact your values and transcend your ego, you can become the kind of inspiring, transcendent leader that people will follow in the face of the most daunting challenges.

Chapter 14
SUPERCONSCIOUS CAPITALISM

RETURN TO THE MARKETPLACE
WITH HELPING HANDS

Unless you have realized [others] as one with yourself, you cannot love them. Your love of others is the result of self-knowledge, not its cause. When you know beyond all doubt that the same life flows through all, [. . .] you will love all naturally.

—Nisargadatta Maharaj

One of the oldest depictions of human evolution is a series of ten images called "The Ox Herding Pictures," from the Zen school of twelfth-century China.[1] In these wood carvings, the spiritual path is represented by the journey of an oxherd. The first three images, in which the herder desperately searches for his ox, represent the unconscious state of the human being. The second three, in which the herder catches and tames the ox, represent the conscious state. The third three, in which the herder realizes he and the ox are one with everything, represent the superconscious state.

The last image offers a surprising insight about enlightenment. The tenth ox-herding picture is called "Entering the Marketplace with Helping Hands." The oxherd, finally awakened, appears as "a jolly rustic whose body is overflowing with life-energy, and whose heart is full of compassionate love." "He enters the town marketplace, doing all the ordinary things that everyone else does. But because he is deeply aware, everything he does is quite extraordinary. He does not retreat from the world, but instead shares his enlightened existence with everyone around him. Not only does he lead fishmongers and innkeepers in the way of the Buddha, but such is his creative energy and the radiance of his life that even withered trees bloom."[2]

Some seekers see the end of their spiritual evolution as a blissful loss of interest in daily affairs. For them, self-transcendence means disappearing from ordinary life. However, according to the Zen masters, enlightenment does not lead to oblivion. On the contrary, it leads back to full, loving participation in the human world. Genuine spirituality does not end in abandonment, but in passionate engagement.

When you "enter the market with open hands," as a transcendent leader, there is no sense of ultimate separation. You find it natural to "love another as thyself" because there is no hard boundary between the other and yourself. Of course, you see your body as separate from other bodies, just as you see one leaf as separate from another leaf on the same tree. But you don't see yourself as emotionally separate from other selves. You can see one wave as separate from other waves, and yet realize that all of them are movements of the same sea. In enlightened awareness, there is only a unified field of wholeness, suffused with wise compassion.

Out of this field arises the impulse to help people flourish through meaningful work, to organize their efforts for a noble purpose, through ethical principles. That's what the marketplace looks like to a superconscious mind. Yet that's not the way it looks to many ordinary minds.

THE FIRST GREAT MISUNDERSTANDING

A client once asked me how I could square an organization's noble purpose with the capitalist ambition to make money, suggesting that capitalism was responsible for many evils in the world.

These days it's fashionable to blame capitalism for a host of problems. A 2016 Harvard University survey of young adults between the ages of eighteen and twenty-nine found that 51 percent of respondents do not support capitalism.[3] For many, capitalism is the territory of greedy, exploitative businesspeople. Capitalists' main occupation, as it appears to them, is to take advantage of the needy, trying to maximize

their profits without any ethical scruples—and in the process destroying human beings and the environment.

Those who criticize capitalism have valid concerns, but I believe
the problem is not capitalism per se—a system of property rights and
free exchange that has conferred great good upon humanity, as I will
explain in a moment—but cronyism. The reason I raise this is that unless you understand the difference, and are able to clarify it for your
coworkers, you will not be able to inspire them. It will be impossible to
perform in the marketplace with open hands if you don't make clear,
and demonstrate, your highest ethical principles in doing so. You have
to be able to show everyone in the organization, and other stakeholders, that you can make a profit and still be proud of yourself and your
business.

Cronyism is a political and economic system in which the government is controlled by corporations and intervenes in the market using
its coercive power on their behalf. Crony businesspeople thrive not because they serve their stakeholders but because they exploit the power
of the state, circumventing the discipline of the free market. While capitalism channels personal ambition into the service of others, cronyism
channels personal greed into abuse.

Crony politicians crush competition by handing out special per-
mits, government grants, and tax breaks to those whom they favor, and
by imposing tariffs and restrictions on their competitors and consumers. Crony corporations take inordinate risks fearlessly, knowing that if
they win, their earnings will be privatized, but if they lose, their losses
will be covered through bailouts and special aid packages. Crony businesses make money not by profiting in the economic market through
their value-adding services, but by profiteering in the political market
through value-destroying takings.[4]

Crony businesspeople fully deserve blame. They are rapacious,
predatory, and immoral. They harm people and the environment in
pursuit of endless greed. They know no limits and trample over people without regard for their rights. Perhaps that's why the Marxist arguments of a century ago about the exploitation of the workers have

found purchase in people's minds. But to me, crony businesspeople are not capitalists; they are Mafiosi.

Capitalism doesn't operate this way. In free markets under the rule of law, businesses don't profit by being callous, manipulative, and greedy—although behaving that way may give them short-term advantages. Businesses really profit over the long run by being empathetic (understanding their customers, employees, and other stakeholders), compassionate (serving them), and equitable (being fair to them). The only reason narcissistic Machiavellian psychopathic companies survive—and promote narcissistic Machiavellian psychopathic leaders—is that they can preempt competition (through their government cronies) from others able to provide better value.

It is a tragedy of our time that capitalism is confused with the behavior of a criminal syndicate. It is not recognized as the great boon to society that it is (as I will explain in a moment). This is like confusing a brutal dictatorship with a republic. The fundamental difference between capitalism and cronyism, like the difference between a dictatorship and a republic, is respect for property rights and the basic freedoms entailed by them. Conscious leaders are the people most responsible for upholding these values.

As Peter Drucker warned, "Tyranny is the only alternative to strong, performing autonomous institutions. Tyranny substitutes one absolute boss for pluralism. It substitutes terror for responsibility." According to Drucker, tyranny subsumes free-market organizations in an all-embracing political bureaucracy—the end of crony capitalism is fascism. It does produce goods and services, but at an enormous cost in suffering, humiliation, and frustration. Drucker wrote, "To make our institutions perform responsibly, autonomously, and on a high level of achievement is thus the only safeguard of freedom and dignity in the pluralist society."[5] Conscious leaders make institutions perform. Conscious leadership is the alternative to tyranny and our best protection against it.

THE SECOND GREAT MISUNDERSTANDING

In addition to blaming capitalism as an economic system, many people react negatively to specific for-profit businesses. A dominant social meme goes something like this: "Businesspeople are not to be trusted. They are exploiters who take advantage of employees and customers." This is a false conclusion, arising from confusion about the source of profit. Some people think it springs from an exploitation of weakness. In fact, it comes from a provision of strength.

Here's an example from an event that happened to me as I was working on this book. I was free-diving off the coast of Belize when I started seeing what looked like a lightning storm in my left eye.[6] It was as though a strobe light started flashing directly into my brain. The cause of the show was a detached retina—as I learned several days later when I was able to reach land. At the urging of a local ophthalmologist, I flew back to the United States that same day and a specialist performed surgery on my eye that very evening. Although my insurance covered the costs, I'm sure the doctor made a good sum of money from the procedure.

I could blame the surgeon for "profiting from my suffering." He benefited from my misfortune and was better off because I was worse off. I could imagine him feeling happy that I had this terrible thing happen to me, as it created a profitable opportunity for him. I know this is not true—his primary focus was in saving my vision and helping me to successfully recover. Yes, he makes his living from his profession, but most of the doctors I know go into the long and arduous training in medicine first and foremost to help people.

The cause of my eye problem is unknown. Perhaps it had to do with my age. Perhaps it was due to the water pressure during my dives. Perhaps it had to do with the Lasik surgery I underwent twenty years ago. Perhaps it was something else. Or perhaps all of the above played a role—I will never know for sure, and it really doesn't matter. What I do know is that the eye doctor had nothing to do with it.

I found myself almost blind in my left eye. I felt lost, confused, scared, and vulnerable. The doctor examined me with great kindness, honestly shared with me the diagnosis, and discussed treatment options. My condition was serious; although the surgery posed some risks, I would almost surely have lost my eye without it.

The doctor didn't profit from my suffering; he profited from *alleviating* it. I paid him because he had prepared himself to help people facing my condition—and he did his work masterfully. I was full of admiration and gratitude. In fact, I would have paid much more than what I did to reclaim my vision.

In the same way, I believe it is unfair, even insulting, to blame food manufacturers for profiting from people's hunger, clothes producers for making money at the expense of people's need for protection from the elements, construction companies for people's need for safe housing, and so on. Food manufacturers, clothes producers, and construction companies provide people with the goods they need to stay alive. Life is not guaranteed in any way by nature; only death is certain. It is our society, and its economic system, that provides the means to sustain and improve our lives. To stay alive and thrive, every being has to toil and provide for his or her needs. It is unfair to argue that those who supply the means to satisfy these needs are the ones who created them.

Although all this might seem obvious, too many businesspeople I've encountered feel guilty, stained by the presumption that they profit from others' misfortune by exploiting those who need jobs. That's why they think that they have to "give back to society" after they make their money.

I've always had a problem with this notion, because the hidden implication behind "giving back" is that the people who made money took something that didn't belong to them. I'm all in favor of *giving* generously, wisely, and compassionately. I'm just opposed to idea that successful businesspeople feel they have to make up for a previous fault.

Bill Gates, for example, earned his wealth fairly and squarely, and he can do whatever he wants with it. His philanthropic works are praiseworthy and generous—but they are not compensatory. For many years Gates amassed a fortune by creating products that people acquired to enhance their lives.[7] Regardless of what you might think of Gates, he didn't violate people's rights by taking their money against their will.

Anyone who bought Microsoft's software did so voluntarily (or bought the computer voluntarily that was preloaded with Microsoft's operating system and applications). He built an astounding amount of wealth. But I would argue his personal wealth is relatively small in comparison to the wealth he produced for all of us who bought Microsoft's products and services.

Most people only acknowledged Bill Gates as an ethical person when he started giving his fortune to charity. I find this odd, because in addition to benefiting its customers, Microsoft grew the national economy, advanced our technological prowess generally, turned the Seattle area into a technology center, and produced many other social benefits. Hundreds of thousands of people and their families have benefited from Microsoft, as employees, and as employees of its network of suppliers, partners, and business customers.

People presume that Gates's intention as a businessman was to make money, and that his intention as a philanthropist is to improve people's lives. But Gates the businessman and Gates the philanthropist are not two separate people. Apparently, some people can't conceive of the possibility that Gates wanted to make money by improving people's lives.[8]

I also take issue with the idea that it is impossible for capitalists and entrepreneurs to make profits without "exploiting" their employees.[9] After I left MIT, I cofounded and led consulting companies that used contractors. We paid these contractors roughly 50 percent of what we charged our clients for their services. (To simplify things, let's disregard all our other costs and assume that we made a 50 percent net margin.) Some would accuse me of exploiting our contractors by buying their services at half of what they were worth in the marketplace— just as they accuse businesses for making profits on the back of their workers.

What's wrong with this argument?

The fallacy lies in the expression "what they are really worth in the marketplace." Contractor services are worth only what someone is willing to pay for them. If the contractors could sell their services in the marketplace for twice as much as my company paid them, why would they sell them to us rather than to our final clients? They sold their services to us because they couldn't sell them for better conditions to other clients. They decided that ours was the best deal they could get. Otherwise they would have used their time, energy, and skills differently. (In fact, there were lots of consultants who did not work with my firm—surely because they thought they were better off striking out on their own or with another consulting firm. I always felt nothing but goodwill toward them as they competed against my company. Competition made us all better.)[10]

Our clients contracted with my company because they trusted us to provide a consistent, scalable, global service, supervised by my partners and me, through proprietary processes and materials that we had developed, and with a logistics and administration structure that could match their own. They trusted us because we had invested in marketing and research materials and had a sales organization that explored what we could do for them. The corporations that engaged us did not want to deal with individual consultants, but with a reliable consulting company with a credible history. And the contractors who engaged with us did not want to sell and deliver their services directly. They wanted a consulting company that would support them. It was a win-win-win deal for the clients, the contractors, and us.

THE GREAT BOON

"The progressive political philosophy I believed in," wrote John Mackey, founder of Whole Foods and coauthor of *Conscious Capitalism*, "had taught me that both business and capitalism were fundamentally based on greed, selfishness, and exploitation: the exploitation of consumers, workers, society, and the environment for the goal of maximizing profits. (. . .) I believed that profit was a necessary evil at best, and certainly not a desirable goal for society as a whole."[11]

Becoming an entrepreneur and starting a business completely

changed Mackey's life. "Almost everything I had believed was proven to be wrong," he wrote. "The most important thing I learned in my first year was that business isn't based on exploitation or coercion at all. Instead, I discovered that business is based on cooperation and voluntary exchange. People trade voluntarily for mutual gain."[12]

Starting and running a business is an opportunity to serve a yet unmet need more efficiently than other existing alternatives, combining factors of production in novel and more profitable ways. Capitalism, as Mackey came to understand, is based on the concept of service. Unless the business serves its customers, it will have no customers. Unless the business serves its employees, it will have no employees. Unless the business serves its suppliers, it will have no suppliers.

Detangled from cronyism, capitalism is the greatest mechanism for social cooperation and human progress the world has ever known. "The record of history is absolutely crystal clear," wrote Nobel laureate Milton Friedman. "There is no alternative way, so far discovered, of improving the lot of the ordinary people that can hold a candle to the productive activities that are unleashed by a free enterprise system."[13]

Capitalism has dramatically improved living conditions, decreased poverty, extended life expectancy, reduced child mortality, increased education, promoted equality of rights, and much more. If you look at the last two hundred years, the amount of good that capitalism has brought to the world is astonishing. Until the 1900s, the average life expectancy worldwide was under twenty-five years (forty-five for the United States); today it is seventy-two years (eighty for the United States).[14] In the 1800s, 85 percent of the world's population lived in extreme poverty (defined as less than $1.25 a day); that number is now less than 10 percent.[15] In fact, average income per capita globally has increased 1,000 percent since 1800.[16] Today, the overall level of global violence around the world is lower, though our awareness of what's happening around the world is higher.[17] Compared to even fifty years ago, things have changed dramatically for the better because entrepreneurs and their companies have developed a myriad of goods and services, from refrigerators to cell phones, from cars to televisions, from indoor plumbing to air-conditioning, that make the lives of even the poor of our developed economies materially better than the royalty of previous centuries.[18, 19]

It took over two hundred thousand years (when it's believed that the first *Homo sapiens* appeared on Earth) for the human population to reach one billion (which happened approximately in 1800). The average annual growth rate from 10,000 BC (when it's estimated that there were around four million humans) was around 0.05 percent. The spread of capitalism, the Industrial Revolution, produced a unique inflection point in history. It took only two hundred years to go from one billion to seven and a half billion people, with an average annual growth rate of around 1 percent—twenty times higher than the rate of the previous ten thousand years. Consider that without capitalism, seven out of every eight people would not be alive today (there's an 85 percent chance that you would not be around).

Plus, depending on your age, the odds of your surviving would have been quite small, because for most of human history life expectancy was around twenty-five years. Before the Industrial Revolution, you would have had only a fraction of the income that you have today, and you would have been in much worse physical health.[20] "The average person of 100,000 BC was better off (in terms of hours of labor required to obtain basic necessities, life expectancy, physical health, etc.) than the average person of 1800," writes the economic historian Gregory Clark. "Indeed, the bulk of the world's population was poorer than their remote ancestors."[21, 22, 23]

As a transcendent leader, it is important to be able to articulate the strengths of capitalism and its power to enhance our lives, and to condemn cronyism.[24] Why? Because ultimately, I believe we human beings are driven by an ethical core. We want to see ourselves and be seen by others as good, as just, as doing the right thing.

UNCONSCIOUS CAPITALISM

It is possible to participate in a free market and to benefit society without any understanding of its principles. The critical rule is that companies and individuals do not encroach on other people's property and fulfill their contracts. As long as this holds, economic interactions serve the greater good.

When a voluntary transaction takes place, each party must receive at least as much (and generally more) satisfaction from what she gets than the one she forgoes through what she gives up. For example, if I want to trade my orange for your apple, I must value your apple more than my orange. Similarly, if you accept the trade, you must value my orange more than your apple. Thus, the transaction is based on two inequalities. This disparity generates a net surplus in satisfaction: both parties expect to be better off after the transaction than they were before.

This is why cronyism is so detrimental to the social good. The safety mechanism of capitalism, the one that disciplines the potentially rapacious ambition of a company or an individual, is the possibility of opting in or out of any transaction—guaranteed by property rights and free exchange. Once legal coercion blocks this safety switch, the whole system derails. If people are coerced (illegally, as in crime, or legally, as in politics) into participating in transactions that they would prefer to avoid, "natural selection" in the ecosystem breaks down.

Capitalism creates a force field that channels personal ambition toward support for others, and it organizes society for cooperation through the division of labor, and through innovation toward the satisfaction of the needs of its members. As Adam Smith explained, "It is not from the benevolence of the butcher, the brewer, or the baker, that we expect our dinner, but from their regard to their own interest." And yet, they are "led by an invisible hand" to promote a socially beneficial end that was no part of their intention.[25]

This is why capitalism works even when people are unconscious and driven by selfish desires. Even if an entrepreneur is no moral hero, capitalism will turn him or her into a servant of society. Property rights and free exchange distill self-interest into service, making it necessary to enter the marketplace with an intention to help.[26] Capitalism is the alchemical crucible in which humanity transforms its base instincts into gold.

CONSCIOUS CAPITALISM

Capitalism works even better if people are conscious. Just as an engineer who knows what she is doing can use a computer more effectively than someone who doesn't understand the technology, a conscious capitalist can participate in a free market more effectively than someone who doesn't understand its economic principles.

Rather than "doing it by accident," conscious capitalists have a deliberate intention to profit by serving others. They pursue their own well-being by promoting the well-being of their investors, their customers, their employees, their vendors, and all those who exchange with their enterprise. They understand that in doing so, they benefit many others they don't even know. Contributing to society is not something they do as a collateral benefit of running their businesses; it is the way they run their businesses.

Several years ago, I asked John Mackey who he thought the biggest beneficiaries of Whole Foods were. He predictably responded that they were its customers. I disagreed. He looked at me quizzically and moved down the list of stakeholders: employees, shareholders, suppliers, and so on. I kept shaking my head. "Of course," I explained to him, "there is a primary impact on the traditional stakeholders. But in the same way that a pebble in a pond creates expanding ripples, a company in an economy—especially if it is led consciously—creates expanding waves of goodness." The more conscious one is, the further one can see the reach of these waves. Two of the less obvious beneficiaries are the competitors' customers and the competitors' employees.

Customers of other grocers benefit because Whole Foods's additional supply puts downward pressure on price and upward pressure on the quality that these competitors have to offer to attract them to their stores. For example, when I lived in Boulder, Colorado, I noticed that the Safeway store in which I shopped raised its quality when a Whole Foods Market opened nearby. Whole Foods's revenue was about $13 billion at the time, while Safeway's was about $36 billion. Many more people shopped at Safeway than at Whole Foods, so the beneficial social impact of the competition went way beyond Whole Foods's direct customers.

Additionally, employees of competitors—that is, of any company that wants to hire people who could work for Whole Foods—benefit because Whole Foods's additional demand puts upward pressure on the monetary and nonmonetary compensation that these competitors have to offer employees to attract them to their workplaces. To attract the employees the competitors need, Safeway and other grocery stores must improve their offer to make themselves more appealing to people who might otherwise decide to work at Whole Foods.

You don't need to be an entrepreneur to be a conscious capitalist. You have the chance to "vote" with your money, investing in or patronizing companies that behave ethically toward those in their supply chain (e.g., the emergence of fair trade, green, treatment of animals, and similar certifications), their employees, their customers, and so on. Capitalism is an economic democracy in which every dollar gives you a right to vote. As Mises remarked, "The real bosses are the consumers. They, by their buying and by their abstention from buying, decide who should own the capital and run the plants. They determine what should be produced and in what quantity and quality. Their attitudes result either in profit or in loss for the enterpriser. They make poor men rich and rich men poor."[27]

Each of us also has the chance to vote with our most precious resource: ourself. We must select in which enterprise to "invest" our energy. Firms compete to offer each of us not only money, benefits, and career opportunities. At the highest level, they offer us a project that gives significance to our life. The ultimate attractor is not money but meaning. Each of us can choose where to work, becoming an employee in a company we admire for its transcendent leadership, noble purpose, and ethical principles.

Finally, as a transcendent leader, you can raise your employees' and colleagues' and customers' consciousness about capitalism and entrepreneurship. You can help them understand why and how freedom and respect in the marketplace work for the betterment of humanity. And you have a chance to participate in public discourse defending these principles in personal as well as in social interactions. And most important, you can become a role model for conscious living, which includes conscious participation in the business world.

SUPERCONSCIOUS CAPITALISM

"Work is love made visible," wrote Khalil Gibran.[28] When an enlightened person with few ego anxieties enters the marketplace, he or she substitutes Adam Smith's invisible hand for the oxherd's helping hand.

I believe it is *agape* (support for others' growth and well-being) that drives what I call a superconscious capitalist. Such a person enters the marketplace with the commitment to alleviate the suffering and to support the flourishing of all sentient beings. Earlier in the process of transformation from unconsciousness to consciousness, service is a means to success; it is necessary to offer value to stakeholders in order to obtain value from them. At this stage, success is a means to service; it is necessary to obtain resources in order to deliver value to more and more people.

During a monthlong meditation retreat in the mountains of Colorado, I took what I called a "business-sattva" vow. I committed to return to the marketplace with helping hands—and with these ideas about leadership. A huge weight lifted from my shoulders. I got a taste of what it felt to be free of the ego anxiety that had made me an overachiever. I realized I had been running on fear, an unclean fuel that clogs mind and heart. And I could envision what it would be like to run on love.

At the end of that retreat, as I walked silently in the snowy mountains, I remembered the story of Moses being banned from entering the promised land. When I learned the story in Hebrew school, I couldn't understand why God punished Moses so severely for just hitting a rock. But at that moment, I could give it a more meaningful interpretation. God had commanded Moses to speak to a rock so it would pour out its water. Instead Moses "struck the rock with his staff" and took the credit in front of the community for bringing forth the water.

That struck me as a perfect metaphor for the ego and enlightenment. The beginning of the search for awakening is always driven by ego. How could it be otherwise? Ego is the master until you wake up and realize your true self. For forty years ego wanders in the desert, striving to reach the land of milk and honey. But when the promised land is finally in sight, ego is not permitted to enter. It cannot cross into the promised land because liberation means its dissolution—or rather, its dis-illusion. Liberation happens when one realizes that there is no ego at the center of awareness, and that there are no hard boundaries within the field of consciousness.

But for the unenlightened mind, "I" (the ego) needs permanent protection and reassurance as it faces a dangerous world that threatens to shatter its self-worth. Typical of ego-defensive patterns are the traits of arrogance and pride. Many of my clients have told me they want their company to be known as "the best and most admired X company in the world," where X stands for their industry. My usual response is to ask them what they would think of me if I told them that I wanted to be renowned as "the best and most admired consultant in the world." They laugh and respond that I would sound arrogant, cocky, and shallow. I laugh, too, and tell them that that's how they sound to me. A healthy goal can't be just to be recognized as the best. The two essential questions are: What would you want to be admired for, and for what purpose?

Those who want to be admired for their financial performance are not at the superconscious stage. If you are at the superconscious stage, you want to be admired because, in addition to being financially healthy, you developed an exemplary culture based on universal human values, because you were able to consistently bring to market new products and services that transform people's lives for the better, and because you lead in a way that inspires people to be and give their best.

If you want to be admired in order to satisfy your cravings for fame, power, status, and wealth, you will have little impact and leave little lasting legacy on the world around you. On the other hand, if you want to be admired in order to have the material means and moral authority to help other organizations emulate yours and mentor other people along their heroes' journeys, "you will make even withered trees bloom."[29]

What would you do if you had enough money (success, power, status, fame, sex appeal, and so on) to extinguish financial and nonfinancial anxiety forever?[30] Of the thousands of people to whom I've posed this question, not one of them has ever responded "I'd retire." Some of them (who actually do have more money than they could ever spend) respond that they would not change anything they are already doing. Others imagine starting businesses or nonprofit organizations to serve humanity.

The interesting thing is that when the material motive is gone, the spiritual one takes over. Peace of mind—which is much more a consequence of ego relaxation than of resource acquisition—triggers a rush of excitement. People feel free to manifest some of their most cherished dreams. They want to do what they love and contribute to the world through it. Instead of seeing the marketplace as a means to prove their superiority over others, they see it as a means to express their love.

When people do business from an enlightened perspective, there is no tension between material and spiritual pursuits. Enlightened business integrates wisdom and compassion in support of human development—through it, spiritual wisdom and practical economics become one and the same.

SELF-TRANSCENDENCE

Our professional activities define our identities. They provide us with a community, offer us a sense of purpose and meaning, provide challenges and opportunities for achievement and integrity, and lend us a sense of power and skill. People feel happy at work when they feel respected, listened to, valued, supported, entrusted with meaningful and challenging work that allows them to contribute to the mission of the organization with autonomy, power, and integrity. This is what the psychologist Abraham Maslow called "self-actualizing work."

Maslow asserted that self-actualization through a commitment to worthwhile work is the realistic path to human happiness in the West—as opposed to sitting full-time in a cave. Self-transcending work is a powerful way to go beyond ego, to free oneself from attachment and self-preoccupation: "The inner and the outer world fuse and become one and the same."[31]

The larger purpose of business, then, is not to win or make money but to flourish through self-transcending service. The enlightened effort to win in the marketplace is subordinated to the commitment to support the flourishing of all human beings. Business success is not the end anymore; it becomes a means to express one's highest nature: love.

And there is much loving to be done. Billions of people alive today are no better off than our ancestors thousands of years ago. For example, about half of the world's population lives with income of less than $2.50 a day.[32] And 71 percent of the world's population lives on less than $10 a day. (The poverty line in the United States is around $35 a day.) These numbers are not just about poverty. They summarize social conditions that affect the sensibilities of anyone who cares about human beings. The opportunities for development are endless, and we have barely begun to tap them.[33]

Connecting people to their highest purpose at work solves the hardest problem there is for individuals (how to achieve symbolic immortality), for organizations (how to align self-interested individuals in pursuit of a shared goal), for societies (how to foster peace, prosperity, and progress), and for humanity (how to avoid self-destruction and coexist in *agape*).

Transcendent leaders build organizations that span the whole spectrum—from economic entities that provide for people's material needs, to temples of meaning that provide for their spiritual ones. Once security and success have been satisfied, significance is what matters. In our age of extreme wealth and extreme poverty, there is a greater onus than ever on business leaders to liberate the workplace as a great force for good in the world.

Humanity has reached the state of consciousness in which we can harness the desire for meaning into a commitment to serve others through the marketplace. Now we need leaders with the superconsciousness required to do it. "When a leader demonstrates that his purpose is noble," notes *Flow* author Mihaly Csikszentmihalyi, "that the work will enable people to connect with something larger—more permanent than their material existence—[then] people will give the best of themselves to the enterprise."[34] When people give the best of themselves in serving a noble purpose, they become the highest selves they can be—and create the best world they can conceive.

EPILOGUE

WHAT TO DO ON MONDAY MORNING

After the ecstasy, the laundry.

—Jack Kornfield

Once you reach clarity about who you really are, then comes the hard daily work of staying conscious. To be a transcendent leader, after the ecstasy of discovering your true nature and coming back from your hero's journey with a gift for your community, you have to do the metaphorical laundry. You need to enact your fundamental commitments every day. You have to manifest your noble purpose, your ethical principles, and your connection to people in every single thing you do. By doing this, you will not only lead your organization, but thanks to the market dynamics, you can bring about a much bigger change.

Any organization that is led from the transcendent heart, in addition to the head, inspires—and compels—others to adopt admirable business models. A company with a great talent brand, one that receives a high score on employee engagement, for example, sets a standard that attracts talent like a magnet and keeps turnover low. This is talent that doesn't go to other organizations that would like to profit from it. Just as competition in the product market benefits consumers, stimulating improvements in innovation, service, quality, and price, competition in the labor market benefits employees, stimulating work-places that support human flourishing.

In exchange, those who do well at work help their organizations do well, too. According to Gallup, the forty organizations that receive its annual "Great Workplace Award" "understand that employee engage-ment is a force that drives real business outcomes" and are rewarded with "higher employee engagement, greater efficiency, higher quality and increased productivity." Gallup claims these organizations average nine engaged employees for every one actively disengaged employee, "which is more than five times the rate in the U.S. and more than 16 times the rate for workforces globally."[1] Such engagement creates a vir-tuous cycle. The companies with higher Gallup engagement scores at-tract the best talent, which makes them more financially successful; this, in turn, allows them to grow and attract more talent, and so on. More important, these companies surpass those who refuse to human-ize their work environments, just as innovators extinguish obsolete competitors in the product market.

For thousands of years, human beings have relied on community as an insurance policy of sorts. You make "deposits" by getting along with your neighbors and helping them, and you count on their reciprocity when you need aid. The same thing happens in an organization. When a leader takes care of his people and offers them an opportunity to tran-scend their mortal shrouds, they reciprocate by taking care of the or-ganization and giving their all to the mission. Taking care of people means giving them a purpose, a mission, a strategy, a sense of commu-nity, respect, kindness, attention, support, pride, and a host of other nonmaterial goods, which end in well-being, flourishing, and lasting happiness.

What does all this imply for your own behavior as a transcendent leader, beginning on Monday morning?

- *Define your organization's noble purpose and stick to it.* Inspire your team to pursue it in accordance with the highest ethical values. Discuss why your organization does what it does, who it benefits, and how you go about doing it. For example, the twelve-thousand-employee ABC Supply Company, an eleven-time winner of the Gallup award that distributes materials like windows, roofing, and siding to building contractors in the United States, is built on a "dream to take care of our customers better than anyone else," says the chairman, Diane Hendricks.[2]

- *Describe the mission of your organization in a way that would make your children proud of you if they told their friends at school about it.* Encourage everybody to explain in his or her own words how this mission gets fulfilled. Make sure everyone understands the organization's noble purpose (ABC, for example, is "dedicated to promoting and preserving the American Dream by helping people accomplish the extraordinary—based on our fundamental belief that every person has within themselves the ability to do great things") and how their specific work contributes to it.

- *Transform compliance into commitment.* Invite people to choose to be a part of the organization because the work it does is also part of their life's mission, not because working there is their job.

- *Distinguish between anyone's role and everyone's job. Clarify that their apparent job is their role, but their real job is to help the team to win.* Constantly reinforce this idea to break down the mirage that optimizing local performance indicators will optimize global performance. Remember the NASA custodian who proudly told President Kennedy he was working to "put a man on the moon."

- *Establish ethical principles that promote the well-being and development of everyone who comes in contact with the organization.* Behave in alignment with those principles in every one of your actions, and demand that everybody affiliated with the company, not just employees but also contractors, vendors, and even clients, does the same. In the words of the Greek philosopher Heraclitus, "Do only those things that are in line with your principles and can bear the light of day. The content of your character [and your organization's culture] is your choice. Day by day, what you think, what you choose, and what you do is who you become. Your integrity is your destiny."[3]

- *Create a mission- and values-driven band of brothers and sisters.* Foster the sense of community through respect, inclusion, and belonging for all those who share the organization's mission and values. Strengthen personal bonds up and down and sideways in the hierarchy, and beyond the organization's legal boundaries, for all those who participate in its project.

- *Ensure that all members of the organization have some measure of autonomy over how they discharge their duties.* Allow them to serve the purpose with as much autonomy as possible. Empower them to own their work environment and deliver results with maximum discretion.

- *Urge people to take up challenges that will stretch and force them to learn new ways of thinking and acting.* Promote a growth mind-set, driving out fear and supporting people to work in a state of flow. Celebrate "intelligent risk-taking," especially when an experiment doesn't pan out. Redeem it as a learning experience and "activate" the lesson as part of the organization's knowledge capital.

- *Compensate people competitively and equitably, but don't rely on financial incentives to motivate them.* Attract missionaries and repel mercenaries, offering a package of material and nonmaterial benefits that appeal to the former but not to the latter. Use money only to take money off the table.

- *Develop a strategy-enabling culture through the Four D's: define the standards, demonstrate the standards, and demand the standards.* Then demand that everyone demand the standards, and that they *delegate the standards* to the next levels.

- *Exemplify, exemplify, exemplify.* Just as your parents' actions told you what was really valued in your family, let your actions tell the people who observe you what your values are. Confront those who appear to deviate from these values with humility rather than blame, asking them for their reasoning. Invite those who think you appear to deviate from these values to confront you with humility, inquiring for your reasoning. Correct any actual deviations.

- *Assume unconditional response-ability in the face of any circumstances you encounter.* Own your part in the problem to be a part of the solution. Focus on those aspects of the situation that are under your control. Explain problems as your inability to respond effectively to the challenge that you face, and consider what you need to learn to expand your ability in the future. Invite everyone else in your organization to adopt this stance.

- *Remember that you can't always guarantee success, but you always have the unconditional power to guarantee integrity*—which is success beyond success. Challenge everybody around you to stop thinking of themselves as victims of circumstance and become masters of their choices.

- *Look at conflicts as strategic disagreements about the best way to reach the goal.* Understand that they are inevitable in any complex organization, because people are dealing with their own subsystemic performance metrics and incomplete information. Remember that every person is touching just one part of the (organizational) elephant, and those who see the elephant from a distance have no appreciation of the details. Resolve these conflicts collaboratively, using the organization's mission and values as the measure of goodness.

- *Open conversations to resolve any conflicts, especially those you've been avoiding because you fear not being liked or upsetting others.* Start these conversations by codefining a shared goal. Understand your counterpart's point of view. Explain your point of view. Develop a mutually agreeable solution, or define the trade-offs for joint escalation. Don't finish the conversation without firm commitments for implementing any agreements.

- *Establish a system of "escalating collaboration"* in which people bring unresolvable conflicts to the attention of senior managers, providing them with the granular information required for making intelligent global decisions. Ensure that such escalations are seen as examples of escalating collaboration rather than escalating conflict. Use this system to preserve working relationships in the face of difficult decisions with decentralized and ambiguous costs and benefits. Use it also to expose any attempts to optimize subsystems to the detriment of the system.

- *Fulfill your promises whenever possible, and when it's not possible to do so, honor your word by letting the other know what the roadblock is and taking care of any consequences of your default.* Establish this as a basic rule of behavior, requiring that any person affiliated with the organization live by it. Remind yourself and others that nothing works without integrity. Consider any repeated transgression as seriously as you would fraud or abusive disrespect.

- *Constantly seek to learn and improve in the It, We, and I dimensions.* Ask others how you yourself can personally do better—and invite others to do the same. Discuss with others—not just your peers but those above and below you in the hierarchy—how you can jointly improve the way you work together, the way you relate, and the way you support each other's well-being.

- *Don't tell people what you expect from them.* Instead, tell them what they have a right to demand from you and your leadership team, including your unabashed honesty and personal support.

- *Remember that a true leader has no followers.* A true leader has "energy investors." Get out of the way and be the way in which people connect to the mission and values. Offer them a platform to play big and achieve symbolic immortality.

- *Tame your ego.* Stop worrying about whether you're the most valuable player, and stop acting aggressively or defensively to appear as such. Disrupt your automatic routines for dealing with your anxiety about your self-worth by noticing and relaxing your "emotional pinches."

- *Die before you die.* Let death, the awareness of our precious and limited time on Earth, dissolve the unimportant and leave only what matters. Wake up from the dream of complacency, and disconnect the autopilot that keeps you stuck in the rut of familiarity. Focus on your legacy, your "symbolic immortality project," and make that the true north star of your existence—and your organization's. Substitute winning for meaning and hedonism (pleasure) for moralism.

- *Take the hero's journey.* Accept the call of adventure in spite of your fears. Go into the underworld, connect with your allies, learn who you are, fight your inner battle, come back to fight the outer battle, and then come back to give your gift of awareness and wisdom to your community. Become an ally, supporting those who undertake their own difficult journeys.

- *Return to the market with helping hands.* Be a superconscious capitalist, profiting from your service to those around you. Inspire people to build a better world through *agape,* the commitment to support the well-being and development of other human beings.

As I've stated from the outset, we all want our lives to matter, to confer meaning in some way, to serve something bigger than ourselves, to do something that leaves a mark and makes a difference in the company of like-minded comrades. We understand that our existence is fleeting and that the future is dauntingly vast. How can we achieve significance with our comparatively little energy in our extremely limited time on Earth? That's the question all human beings must confront and answer if they want to fully live.

As a transcendent leader, you will inspire the internal commitment of people to fulfill their hunger for meaning through a collective mission, which is pursued through ennobling values that create a community of purpose.

If you do the things I've advocated in this book, people will give their very best to you and to your organization, and you will find happiness beyond your wildest dreams. As you let go of your performance anxiety and focus on the noble mission, you will gain the meaning that makes you immortal. In the words of Viktor Frankl: "Don't aim at success. The more you aim at it and make it a target, the more you are going to miss it. For success, like happiness, cannot be pursued; it must ensue, and it only does so as the unintended side effect of one's personal dedication to a cause greater than oneself."[4]

FROM SLAVERY TO SERVICE

While I was working on this book, I took a cruise down the Nile. I had been to Egypt many years ago, but not with my partner, Magda, who always dreamt of visiting the great pyramids and temples. We flew to Alexandria and boarded the riverboat. I braced myself for a less than exciting time, since I had done the tour before. *It's a gesture of love*, I consoled myself. *It'll be good for our relationship and for my soul.* To my great surprise, though, I found the trip even more interesting than it was the first time. I saw everything through both Magda's and Ernest Becker's eyes. I saw immortality projects everywhere: the architecture, the monuments, the rituals, the hieroglyphics, the temples, the mummies, the pyramids, the obelisks were all attempts to manage death anxiety.

What impressed me the most were the graffiti carved by the Napoleonic soldiers on a temple built by Ramses II. English soldiers carved their names on it, too. Wildly different people sent the same message: "I was here." The Egyptians built the temple five thousand years ago as proof of their imperial superiority, and the French and English conquered the place millennia later, inscribing their names to prove their imperial superiority. Although they were all separated by a cultural chasm, the ancient Egyptians and the modern Europeans had the same desire: to be seen, admired, and remembered as people of significance. While I mused about the human pursuit of symbolic immortality, feeling proud of my objective analysis of past civilizations, I was jolted by a voice in my head: *Don't feel so smug, Fred. Isn't this also why you are writing your book?*

A meaning revolution is brewing in the crucible of superconscious capitalism. Transcendent leaders are its catalytic converters, developing immortality projects aimed at the flourishing of all sentient beings. The same free market that transforms self-interest into service can, operating at a higher level of consciousness, transform conquest into community, separation into union, and ego fear into soul love. This revolution will require transcendent leaders who can engage people in a fantastic project: creating socioeconomic structures in which radical respect for every being ushers in a new era for humanity.

Are you ready to join the revolution?

ACKNOWLEDGMENTS

Thanks to:

Jeff Weiner, who inspired and supported me.

Reid Hoffman, who expanded and refined my ideas.

Sheryl Sandberg, who shared her truth heroically.

Mike Gamson, who helped me cross the finish line.

Bronwyn Fryer, who helped me write.

Steve Ross, who helped transform this idea into matter.

Roger Scholl, who let me run with it.

LinkedIn is a company of over 10,000 human beings who all make mistakes; it's not a perfect culture, but it is trying to get there and it's better than most I've dealt with. One of the reasons that makes LinkedIn a great place to work is that it supports employees in their professional development. I'm appreciative of LinkedIn's permission to candidly share my experiences with a broader audience outside the company. It's important for me to mention that the content of this book represents my own personal views and interpretations and not necessarily those of LinkedIn.

NOTES

CHAPTER 1: A HOT WORKSHOP

1. You can hear the SoundCloud clip here: https://soundcloud.com/ryan-block-10/comcastic-service.

2. https://brainyquote.com/quotes/w_edwards_demiry_672627.

3. David Gelles, "At Aetna, a C.E.O.'s Management by Mantra," *New York Times*, February 27, 2015, http://www.nytimes.com/2015/03/01/business/at-aetna-a-ceos-management-by-mantra.html.

4. Roy F. Baumeister, Kathleen D. Vohs, Jennifer L. Aaker, and Emily N. Garbinsky, "Some Key Differences Between a Happy Life and a Meaningful Life," *The Journal of Positive Psychology* 8, no. 6 (2013): 505–16.

5. I've personally experienced the "authorhood paradox" multiple times. I'm very happy I wrote *Metamanagement* (3 vols., in Spanish), *Conscious Business*, and *The Meaning Revolution*, but I can't say I enjoyed writing them. It was like nine months of labor after years of mental pregnancy. For me, writing books decreases happiness but increases meaning.

6. Baumeister, Vohs, Aaker, and Garbinsky, "Some Key Differences Between a Happy Life and a Meaningful Life."

7. https://blogs.scientificamerican.com/beautiful-minds/the-differences -between-happiness-and-meaning-in-life/.

8. Baumeister, Vohs, Aaker, and Garbinsky, "Some Key Differences Between a Happy Life and a Meaningful Life."

9. http://news.gallup.com/poll/154607/Americans-Emotional-Health -Reaches-Four-Year-High.aspx?utm_source=alert&utm_medium= email&utm_campaign=syndication&utm_content=morelink&utm _term=USA%20-%20Wellbeing%20-%20Well-Being%20Index.

10. http://onlinelibrary.wiley.com/doi/10.1111/j.1758-0854.2010.01035.x /abstract.

11. http://www.huffingtonpost.com/todd-kashdan/whats-wrong-with -happines_b_740518.html.

12. Viktor Frankl, *Man's Search for Meaning* (Boston: Beacon Press, 1946, 2006).

CHAPTER 2: DISENGAGEMENT

1. Brian Solomon, "Yahoo Sells to Verizon in Saddest $5 Billion Deal in Tech History," *Forbes*, July 25, 2016, http://www.forbes.com/sites /briansolomon/2016/07/25/yahoo-sells-to-verizon-for-5-billion-marissa -mayer/#62c080fd71b4.

2. Arjun Kharpal, "Verizon Completes Its $4.48 Billion Acquisition of Yahoo; Marissa Mayer Leaves with $23 Million," CNBC, June 13, 2017, https://www.cnbc.com/2017/06/13/verizon-completes-yahoo -acquisition-marissa-mayer-resigns.html.

3. Todd Spangler, "Yahoo's False Prophet: How Marissa Mayer Failed to Turn the Company Around," *Variety*, May 24, 2016, http://variety .com/2016/digital/features/marissa-mayer-yahoo-ceo-1201781310/.

4. Miguel Helft, "The Last Days of Marissa Mayer?," *Forbes*, November 19, 2015, http://www.forbes.com/sites/miguelhelft/2015/11/19 /the-last-days-of-marissa-mayer/#5463c48b6bff.

5. Mike Myatt, "Marissa Mayer: A Case Study in Poor Leadership," *Forbes*, November 19, 2015, http://www.forbes.com/sites /mikemyatt/2015/11/20/marissa-mayer-case-study-in-poor-leadership /#56d238e93795.

6. Teresa Amabile and Steven Kramer, "How Leaders Kill Meaning at Work," *McKinsey Quarterly*, January 2012, http://www.mckinsey .com/global-themes/leadership/how-leaders-kill-meaning-at-work.

7. Murray Rothbard, "The Mantle of Science," in *Scientism and Values*, ed. Helmut Schoeck and James W. Wiggins (Princeton: D. Van Nostrand, 1960).

8. "Louise Bush-Brown," Bartleby.com, last modified 2015, http://www.bartleby.com/73/458.html.

9. Amy Adkins, "Majority of U.S. Employees Not Engaged Despite Gains in 2014," Gallup, January 28, 2015, http://www.gallup.com/poll/181289/majority-employees-not-engaged-despite-gains-2014.aspx.

10. "State of the American Workplace Report 2013," Gallup, http://www.gallup.com/services/178514/state-american-workplace.aspx?g_source=EMPLOYEE_ENGAGEMENT&g_medium=topic&g_campaign=tiles.

11. Brandon Rigoni and Bailey Nelson, "Millennials Not Connecting with Their Company's Mission," Gallup, November 15, 2016, http://www.gallup.com/businessjournal/197486/millennials-not-connecting-company-mission.aspx?g_source=EMPLOYEE_ENGAGEMENT&g_medium=topic&g_campaign=tiles.

12. Gallup, "State of the American Workplace Report 2013."

13. Robyn Reilly, "Five Ways to Improve Employee Engagement Now," Gallup, January 7, 2014, http://www.gallup.com/businessjournal/166667/five-ways-improve-employee-engagement.aspx.

14. Ibid.

15. Les McKeown, "A Very Simple Reason Employee Engagement Programs Don't Work," *Inc.*, September 10, 2013, http://www.inc.com/les-mckeown/stop-employee-engagement-and-address-the-real-problem-.html.

16. "Chaplin Modern Times Factory Scene," YouTube, September 5, 2015, https://www.youtube.com/watch?v=HPSK4zZtzLI.

17. Elaine Hatfield, John Cacioppo, and Richard Rapson, "Emotional Contagion," *Current Directions in Psychological Sciences* 2, no. 3 (June 1993): 96–99.

18. Amy Adkins, "U.S. Employee Engagement Flat in May," Gallup, June 9, 2015, http://www.gallup.com/poll/183545/employee-engagement-flat-may.aspx.

19. "How Seligman's Learned Helplessness Theory Applies to Human Depression and Stress," Study.com, last modified 2017, http://study.com

/academy/lesson/how-seligmans-learned-helplessness-theory-applies
-to-human-depression-and-stress.html.

20. The goal of a nonprofit could be to care for the sick, feed the hungry, or educate children, but it still needs to fulfill the demand of its stakeholders and donors.

21. Susie Cranston and Scott Keller, "Increasing the 'Meaning Quotient' of Work," *McKinsey Quarterly*, January 2013, http://www.mckinsey.com/business-functions/organization/our-insights/increasing-the-meaning-quotient-of-work.

22. James C. Collins, *Good to Great: Why Some Companies Make the Leap . . . and Others Don't* (New York: HarperBusiness, 2001).

23. "Quotes, Authors, Humberto Maturana," AZ Quotes, last modified 2017, http://www.azquotes.com/quote/703356.

24. "What Drives Employee Engagement and Why It Matters," Dale Carnegie Training, 2012, https://www.dalecarnegie.com/assets/1/7/drive engagement_101612_wp.pdf.

25. Campbell Soup Company was founded in 1869.

26. Terry Waghorn, "How Employee Engagement Turned Around at Campbell's," *Forbes*, June 23, 2009, http://www.forbes.com/2009/06/23/employee-engagement-conant-leadership-managing-turnaround.html.

27. Doug Conant (@DougConant), "To win in the marketplace you must first win in the workplace," Twitter, August 29, 2015, https://twitter.com/dougconant/status/373155799222480896.

28. Waghorn, "How Employee Engagement Turned Around at Campbell's."

CHAPTER 3: DISORGANIZATION

1. See Uri Gneezy, Ernan Haruvy, and Hadas Yafe, "The Inefficiency of Splitting the Bill," *The Economic Journal* 114, no. 495 (April 1, 2004): 265–80, doi:10.1111/j.1468-0297.2004.00209.x.

2. Richard J. Maybury, "The Great Thanksgiving Hoax," Mises Institute, November 27, 2014. https://mises.org/library/great-thanksgiving-hoax-1.

3. Chris Argyris, "Teaching Smart People How to Learn," *Harvard Business Review*, May–June 1991, https://hbr.org/1991/05/teaching -smart-people-how-to-learn.

CHAPTER 4: DISINFORMATION

1. A full tank has 3,000 PSI of oxygen, which allows a bottom time of almost an hour in a normal dive. Dive masters require that divers come up to the surface when the tank falls below 1,000 PSI, so that the diver has enough air for a safety stop. The absolute limit is 500 PSI, at which point the gauge goes red and screams "Danger!"

2. I told a version of this story in *Conscious Business: How to Build Value Through Values* (Boulder, CO: Sounds True Publishing, 2006).

3. Friedrich A. von Hayek, *The Fatal Conceit: The Errors of Socialism* (Chicago: University of Chicago Press, 1988).

4. I base this on the famous Schrödinger's cat experiment, a paradox explained very simply here: http://astronimate.com/article /schrodingers-cat-explained/.

5. Friedrich A. von Hayek, "The Use of Knowledge in Society," *The American Economic Review* 35, no. 4 (September 1945): 519–30.

6. Ludwig von Mises, *Socialism: An Economic and Sociological Analysis* (New Haven: Yale University Press, 1951).

7. Alfred Chandler Jr., *The Visible Hand: The Managerial Revolution in American Business* (1977; repr., Cambridge: Belknap Press of Harvard University Press, 1993).

8. Murray Rothbard, "Man, Economy, and State, with Power and Market," *Mises Institute*, 2004, https://mises.org/library/man-economy -and-state-power-and-market/html/pp/1038.

9. Isaac Asimov, "The Machine That Won the War," Scribd.com, last modified 2017, https://www.scribd.com/doc/316453610/The-Machine -That-Won-the-War.

CHAPTER 5: DISILLUSION

1. "Volkswagen Executives Describe Authoritarian Culture Under Former CEO," *The Guardian*, October 10, 2015, https://www.the

guardian.com/business/2015/oct/10/volkswagen-executives-martin
-winterkorn-company-culture.

2. Joann Muller, "How Volkswagen Will Rule the World," *Forbes*,
   May 6, 2013, https://www.forbes.com/sites/joannmuller/2013/04/17
   /volkswagens-mission-to-dominate-global-auto-industry-gets-noticeably
   -harder/.

3. "Volkswagen Executives Describe Authoritarian Culture Under Former CEO."

4. "Former VW CEO Quits as Audi Chair as Emission-Scandal Probes
   Continue," Reuters, November 12, 2015, http://www.reuters.com
   /article/us-volkswagen-emissions-audi-idUSKCN0T10MR20151112#
   uO2kaAmSzGO27E4g.97.

5. Mark Thompson and Chris Liakos, "Volkswagen CEO Quits over
   'Grave Crisis'," CNN Money, September 23, 2015, http://money.cnn
   .com/2015/09/23/news/companies/volkswagen-emissions-crisis/index
   .html?iid=EL.

6. Paul R. La Monica, "Volkswagen Has Plunged 50%. Will It Ever Recover?" CNN Money, September 25, 2015, http://money.cnn.com
   /2015/09/24/investing/volkswagen-vw-emissions-scandal-stock/.

7. Sarah Sjolin, "Volkswagen Loses €14 Billion in Value as Scandal Related to Emissions Tests Deepens," MarketWatch, September 21, 2015,
   http://www.marketwatch.com/story/volkswagen-loses-14-billion-in
   -value-as-scandal-related-to-emissions-tests-deepens-2015-09-21.

8. Hiroko Tabuchi, Jack Ewing, and Matt Apuzzo, "6 Volkswagen Executives Charged as Company Pleads Guilty in Emissions Case," *New
   York Times*, January 11, 2017, https://www.nytimes.com/2017/01/11
   /business/volkswagen-diesel-vw-settlement-charges-criminal.html
   ?ref=todayspaper&_r=1.

9. Peter Campbell, "Volkswagen's Market Share Falls After Scandal," *Financial Times*, July 15, 2016, https://www.ft.com/content/35575f80
   -4a75-11e6-b387-64ab0a67014c.

10. Ben Webster, "Volkswagen Emissions Scam 'Means Early Death for
    Thousands in Europe,'" *The Times*, March 4, 2017, http://www.the
    times.co.uk/edition/news/volkswagen-emissions-scam-means-early
    -death-for-thousands-in-europe-rmhcgsnrx?CMP=TNLEmail_118918
    _1415750.

11. Thompson and Liakos, "Volkswagen CEO Quits over 'Grave Crisis.' "

12. Tabuchi, Ewing, and Apuzzo, "6 Volkswagen Executives Charged as Company Pleads Guilty in Emissions Case."

13. Elizabeth Anderson, "Volkswagen Crisis: How Many Investigations Is the Carmaker Facing?" *The Telegraph*, September 29, 2015, http://www.telegraph.co.uk/finance/newsbysector/industry/11884872/Volkswagen-crisis-how-many-investigations-is-the-carmaker-facing.html.

14. Harvard professor Amy Edmondson has done a lot of research into psychological safety. See Amy Edmonson, "Managing the Risk of Learning: Psychological Safety in Work Teams," Harvard Business School, March 15, 2002, http://www.hbs.edu/faculty/Publication%20Files/02-062_0b5726a8-443d-4629-9e75-736679b870fc.pdf; and Amy Edmonson, "Building a Psychologically Safe Workplace," TEDx Talks, May 4, 2011, https://www.youtube.com/watch?v=LhoLuui9gX8.

15. Behavioral economists have found that just thinking about money can lead to dishonest behavior. See Gary Belsky, "Why (Almost) All of Us Cheat and Steal," *Time*, June 18, 2012, http://business.time.com/2012/06/18/why-almost-all-of-us-cheat-and-steal/. See Dan Ariely, *The (Honest) Truth About Dishonesty: How We Lie to Everyone, Including Ourselves* (New York: HarperCollins, 2015).

16. Eric Newcomer, "In Video, Uber CEO Argues with Driver over Falling Fares," *Bloomberg*, February 28, 2017, https://www.bloomberg.com/news/articles/2017-02-28/in-video-uber-ceo-argues-with-driver-over-falling-fares.

17. Mike Isaac, "Uber Flunks the Better Business Bureau Test," *New York Times*, October 9, 2014, https://bits.blogs.nytimes.com/2014/10/09/uber-flunks-the-better-business-bureau-test/?_r=0.

18. Mike Isaac, "Inside Uber's Aggressive, Unrestrained Workplace Culture," *New York Times*, February 22, 2017, https://www.nytimes.com/2017/02/22/technology/uber-workplace-culture.html.

19. Mike Isaac, "Uber Founder Travis Kalanick Resigns as C.E.O.," *New York Times*, June 21, 2017, https://www.nytimes.com/2017/06/21/technology/uber-ceo-travis-kalanick.html.

20. Pascal-Emmanuel Gobry, "How You Know the CEO Is a Goner," *Bloomberg*, June 23, 2017, https://www.bloomberg.com/view/articles/2017-06-23/uber-s-boss-wasn-t-fired-for-bad-behavior.

21. Isaac, "Inside Uber's Aggressive, Unrestrained Workplace Culture."

22. "'Squish like Grape' from *Karate Kid*," YouTube, May 29, 2010, https://www.youtube.com/watch?v=Y3lQSxNdr3c.

23. "Marriage and Men's Health," *Harvard Men's Health Watch*, July 2010, http://www.health.harvard.edu/newsletter_article/marriage-and-mens-health.

24. Here is Professor Chatman's fuller quote: "Leaders who emphasize values should expect employees to interpret those values by adding their own layers of meaning to them. Over time, an event inevitably will occur that puts the leader at risk of being viewed as acting inconsistently with the very values he or she has espoused. Employees are driven by (. . .) the human tendency to explain one's own behavior generously (. . .) and to explain others' behavior unsympathetically (. . .). When leaders behave in ways that appear to violate espoused organizational values, employees conclude that the leader is personally failing to 'walk the talk.' In short, organization members perceive hypocrisy and replace their hard-won commitment with performance-threatening cynicism. Worse yet, because such negative interpersonal judgments are inherently threatening, employees say nothing publicly, precluding a fair test of their conclusions and disabling organizational learning from the event. The process cycles as subsequent events are taken to confirm hypocrisy, and eventually a large number of employees may become disillusioned." See Jennifer A. Chatman and Sandra Eunyoung Cha, "Leading by Leveraging Culture," *California Management Review* 45, no. 4 (2003): 20–34, doi:10.2307/41166186.

25. Dwight Morrow, U.S. Ambassador to Mexico, 1930.

26. Victor Harris and Edward Jones, "The Attribution of Attitudes," *Journal of Experimental Social Psychology* 3, no. 1 (1967): 1–24, doi:10.1016/0022-1031(67)90034-0. For more on attribution error, see https://en.wikipedia.org/wiki/Fundamental_attribution_error.

27. http://gandalfquotes.com/dont-tempt-me-frodo/.

28. Dacher Keltner, *The Power Paradox: How We Gain and Lose Influence* (New York: Penguin Random House, 2016).

29. Lisa J. Cohen, "What Do We Know About Psychopathy?" *Psychology Today*, March 14, 2011, https://www.psychologytoday.com/blog/handy-psychology-answers/201103.

30. David Larcker and Brian Tayan, "We Studied 38 Incidents of CEO Bad Behavior and Measured Their Consequences," *Harvard Business Review*, June 9, 2016.

31. There are many citations of this truism. For example, see Victor Lipman, "People Leave Managers, Not Companies," *Forbes*, August 4, 2015, https://www.forbes.com/sites/victorlipman/2015/08/04/people-leave-managers-not-companies/#464f55c347a9; "How Managers Trump Companies," Gallup, August 12, 1999, http://www.gallup.com/businessjournal/523/how-managers-trump-companies.aspx; "Why People Leave Managers, Not Companies," Lighthouse, https://getlighthouse.com/blog/people-leave-managers-not-companies/.

32. I share this story, as well as others later in the text, with Jeff's permission.

33. "Glassdoor Announces Highest Rated CEOs for 2016, Employees' Choice Award Winners," MarketWatch, June 8, 2016, http://www.marketwatch.com/story/glassdoor-announces-highest-rated-ceos-for-2016-employees-choice-award-winners-2016-06-08-7160029.

CHAPTER 6: MOTIVATION

1. Jack Zenger, Joe Folkman, and Scott Edinger, "How Extraordinary Leaders Double Profits," *Chief Learning Officer* (July 2009): 30–35, 56; Daniel H. Pink, *Drive: The Surprising Truth About What Motivates Us* (New York: Riverhead Books, 2009).

2. Cited by Daniel H. Pink, *What Matters? Ten Questions That Will Shape Our Future*, ed. Rik Kirkland (New York: McKinsey and Co., 2009), 80.

3. Marcus Buckingham and Curt Coffman, *First Break All the Rules* (London: Simon & Schuster, 2000).

4. Kathy Gurchiek, "Millennial's Desire to Do Good Defines Workplace Culture," Society for Human Resource Management, July 7, 2014, https://www.shrm.org/ResourcesAndTools/hr-topics/behavioral-competencies/global-and-cultural-effectiveness/Pages/Millennial-Impact.aspx.

5. Whitney Daily, "Three-Quarters of Millennials Would Take a Pay Cut to Work for a Socially Responsible Company, According to the Research from Cone Communications," Cone Communications,

November 2, 2016, http://www.conecomm.com/news-blog/2016 -cone-communications-millennial-employee-engagement-study-press -release.

6. Adam Smith, *An Inquiry into the Nature and Causes of the Wealth of Nations* (London: Methuen & Co., 1776), http://www.econlib.org /library/Smith/smWN1.html.

7. Frederick Herzberg, Bernard Mausner, and Barbara B. Snyderman, *The Motivation to Work*, 2nd ed. (New York: John Wiley & Sons, 1959).

8. Daniel H. Pink, *Drive: The Surprising Truth About What Motivates Us*, 35, Kindle edition.

9. Frank Newport, "In U.S., Most Would Still Work Even If They Won Millions," Gallup, August 14, 2013, http://www.gallup.com/poll /163973/work-even-won-millions.aspx.

10. Alfie Kohn, *Punished by Rewards: The Trouble with Gold Stars, Incentive Plans, A's, Praise, and Other Bribes* (New York: Mariner Books, 1995).

11. Barry Schwartz, *Why We Work* (London: Simon & Schuster, 2015), 53.

12. Uri Gneezy and John List, *The Why Axis: Hidden Motives and the Undiscovered Economics of Everyday Life* (New York: Public Affairs, 2013), 19–21. See also Uri Gneezy and Aldo Rustichini, "A Fine Is a Price," *Journal of Legal Studies* 29, no. 1 (2000): 1–17.

13. "Gresham's law," Wikipedia, last modified August 27, 2017, https:// en.wikipedia.org/wiki/Gresham%27s_law.

14. Fred Kofman, *Conscious Business: How to Build Value Through Values* (Louisville, CO: Sounds True Publishing, 2013), ch. 3, "Essential Integrity."

15. Mistakenly translated as "happiness," *eudaemonia* also means "activity that produces human peace of mind and flourishing." See "Eudaemonism," *Encyclopaedia Britannica,* https://www.britannica.com /topic/eudaemonism#ref273308.

16. Jo Cofino, "Paul Polman: 'The Power Is in the Hands of the Consumers,'" *The Guardian*, November 21, 2011, http://www.theguardian .com/sustainable-business/unilever-ceo-paul-polman-interview.

17. Ibid.

18. Sam Harris, *The Moral Landscape* (London: Simon & Schuster, 2010), 1.

19. Dee Hock, "The Chaordic Organization: Out of Control and into Order," Ratical, https://www.ratical.org/many_worlds/ChaordicOrg .pdf.

20. Barry Brownstein, *The Inner-Work of Leadership* (Thornton, NH: Jane Philip Publications, 2010), 54, Kindle edition.

21. This strategy has stringent limitations, though, as the natural group with which we can maintain stable social relationships given our cognitive limits can grow up to roughly 150 people—this is called the Dunbar number. See "Dunbar's number," Wikipedia, last modified August 20, 2017, https://en.wikipedia.org/wiki/Dunbar%27s_number.

22. Yuval Noah Harari, *Sapiens: A Brief History of Humankind* (New York: HarperCollins, 2015), 27.

23. Richard Dawkins, *The Selfish Gene* (Oxford: Oxford University Press, 1990).

24. Harari, *Sapiens: A Brief History of Humankind*, 27.

25. Bob Chapman and Raj Sisodia, *Everybody Matters: The Extraordinary Power of Caring for Your People like Family* (New York: Portfolio/Penguin, 2015).

26. Ibid., 54.

27. Simon Sinek, *Leaders Eat Last: Why Some Teams Pull Together and Others Don't* (New York: Portfolio/Penguin, 2017), ch. 2.

28. Ibid.

29. Reed Hastings, "Culture," SlideShare, August 1, 2009, https://www .slideshare.net/reed2001/culture-1798664.

30. Ben Casnocha, Reid Hoffman, and Chris Yeh, "Your Company Is Not a Family," *Harvard Business Review,* June 17, 2004, https://hbr .org/2014/06/your-company-is-not-a-family; and Reid Hoffman, Ben Casnocha, and Chris Yeh, *The Alliance: Managing Talent in the Networked Age* (Boston: Harvard Business Review Press, 2014).

31. According to C. S. Lewis, *agape* is a Christian virtue to develop. C. S. Lewis, *The Four Loves* (London: Geoffrey Bles, 1960).

32. See Lee Cockerell, *Creating Magic: 10 Common Sense Leadership Strategies from a Life at Disney* (New York, Doubleday, 2008).

33. "Our Client Organizations," Gorowe, http://www.gorowe.com/rowe -certified-organizations/.

34. Author interview.

35. Edward L. Deci and Richard M. Ryan, "Facilitating Optimal Motiva- tion and Psychological Well-Being Across Life's Domains," *Canadian Psychology* 49, no. 1 (February 2008): 14. Quoted in Pink, *Drive: The Surprising Truth About What Motivates Us*, 225.

36. Pink, *Drive: The Surprising Truth About What Motivates Us*, 91.

37. "Russell L. Ackoff," Informs, https://www.informs.org/Explore /History-of-O.R.-Excellence/Biographical-Profiles/Ackoff-Russell-L.

CHAPTER 7: CULTURE

1. "United Airlines Passenger Forcibly Removed from Overbooked Flight—Video," *The Guardian*, April 11, 2017, https://www.the guardian.com/world/video/2017/apr/11/united-airlines-passenger- forcibly-removed-from-overbooked-flight-video.

2. This is not the first time United has had to deal with embarrassing viral videos. See "United Breaks Guitars," YouTube, July 6, 2009, https:// www.youtube.com/watch?v=5YGc4zOqozo.

3. Ed Mazza, "Jimmy Kimmel Creates a Brutally Honest New Com- mercial for United Airlines," Huffington Post, April 11, 2017, http:// www.huffingtonpost.com/entry/jimmy-kimmel-united-commercial _us_58ec7654e4b0df7e2044b81e.

4. As it turned out, the flight was not, in fact, overbooked. See John Bacon and Ben Mutzabaugh, "United Airlines Says Controversial Flight Was Not Overbooked; CEO Apologizes Again," *USA Today*, April 12, 2017, https://www.usatoday.com/story/news/nation/2017/04/11/united -ceo-employees-followed-procedures-flier-belligerent/100317166/.

5. Lauren Thomas, "United CEO Said Airline Had to 'Re-Accommodate' Passenger and the Reaction Was Wild," CNBC, April 11, 2017, http://www.cnbc.com/2017/04/10/united-ceo-says-airline-had-to-re -accommodate-passenger-and-twitter-is-having-a-riot.html.

6. No one really knows the origin of this saying. See "Did Peter Drucker Actually Say 'Culture Eats Strategy for Breakfast'—and If So, Where/ When?" Quora, https://www.quora.com/Did-Peter-Drucker-actually -say-culture-eats-strategy-for-breakfast-and-if-so-where-when.

7. Ram Charan and Geoffrey Colvin, "Why CEOs Fail," *Fortune*, June 21, 1999, 68–78.

8. Edgar Schein, *Organizational Culture and Leadership* (San Francisco: Jossey-Bass, 1996).

9. Jeffrey Pfeffer, *The Human Equation: Building Profits by Putting People First* (Cambridge: Harvard University Press, 1998).

10. Christopher Elliott, "Southwest Airlines Pilot Holds Plane for Murder Victim's Family," Elliott, January 10, 2011, http://elliott.org/blog/southwest-airlines-pilot-holds-plane-for-murder-victims-family/.

11. Elias Parker, "7 Companies with Crushworthy Customer Experience," ICMI, February 17, 2016, http://www.icmi.com/Resources/Customer-Experience/2016/02/7-Companies-with-Crushworthy-Customer-Experience.

12. C. O'Reilly, "Corporations, Culture, and Commitment: Motivation and Social Control in Organizations," *California Management Review* 31, no. 4 (Summer 1989): 9–25.

13. Ken Makovsky, "Behind the Southwest Airlines Culture," *Forbes*, November 21, 2013, https://www.forbes.com/sites/kenmakovsky/2013/11/21/behind-the-southwest-airlines-culture/#4f7273833798.

14. "What Are the Funniest Things Southwest Flight Attendants Have Said," Quora, https://www.quora.com/What-are-the-funniest-things-Southwest-flight-attendants-have-said.

15. Carmine Gallo, "How Southwest and Virgin America Win by Putting People Before Profit," *Forbes*, September 10, 2013, https://www.forbes.com/sites/carminegallo/2013/09/10/how-southwest-and-virgin-america-win-by-putting-people-before-profit/#3338b574695a.

16. It's important to notice that an effective culture is focused. That is, although it appreciates all the factors that contribute to strategic success, it emphasizes the most essential one with determination. If a leader tries to establish a culture with all the above attributes, it will end up diluting each one of them creating a hodgepodge that yields only average performance.

17. Schein, *Organizational Culture and Leadership*.

18. John Kotter and James Heskett, *Corporate Culture and Performance* (New York: Free Press, 1992).

19. https://www.bizjournals.com/columbus/news/2016/06/01/japans-big -3-automakers-built-more-cars-in-u-s.html.

20. Jennifer Chatham, David Caldwell, Charles O'Reilly, and Bernadette Doerr, "Parsing Organizational Culture: How the Norm for Adaptability Influences the Relationship Between Culture Consensus and Financial Performance in High-Technology Firms," *Journal of Organizational Behavior* 35 (February 12, 2014): 785–808, doi:10.1002/job.1928.

21. Mike Gamson, "Take Intelligent Risks," LinkedIn, February 23, 2015, https://www.linkedin.com/pulse/take-intelligent-risks-mike -gamson/.

22. George Parker, "Lessons from IBM's Near-Implosion in the Mid-1990s,"Quartz, November 9, 2012, https://qz.com/26018/it -companies-could-learn-how-ibm-turned-around-in-the-nineties/.

23. Paul Hemp and Thomas Stewart, "Leading Change When Business Is Good," *Harvard Business Review,* December 2004, https://hbr.org /2004/12/leading-change-when-business-is-good.

24. It seems Palmisano was able to combine material and non-material incentives without conflict.

25. Laura Lorenzetti, "Pfizer and IBM Launch Innovative Research Project to Transform Parkinson's Disease Care," *Fortune,* April 6, 2016, http://fortune.com/2016/04/07/pfizer-ibm-parkinsons/.

26. Hemp and Stewart, "Leading Change When Business Is Good."

27. Collins, *Good to Great.*

28. "Zappos.com, No. 86 in 100 Best Companies to Work for 2015," *Fortune,* http://fortune.com/best-companies/2015/zappos-com-86/.

29. Keith Tatley, "Zappos—Hiring for Culture and the Bizarre Things They Do," RecruitLoop, July 13, 2015, http://recruitloop.com/blog /zappos-hiring-for-culture-and-the-bizarre-things-they-do/.

30. Ibid.

31. Jennifer Chatman, "Matching People and Organizations: Selection and Socialization in Public Accounting Firms," *Administrative Science Quarterly* 36 (1991): 459–84.

32. Jennifer Chatman and Sandra Eunyoung Cha, "Leading by Leveraging Culture," *California Management Review* 45, no. 4 (Summer 2003): 5–6.

CHAPTER 8: RESPONSE-ABILITY

1. See Charles Duhigg, *Smarter Faster Better: The Transformative Power of Real Productivity* (New York: Random House, 2016), https://www.amazon.com/Smarter-Faster-Better-Transformative-Productivity-ebook/dp/B00Z3FRYB0; and Charles Duhigg, "The Power of Mental Models: How Flight 32 Avoided Disaster," Lifehacker, March 16, 2016, https://lifehacker.com/the-power-of-mental-models-how-flight-32-avoided-disas-1765022753.

2. This section builds on Kofman, *Conscious Business*, ch. 2.

3. The psychological term for this impulse is "self-serving bias," which is the belief that individuals tend to ascribe success to their own abilities and efforts, but ascribe failure to external factors. See W. Keith Campbell and Constantine Sedikides, "Self-Threat Magnifies the Self-Serving Bias: A Meta-Analytic Integration," *Review of General Psychology* 3, no. 1 (1999): 23–43.

4. Jocko Willink and Leif Babin, *Extreme Ownership: How U.S. Navy SEALs Lead and Win* (New York: St. Martin's Press, 2015), 17–18.

5. Ibid., 22.

6. Ibid., 24.

7. Ibid., 25–26.

8. Ibid., 26–27.

9. Ibid., 30.

CHAPTER 9: COLLABORATION

1. https://www.ncbi.nim.nih.gov//pmc/articles/pmc2791717.

2. I've explained them at conscious.linkedin.com.

3. See Kofman, *Conscious Business*, ch. 5; and conscious.linkedin.com (section on communication).

CHAPTER 10: INTEGRITY

1. https://www.brainyquote.com/authors/mike_tyson.

2. Peanuts can cause severe allergies in some people.

3. You can find examples of these role plays in my coaching sessions at conscious.linkedin.com. For example, Kofman, "How to Establish and Maintain Commitments: A Coaching Conversation (8.6)," LinkedIn, October 9, 2015, https://www.linkedin.com/pulse/how-establish-maintain-commitments-coaching-86-fred-kofman.

4. Francis Fukuyama, *Trust: The Social Virtues and the Creation of Prosperity* (New York: Free Press, 1995).

CHAPTER 11: GET OVER YOURSELF

1. Brandon Black and Shayne Hughes, *Ego Free Leadership: Ending the Unconscious Habits That Hijack Your Business* (Austin, TX: Greenleaf Book Group Press, 2017).

2. George Wald's letter is cited in Jack Kornfield, *A Path with Heart: A Guide Through the Perils and Promises of Spiritual Life* (New York: Bantam, 1993).

3. Black and Hughes, *Ego Free Leadership*.

4. Ibid.

5. Ibid.

6. In *Good to Great*, Collins found that the keystone of a great organization is "Level 5 leadership." Level 5 leaders are those who are, among other qualities, humble. "Level 5 leaders channel their ego needs away from themselves and into the larger goal of building a great company," Collins wrote. "It's not that Level 5 leaders have no ego or self-interest. Indeed, they are incredibly ambitious—but their ambition is first and foremost to the institution, not themselves." The irony is that transcendent leadership is the complete opposite of what most people assume it means to be a leader. See also Jim Collins, "Level 5 Leadership: The Triumph of Humility and Fierce Resolve," *Harvard Business Review*, July–August 2005, https://hbr.org/2005/07/level-5-leadership-the-triumph-of-humility-and-fierce-resolve.

7. Mihaly Csikszentmihalyi, *Good Business: Leadership, Flow, and the Making of Meaning* (New York: Penguin Books, 2003).

8. One might call people and institutions that have plenty of soul "magnanimous" (*magnus, animus,* or "great soul") and those with little of it "pusillanimous" (*pusilus,* meaning "petty"). Synonyms for *magnanimous* include: generous, high-minded, noble, worthy, upright, benev-

olent, altruistic, considerate, and kindly. Synonyms for *pusillanimous* include: cowardly, nervous, spineless, faint-hearted, tremulous, spiritless, and miserly.

9. "First Follower: Leadership Lessons from Dancing Guy," YouTube, February 11, 2010, https://www.youtube.com/watch?v=fW8amMCVAJQ.

10. Author interview.

11. Author interview.

CHAPTER 12: DIE BEFORE YOU DIE

1. Steve Jobs, " 'You've Got to Find What You Love,' Jobs says," *Stanford News*, June 14, 2005, http://news.stanford.edu/2005/06/14/jobs -061505/.

2. Del Jones, "CEOs Show How Cheating Death Can Change Your Life," *USA Today*, March 9, 2009, http://usatoday30.usatoday.com/money /companies/management/2009-03-09-near-death-executives_n.htm.

3. Rand Leeb-du Toit, "How Dying Redefined My Career," Thread Publishing, http://threadpublishing.com/stories/how-dying-redefined -my-career/.

4. Ernest Becker, *The Denial of Death* (New York: Free Press, 1997).

5. For more on the way humans manage the terror of death (also known as "terror management"), see Sheldon Solomon, Jeff Greenberg, and Tom Pysczynski, *The Worm at the Core: On the Role of Death in Life* (New York: Random House, 2015); and Ernest Becker, *The Birth and Death of Meaning* (New York: Simon & Schuster, 1962).

6. https://www.brainyquote.com/quotes/quotes/w/williamjam101063 .html.

7. Susan Dominus, "Is Giving the Secret to Getting Ahead?" *New York Times*, March 27, 2013, http://www.nytimes.com/2013/03/31 /magazine/is-giving-the-secret-to-getting-ahead.html. In Chapter 14, "Superconscious Capitalism," I will argue that the free market is a ground in which business immortality projects, unlike religions and nation-states, can actually compete constructively and peacefully. A free market transforms self-interest into service and conflict into competition. The way to win is to be the most efficient provider of goods and services that improve human life. That's why I claim that business is the best way to bring back meaning to the world.

8. Adam Grant and Kimberly Wade-Benzoni, "The Hot and Cool of Death Awareness at Work: Mortality Cues, Aging and Self-Protective and Prosocial Motivations," *Academy of Management Review* 34, no. 4 (2009): 600–22.

9. Csikszentmihalyi, *Good Business: Leadership, Flow, and the Making of Meaning.*

10. Michael Pollan, "The Trip Treatment," *The New Yorker*, February 9, 2015, http://www.newyorker.com/magazine/2015/02/09/trip -treatment.

11. Ibid.

12. "Carlos Casteneda," Wikipedia, last modified September 14, 2017, https://en.wikipedia.org/wiki/Carlos_Castaneda.

13. I later discovered much safer and equally effective methods of accessing these extraordinary states through meditation and "Holotropic Breathwork," a technique developed by the psychiatrist Stanislav Groff (http://www.stanislavgrof.com/). Meditation, I'd recommend for everybody; breathwork, I'd be more cautious because it's psychologically demanding; I wouldn't recommend psychedelics unless under the supervision of a specialized therapist or teacher.

14. Sam Harris, *Waking Up: A Guide to Spirituality Without Religion* (New York: Simon & Schuster, 2014), p. 4.

15. Pollan, "The Trip Treatment."

16. Mona Simpson, "A Sister's Eulogy for Steve Jobs," *New York Times*, October 30, 2011, http://www.nytimes.com/2011/10/30/opinion /mona-simpsons-eulogy-for-steve-jobs.html.

CHAPTER 13: BE A HERO

1. The Argentinean Nationalist general and president Juan Domingo Perón's friendship with Mussolini and Hitler was no secret.

2. For background on Argentina's Dirty War, see "Dirty War," Wikipedia, last modified September 11, 2017, https://en.wikipedia.org/wiki /Dirty_War#Casualty_estimates.

3. Vladimir Hernandez, "Painful Search for Argentina's Disappeared," BBC News, March 24, 2013, http://www.bbc.com/news/world-latin -america-21884147. Many books and movies have been made that de-

scribe the horrors of the Dirty War, among them *The Official Story*, which won the 1982 Oscar for best foreign film, and *Kiss of the Spider Woman*. Books include *Guerillas and Generals* by Paul Lewis; *The Little School: Tales of Disappearance and Survival* by Alicia Partnoy; *Revolutionizing Motherhood: The Mothers of the Plaza de Mayo* by Marguerite Guzman Bouvard; *Nunca Mas/Never Again: A Report by Argentina's National Commission on Disappeared People* by Argentina Comision Nacional sobre la Desaparicion de personas; *A Lexicon of Terror: Argentina and the Legacies of Torture* by Marguerite Feitlowitz; *God's Assassins: State Terrorism in Argentina in the 1970s* by Patricia Marchak.

4. Ka-Tzetnik, *Shivitti: A Vision* (New York: Harper and Row, 1989).

5. "Psychedelic therapy," Wikipedia, last modified September 14, 2017, https://en.wikipedia.org/wiki/Psychedelic_therapy.

6. Yiddish is closely related to German; it's fairly easy for German speakers to understand.

7. Before he became CEO of Campbell Soup Company, Doug Conant faced such a situation at RJR Nabisco during a bidding war for the company (a situation made famous in the book and the movie called *Barbarians at the Gate: The Fall of RJR Nabisco*).

8. I share this with Jeff's permission.

9. Warren Bennis and Robert J. Thomas, "Crucibles of Leadership," *Harvard Business Review*, September 2002, https://hbr.org/2002/09/crucibles-of-leadership.

10. "Sheryl Sandberg," Wikipedia, last modified September 17, 2017, https://en.wikipedia.org/wiki/Sheryl_Sandberg.

11. "Sheryl Sandberg posts," Facebook, June 3, 2015, https://www.facebook.com/sheryl/posts/10155617891025177:0.

12. Author interview.

13. "How Sheryl Sandberg's Sharing Manifesto Drives Facebook," *Bloomberg Businessweek*, April 27, 2017, https://www.bloomberg.com/news/features/2017-04-27/how-sheryl-sandberg-s-sharing-manifesto-drives-facebook.

14. See Kofman, *Conscious Business*, ch 9.

15. "What Is Servant Leadership," Greenleaf Center for Servant Leadership, https://www.greenleaf.org/what-is-servant-leadership/.

16. See Act 4, scene 3. "The Life of King Henry the Fifth, Scene III, The English Camp," MIT, http://shakespeare.mit.edu/henryv/ henryv.4.3.html.

CHAPTER 14: SUPERCONSCIOUS CAPITALISM

1. You can find the images in Kakuan Shien, "The Ten Oxherding Pictures with Commentary and Verses," Es (abs.), Nicht, https://sites .google.com/site/esabsnichtenglisch/kakuan-shien-the-ten-oxherding -pictures-with-commentary-and-verses.

2. John Koller, *Asian Philosophies* (Upper Saddle River, NJ: Prentice Hall, 2001), 253. John Koller, "Ox-Herding: Stages of Zen Practice," Department of Cognitive Science, Rensselaer Polytechnic Institute, http:www.columbia.edu/cu/weai/exeas/resources/oxherding.html.

3. Max Ehrenfreund, "A Majority of Millennials Now Reject Capitalism, Poll Shows," *Washington Post*, April 26, 2016, https://www .washingtonpost.com/news/wonk/wp/2016/04/26/a-majority -of-millennials-now-reject-capitalism-poll-shows/?utm_term =.526aa75dfde7.

4. Frederick Bastiat penned a satirical "petition of the candlemakers" to the French parliament to stop the "ruinous competition" of the sun. It can be found at http://bastiat.org/en/petition.html.

5. Peter Drucker, *Management: Tasks, Responsibilities, Practices* (William Heinemann Limited, London, 1973), ix.

6. I was diving without any breathing apparatus, that is, holding my breath.

7. Full disclosure: LinkedIn, the company I work for, is now a wholly owned subsidiary of Microsoft.

8. This is not wise, but it is understandable if one believes that intentions translate into consequences. This is not the case in general (the road to hell is paved with good intentions), and especially in capitalism. "Thomas Hobbes Quotes from *Leviathan* 1651," Richard Geib's personal website, http://www.rjgeib.com/thoughts/nature/hobbes -quotes.html.

9. For an appealing (and dangerously wrong) Marxist perspective of exploitation, see Richard Wolff, "Marx's Labour Exploitation Theory (in Under Four Minutes)," YouTube, March 27, 2016, https://www.you tube.com/watch?v=-XED2nmCFNk.

10. As stated by Mises, "Competitors aim at excellence and preeminence in accomplishments within a system of mutual cooperation. The function of competition is to assign to every member of the social system that position in which he can best serve the whole of society and all its members" (Ludwig von Mises, *Human Action* [New Haven: Yale University Press, 1949], 117). "It is merely a metaphor to call competition competitive war, or simply, war. The function of battle is destruction; of competition, construction" (Ludwig von Mises, *Socialism: An Economic and Sociological Analysis* [New Haven: Yale University Press, 1951], 285).

11. John Mackey and Raj Sisodia, *Conscious Capitalism* (Boston: Harvard Business Review Press, 2013), 13.

12. Ibid.

13. https://www.brainyquote.com/quotes/quotes/m/miltonfrie412622 .html.

14. John R. Wilmoth, "Increase of Human Longevity: Past, Present and Future," Department of Demography, UC Berkeley, 2009, http://www .ipss.go.jp/seminar/j/seminar14/program/john.pdf; "List of countries by life expectancy," Wikipedia, last modified September 15, 2017, https://en.wikipedia.org/wiki/List_of_countries_by_life_expectancy.

15. Marian Tupy, "For the First Time in History, Less Than 10% of Humanity Lives in Extreme Poverty," Postlight Mercury, October 6, 2015, https://mercury.postlight.com/amp?url=https://fee.org/articles /the-end-of-extreme-poverty-and-the-great-fact/.

16. "Last 2,000 Years of Growth in World Income and Population (REVISED)," Visualizing Economics, November 21, 2007, http:// visualizingeconomics.com/blog/2007/11/21/last-2000-of-growth-in -world-income-and-population-revised.

17. Steven Pinker, "Now for the Good News: Things Really Are Getting Better," *The Guardian*, September 11, 2015, http://www.theguardian .com/commentisfree/2015/sep/11/news-isis-syria-headlines-violence -steven-pinker.

18. Chapter 1 of Mackey and Sisodia, *Conscious Capitalism*, has much to say about this, as does John Mackey and Michael Strong, *Be the Solution* (Hoboken: John Wiley & Sons, 2009).

19. Today, 99 percent of Americans officially designated as "poor" have electricity, running water, flush toilets, and a refrigerator; 95 percent

have a television, 88 percent a telephone, 71 percent a car, and 70 percent air-conditioning. Cornelius Vanderbilt, as author Matt Ridley points out, had none of these. Matt Ridley, *The Rational Optimist* (New York: Harper, 2010).

20. https://justsomeideascom.files.wordpress.com/2016/05/worldgdpper capita500bc.jpg?w=656, sourced from J. Bradford De Long, "Estimates of World GDP, One Million B.C.–Present," Department of Economics, UC Berkeley, 1998, http://delong.typepad.com/print/20061012_LR WGDP.pdf.

21. Gregory Clark, *A Farewell to Alms* (Princeton: Princeton University Press, 2007).

22. The premise about the exploitation of workers by capitalists has been entrenched by "fake historians." Take, for example, the case of the Industrial Revolution, falsely chronicled by anticapitalists such as Thomas Carlyle and Frederick Engels. These political ideologues spread the now dominant myth that capitalism was a curse to the working poor, that it imprisoned them into "dark satanic mills" for the benefit of equally satanic industrialists. That was not the case, as Mises argued passionately: "Of course, from our viewpoint, the workers' standard of living was extremely low; conditions under early capitalism were absolutely shocking, but not because the newly developed capitalistic industries had harmed the workers. The people hired to work in factories had already been existing at a virtually subhuman level. The famous old story, repeated hundreds of times, that the factories employed women and children and that these women and children, before they were working in factories, had lived under satisfactory conditions, is one of the greatest falsehoods of history. The mothers who worked in the factories had nothing to cook with; they did not leave their homes and their kitchens to go into the factories, they went into factories because they had no kitchens, and if they had a kitchen they had no food to cook in those kitchens. And the children did not come from comfortable nurseries. They were starving and dying. And all the talk about the so-called unspeakable horror of early capitalism can be refuted by a single statistic: precisely in these years in which British capitalism developed, precisely in the age called the Industrial Revolution in England, in the years from 1760 to 1830, precisely in those years the population of England doubled, which means that hundreds or thousands of children—who would have died in preceding times—survived and grew to become men and women."

23. The correlation between capitalism and prosperity is not only obvious over time, it is equally clear in cross-section studies, where economic freedom is very highly correlated with wealth and economic development. But perhaps the most dramatic evidence of the boon of capitalism comes from two "controlled experiments" in political economy: Korea and Germany. At some point in their histories, these two countries split up into a more capitalistic part and a more socialistic part. One of them, Germany, reintegrated in 1989. The data is incontrovertible. The socialist portions of these countries suffered terrible setbacks, while the capitalist portions thrived to become some of the most powerful economies of the world. (See "South v. North Korea: How Do the Two Countries Compare? Visualised," *The Guardian*, April 8, 2013, https://www.theguardian.com/world/datablog/2013/apr/08/south-korea-v-north-korea-compared; and "Germany's Reunification 25 Years On," *The Economist*, October 2, 2015, https://www.economist.com/blogs/graphicdetail/2015/10/daily-chart-comparing-eastern-and-western-germany.)

24. Dan Sanchez, "Mises in Four Easy Pieces," Mises Institute, January 22, 2016, https://mises.org/library/mises-four-easy-pieces; Robert Murphy's *The Politically Incorrect Guide to Capitalism* (Washington, DC: Regnery, 2007); and Matt Ridley's *The Rational Optimist* are excellent introductions.

25. "Every individual . . . neither intends to promote the public interest, nor knows how much he is promoting it . . . he intends only his own security; and by directing that industry in such a manner as its produce may be of the greatest value, he intends only his own gain, and he is in this, as in many other cases, led by an invisible hand to promote an end which was no part of his intention." Adam Smith, *The Wealth of Nations* (London: W. Strahan and T. Cadell, 1776), book IV, chapter II, 456.

26. As Adam Smith said, "The most likely to prevail [in the marketplace] are those who can draw others' self-love in their favor. (. . .) 'Give me what I want, and you will have what you want,' is the meaning of every offer." "Every act of commerce is an act of mutual service. Regardless of the level of consciousness of business organization, the market system will direct self-centered energy towards helping others." "Adam Smith—Quotes," Goodreads, https://www.goodreads.com/author/quotes/14424.Adam_Smith.

27. Ludwig von Mises, *Bureaucracy* (1944; repr., Indianapolis: Liberty Fund, 2007).

28. Kahlil Gibran, *The Prophet* (New York: Alfred A. Knopf, 1923).

29. The phrase comes from a Japanese fairy tale, "The Story of the Old Man Who Made Withered Trees to Flower" by Yei Theodora Ozaki. See http://etc.usf.edu/lit2go/72/japanese-fairy-tales/4879/the-story -of-the-old-man-who-made-withered-trees-to-flower/.

30. Admittedly, ego desires are infinite. They can't be satisfied by any amount of success. The egocentric person simply keeps comparing him- or herself with richer, more successful, more famous, more powerful, or more attractive peers against whom he or she is always at risk of not being the best. The competitive anxiety to prove one's self-worth is not something that can be relaxed through achievements.

31. Abraham H. Maslow, *The Maslow Business Reader*, ed. Deborah C. Stephens (New York: John Wiley & Sons, 2000), p. 13.

32. "Bottom of the pyramid," Wikipedia, last modified August 24, 2017, https://en.wikipedia.org/wiki/Bottom_of_the_pyramid.

33. As Michael Spence, Nobel laureate in economics and chair of the UN Commission for Growth and Development, declared: "We focus on (economic) growth because it is a necessary condition for the achievement of a wide range of objectives that people care about. One of them is poverty reduction, but there are even deeper ones. Health, productive employment, the opportunity to be creative, all kinds of things that really matter to people depend heavily on the availability of resources and income, so that they don't spend most of their time desperately trying to keep their families alive." United Nations Commission on Growth and Development, *The Growth Report: Strategies for Sustained Growth and Inclusive Development*, 2008.

34. Mihaly Csikszentmihalyi, *Good Business: Leadership, Flow, and the Making of Meaning*.

EPILOGUE

1. "Current and Previous Gallup Great Workplace Award Winners," Gallup, last modified 2017, http://www.gallup.com/events/178865 /gallup-great-workplace-award-current-previous-winners.aspx.

2. "ABC Supply Co. Inc. Becomes 10-Time Recipient of Prestigious Gallup Great Workplace Award," ABC Supply Co. Inc., May 16, 2016,

https://www.abcsupply.com/news/abc-supply-co.-inc.-becomes-10-time-recipient-of-prestigious-gallup-great-workplace-award.

3. "Heraclitus—Quotes," Goodreads, https://www.goodreads.com/author/quotes/77989.Heraclitus.

4. "Viktor E. Frankl—Quotes," Goodreads, https://www.goodreads.com/quotes/34673-don-t-aim-at-success-the-more-you-aim-at-it.

INDEX

ABOUT THE AUTHOR

FRED KOFMAN is the vice president of executive development and leadership philosopher at LinkedIn. As an executive coach, he works with CEOs and executives in Silicon Valley and around the world. Born in Argentina, Kofman came to the United States as a graduate student, where he earned his PhD in advanced economic theory at UC Berkeley. He taught management accounting and finance at MIT for six years before forming his own consulting company, Axialent, from which he designed and taught leadership workshops to more than fifteen thousand executives. Sheryl Sandberg writes about him in her book *Lean In*, claiming Kofman "will transform the way you live and work."